ÁCOMA

University of New Mexico Press
Albuquerque

ÁCOMA

PUEBLO IN THE SKY

Ward Alan Minge   Revised Edition

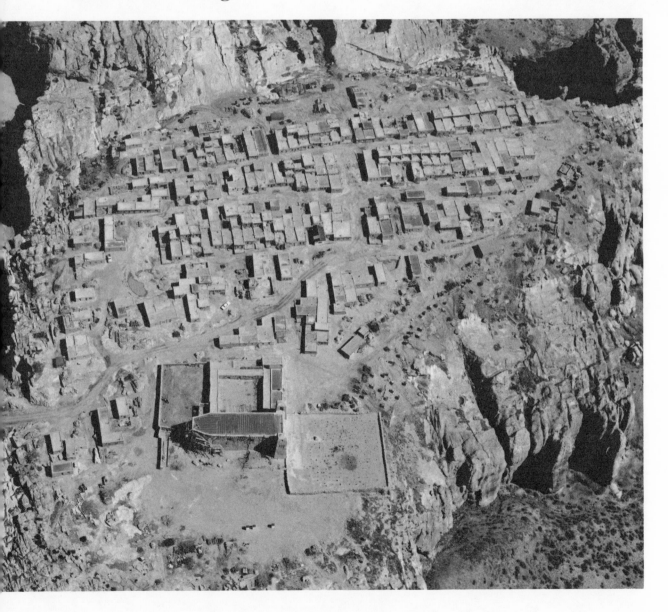

Library of Congress Cataloging-in-Publication Data

Minge, Ward Alan.
    Ácoma: pueblo in the sky/Ward Alan Minge.—Rev. ed., 2nd ed.
      p.   cm.
    Includes bibliographical references and index.
    ISBN 8263-1301-9
    1. Acoma Indians—History.   2. Acoma (N.M.)—History.   3. Acoma Indians—Land
tenure. I. Title.
E99.A16M56 1991   91–20689
978.9'92—dc20   CIP

The research and writing for this book were done under a grant from the National Endowment for the Humanities, No. ES-8593-73-431.

Cover photo courtesy of Dick Kent Photography.

Originally published by the University of New Mexico Press, 1976.

In loving memory and highest regard, this book is dedicated to the Ácoma Land Claims Committee members: Joe A. Chino, Jose Ulario Garcia, Joe C. Ray, and Syme Sanchez

Contents

List of Illustrations

List of Tables

List of Public Events at Ácoma

These are annual Ácoma events to which the public is invited:
February—Governor's Feast Day at Old Ácoma
April—Easter celebrations at Acomita and McCarty's
May—First Sunday, Santa Maria Feast Day at McCarty's
June 24—San Juan Day, rooster pull at Old Ácoma
June 29—Saint Peter and Paul Day, rooster pull at Old Ácoma
July 26—Santiago Feast Day, rooster pull at Old Ácoma
August 10—San Lorenzo Feast Day, celebrations at Acomita
September 2—St. Stephen Feast Day, corn dances and more at Sky City
December 24–28—Christmas festivals at San Estevan del Rey Mission

Days Sky City closed to non-Indians:
July 10–14
October—First weekend

(Source: Calendar of Events, Office of the Governor, Pueblo of Ácoma, no date.)

Foreword

In 1973, the National Endowment for the Humanities made a demonstration grant to four tribes to work in conjunction with the American West Center University of Utah, to produce tribal histories. In each case, an archive of material relating to the tribe's past was completed and placed in possession of the particular tribe. One of the tribes chosen was Pueblo de Ácoma.

Karen Garcia was selected by the Tribal Council of that Pueblo to be trained in research methods. She worked with the American West Center and Dr. Ward Alan Minge in collecting and organizing the archival material. When Miss Garcia returned to her university education, Dr. Minge completed the writing of the manuscript.

The Tribal Council, under three different governors, worked with the project. Theirs was also the final responsibility for management and content. The original funding was applied for during the administration of Governor Harry L. Martinez; the research was done during the administration of Governor Clyde Sanchez; and the printing was approved during the administration of Governor Merle Garcia.

The author, Dr. Minge, has been involved in research relating to the history of the people of Ácoma for many years.

The staff of the American West Center assisted with research and coordinated the efforts of the various participants. The experience was most rewarding and enjoyable. The result of the combined efforts is this book, which speaks for itself.

Floyd A. O'Neil, Assistant Director
American West Center
University of Utah

Introduction

Who are the Ácomas? Where did they come from? In recent years, the Ácoma people have been asking these questions—and others: how long have Ácomas lived at Sky City, what lands were theirs, and how was the land used?

Not too long ago, Ácoma children learned all there was to know about their land and their people as they grew up. They lived at Sky City (Old Ácoma) and spoke the Ácoma language. They heard the old legends and knew the Ácoma name for everything in the sky and on the ground and even underneath the ground.

One of the first stories they learned about their people told of human beings coming from an underground place called Shipapu. The first two people were sisters, Nautsiti and Iatiku. All the people and other living things came to life with these two girls—everything at Ácoma awakened to the sun and to the world and the sisters received husbands and multiplied. Then Nautsiti disappeared to the east but Iatiku remained and gave each girl child a clan name when she was born. That is the reason the first clan mothers were ranked in this order, the oldest named in loving memory of Nautsiti, who had called herself of the Sun Clan:

Sun Clan (osach hano)
Sky Clan (hoaka hano)
Water Clan (ts'its hano)
Badger Clan (dyup hano)
Fire Clan (hakanyi hano)
Antelope Clan (ku'uts hano)
Deer Clan (diehni hano)
Bear Clan (kohaiya hano)
Red Corn Clan (kuganish yaka hano)
Yellow Corn Clan (kuuchnish yaka hano)

Blue Corn Clan (kuiskkush yaka hano)
White Corn Clan (kashaish yaka hano)
Oak Clan (hopani hano)
Squash Clan (tanyi hano)
Roadrunner Clan (shoaska hano)
Eagle Clan (dyami hano)
Turkey Clan (tsina hano)
Isthe Clan (isthe hano)

Throughout the years, some of these clans died out and the body of knowledge and beliefs about Ácoma began to shrink and fade away with the death of each tribal elder.[1]

By 1946 many things about Ácoma had been forgotten by the people who still lived there. But, in that year, the Government of the United States formed the Indian Claims Commission to hear and determine claims made by many tribes and groups of Indians which lived all over the country. Within a year, Ácomas filed their petition with the Commission to "determine title to land claimed by, and to recover the value . . . of land taken from, the Pueblo of Ácoma." From that time on, the Ácoma Councils have relied upon a committee of Ácoma tribal members to guide the people in achieving a just settlement of their claims. The importance of their work caused the Claims Committee to seek answers to many questions about the history of the Ácoma people.[2] The original edition and new revision of this book represent part of the ongoing process of answering these questions.

Descendants of the sister Nautsiti showed up at Ácoma in the sixteenth century and intrusion from outsiders really began in 1629 with the arrival of the priest Juan Ramirez. He was dropped off at Sky City sometime during July as a Spanish expedition stopped over on its way to visit the Pueblo of Zuñi. He helped the Ácoma rebuild their village, which had been destroyed by Vicente de Zaldivar and seventy soldiers in January 1599. Along with an Indian-Spanish style village with two- and three-story row houses, the people built the mission-convent-cemetery complex over a ten- to fifteen-year period. With its mission, Sky City then symbolized a peaceful resolution to intrusions from outsiders.

Would that all human tragedies could be resolved as this one was by those Ácoma ancestors who learned to accept the Spaniards and the priest Ramirez. In working with the Ácoma people over many years, I am convinced that a fundamental pacifism underlies their Indian ways and strongly influences, even dominates, decision making at all levels. The concept contradicts earliest Spanish impressions of the Ácoma as a warlike people feared throughout the region. The modern history of Ácoma, however, belies these negative impressions. Fortunately for all outsiders (and ultimately for Ácoma), the people have always sought peaceful means for settling confrontations. There exists among the Ácoma a concept of world harmony in which people themselves are responsible components. For that reason, it was astonishing to watch the Ácoma openly demonstrate over land issues on State Road 117 in 1987 when a more predictable option was to negotiate peacefully with the United States in the presence of the tribe's Abraham Lincoln cane of authority. But sad and embarrassing to many were the insensitive reactions these past few years from federal officials. One can hope a review of the Ácoma land issues will generate more peaceful resolutions in future relationships with governmental officials.

A continuing purpose in assembling this revision of *Ácoma* is to remind us all of our commitments. Past experience has demonstrated that Ácoma officers rarely serve for long periods, and lack of continuity has been a problem. Also, oral traditions are losing out at a fast pace to computers and modern technology. We hope the perspectives amplified by this new edition to Ácoma's history will be of use as well as of interest to the Ácoma people and their friends. Please note that chapter 6 is an epilogue to the 1976 edition of *Ácoma*. Many of the issues discussed in chapter 5 were resolved during the fifteen years between the two editions and are fully detailed in the final chapter of this book.

Over the past several years, friends at Ácoma have wished to see this history back in print. Through the efforts of the current Governor Ray A. Histia and added encouragement from the tribal attorney, Peter C. Chestnut, steps were taken to bring this about. After several meetings, all agreed the new edition should include not only the recent past of Ácoma, but also more illustrations. With assurances from Governor Histia, I was to have complete access to Ácoma's official files and archives. Working through Lieutenant Governor Tony B. Chino I, Second Lieutenant Governor Reginald Pasqual, Records Coordinator Laura Watchempino, and Gilbert Ortiz, who headed the Ácoma Land Office, I was assured full tribal cooperation.

Thanks to these people, spring and summer of 1990 turned into one of the more inspiring periods of my life. First, it's always the greatest pleasure to spend time at Ácoma amidst such dramatic surroundings and interesting people. Second, the cache of tribal archives and files maintained over recent years by the Administrative Office and tribal officials made my task easier and generated more information than space here will allow. The Ácoma archives are fast becoming, if they don't already represent, one of the most exemplary Indian collections maintained anywhere. Finally, I felt among my Ácoma friends an optimism, even great happiness. As is reflected in the Epilogue, the current generation has indeed moved forward. For helping to reveal these conditions, special credits go to Mrs. Watchempino and Gwyndolen A. Garcia, of the Tribal Administrative Files, who gave so generously of their time and assisted in locating key personnel.

Also contributing directly to this edition were James Toya, Director; Calvin J. Aragon, Assistant Director; and Victoria E. Johnson, Medical Records Librarian—all of the Ácoma-Canoncito-Laguna Hospital. For overviews and perspectives on the court, Bonnie Martinez and Clyde Sanchez, who was past tribal governor and is currently the coordinating officer for the court, were invaluable.

Juan S. Juanico, Bilingual Director, was especially sensitive to and acquainted with Ácoma school children and conditions in the school system, and David Fred Garcia, head of the Ácoma Enrollment Office while working on a new constitution for the tribe, provided necessary insight. The reports of Lloyd Tortalita, Higher Education Officer, were especially helpful, as were those from Flo Hazen, Social Services Director. Caroline Torres, Director of the Senior Center, was also important to the project, and with her warm personality and talents is accomplishing great things for Ácoma senior citizens.

On the delicate conditions surrounding production of Ácoma pottery, I want to acknowledge help from Mary Tenorio, Ácoma Visitors

The Evidence of Archeology and History

Between the calculations of the elder tribesmen and those of archeologists who depend upon evidence of tribal migration, there is a great difference of opinion about the age of the Ácoma Nation. As yet, there is no definite proof of how long the Ácomas have occupied Sky City or the other old settlements, many now in ruins, which surround it.

During the early years of their claims case, the Ácoma council allowed some archeological digs in an effort to establish the age of some sites. The most significant excavation was made on Ácoma Mesa, just north and east of the present mission church. Although the results were far from conclusive, they tended to support tribal legends which state that Ácoma was inhabited before the time of Christ. In fact, the elders claim that the word "Ácoma"—along with other spellings which are equally correct and historically applicable, including *Akome, Acu, Acuo, Acuco,* and *Ako*—all denote a "place that always was" in the sense of a home or even an eternal resting place.[1]

Archeologists do agree that Old Ácoma was inhabited at least from A.D. 1200 to the present, possibly beginning with the extensive Indian migrations of the thirteenth century. In addition to Old Ácoma, they have identified other villages where Ácomas lived: Casa Blanca, now a Laguna village; Kashkachuti; Washpashuka, about 60 miles north of Old Ácoma; Kuchtya; Tsiama (Seama); Tapitsiama (there are two possible settlements by this name; one northwest of Old Ácoma between Crown Point and Coyote Trap, and the other about three miles north of Old Ácoma); Katzima (Enchanted Mesa believed by Ácomas to have been occupied at one time); Heashkowa, two miles southeast of Old Ácoma; and Kowina, about 15 miles west of Old Ácoma and south of Grants. The location of some of these very old villages tends to support the theory that Ácomas took part in early migrations out of the Mesa Verde area of southwestern Colorado. There is also evidence of many farming places, herding areas, and campsites all around and throughout the Ácoma region, but it is not known whether these lands were occupied continuously by Ácomas or, if not, during what periods.[2]

In modern times, it has been observed that so little is known about the Ácomas that their origin "is still wrapped in mysterious and romantic legend." Scholars have done little to clear up the mystery. They agree that the Ácomas are a tribe of Keres (or Queres), composed of clans, some of which appear to have connections with the Hopi and Zia Pueblos. They claim that the Ácomas entered their great valley from the Gila country and were joined by other clans. From the first, Ácomas were in continual conflict with other peoples. Forced to defend themselves, they selected the top of the most inaccessible mesa for the site of Old Ácoma. Much of this, however, is pure speculation.[3]

The Ácoma Indians themselves question whether present Ácoma resulted entirely from migrations. They claim that they have always lived on their mesa, and that they have always hospitably received wandering tribes to share their valley which, at one time, had plenty of water and was excellent for farming.[4]

Contemporary historical evidence about the "Kingdom of Acus" exists because of early and extensive Spanish exploration far north of Mexico City. It was the southwestern region of the present-day United States which came to be known in the Spanish world as the Rio Grande drainage area. Investigation of the region began by chance when Alvar Nuñez Cabeza de Vaca and three companions abandoned an ill-fated expedition to the Florida coast and wandered through much of the modern state of Texas, and northern Mexico, before reaching the Spanish outposts at Sinaloa in 1536. Cabeza de Vaca's news of settlements to the north and west of the confluence of two rivers and his report that "in some high mountains toward the north . . . there were villages with many people and very big houses" stirred the imagination of others.[5]

Vague rumors and speculation about the possibility of another rich Aztec or Inca kingdom on the northern borders of unknown regions excited other potential explorers. The first viceroy to New Spain, Antonio de Mendoza, had little trouble forming an embassy of Spaniards to undertake an *entrada,* or entrance, into the north country. So it was that in 1538 a small party, led by Franciscan Fray Marcos de Niza, made its way into present-day Arizona and western New Mexico. Niza and his men probably did not visit Ácoma although an original description of their journey indicated that they did reach the fabled Seven Cities of Cibola (Zuñi Pueblo). It added that "beyond the Seven Cities of Cibola there were three kingdoms called Marata, Acus, and Tonteac, and the people of these wore turquoises hanging from their ears and noses. By these Indians Fray Marcos was very well received. They gave him skins from Cibola [buffalo], well tanned."[6] However, after a member of his company was killed by Indians,* the friar reported in his own words that he inspected one of the Seven Cities of Cibola—from a distance—and took possession of the kingdom in the name of the viceroy and the King of Spain, along with the "kingdoms of Tontonteac, of Acus, and of Marata." He did not go forward to them, he said, because he did not want to delay reporting to the viceroy what had been seen and done.[7]

The next historic reference to Ácoma is found in a letter from don Francisco de Coronado, then leading a second and larger expedition into the area. Dated August 3, 1540, Coronado informed Viceroy Mendoza about places he had heard of which were supposed to be near Cibola (Zuñi). One of these was Acus, which Fray Marcos had called a kingdom. Both Marcos and Coronado distinguished Acus from Ahacus, or Hawikuh, one of the Seven Cities of Zuñi. Furthermore, Coronado reported, "They tell me there are some other small kingdoms not far

---

*The murder of Estevan, heading an advanced group on this expedition, is pertinent to the Zuñis' history but news of the death traveled among the Indians and is remembered by the Ácomas.

from this settlement [Acus] and situated on a river that I have not seen but of which the Indians told me."[8]

Coronado mentioned two of these other kingdoms. According to the Indians at Zuñi, the Kingdom of Tontonteac (or Tonteac) was located at a "hot lake" where five or six houses could be found along the edge. The Kingdom of Marata could not be further identified and, in fact, was never located by Coronado.[9]

The first Europeans to see and describe the Ácomas were Captain Hernando de Alvarado and his companion, Fray Juan Padilla. Along with a body of soldiers, they were sent by Coronado to explore eastward from Zuñi. Setting out on Sunday, August 29, 1540, they traveled straight east, more or less, from Hawikuh, crossing trackless country where lava beds damaged the horses' hooves. After going seventy-five miles, they arrived at Ácoma, apparently missing any other settlements en route.[10]

Alvarado described Ácoma Pueblo as one of the "strongest ever seen, because the city was built on a high rock. The ascent was so difficult that we repented climbing to the top. The houses are three and four stories high. The people [are] of the same type as those in the province of Cibola [Zuñi], and they have abundant supplies of maize, beans, and turkeys like those of New Spain." Another member of the same party called Ácoma "the greatest stronghold ever seen in the world. The natives . . . came down to meet us peacefully, although they might have spared themselves the trouble and remained on their rock, for we would not have been able to disturb them in the least."[11] When they left Ácoma, the troops withdrew a few miles northeast. Proceeding through the Cañada de la Cruz, they found a pretty lagoon, surrounded by trees, which was fed by the Rio San Jose.[12]

Two other eyewitnesses of the Coronado expedition wrote about it some time after the event, yet agreed about the essentials. One was a soldier in the ranks, Castañeda de Najera; the other was an officer, Juan Jaramillo. Jaramillo, who was aware of the overall significance of the Coronado expedition, wrote a brief account, but Castañeda reported what happened in considerable detail. He saw Ácoma as an inaccessible stronghold. After Captain Alvarado's encounter there, Castañeda estimated that there were two hundred warriors, feared throughout the land, on Ácoma Mesa. The pueblo was strong because of its location atop the rock mesa, which had sheer sides so high that a good musket was needed "to land a ball on top." This position helped to make them bold. "They came down to the valley in a warlike mood and no amount of entreaties was of any avail to them." Ultimately, however, peaceful exchanges of turkeys, bread, dressed deerskins, piñon nuts, flour, and maize were made.[13] Later in 1540, when Captain Alvarado marched the main army past Ácoma en route to winter quarters on the Rio Grande, they found the pueblo to be entirely peaceful.[14]

By October 1541, Coronado had given up the quest for Gran Quivira which he thought was somewhere in the Great Plains to the east. Early in the spring of 1542 his army returned to Mexico. Several friars and Mexican Indians were left behind in New Mexico, but their fate is unknown to this day. Although certain disappointments arising from the Coronado expedition dampened further efforts to explore or even to colonize areas along the Rio Grande, rumors and stories about populated, maybe even rich regions of the north, continued to circulate in Mexico.

Such rumors inspired the expedition of Fray Agustin Rodriguez some forty years after that of Coronado. Rodriguez organized a religious expedition with the help of Fray Francisco Lopez and Fray Juan de Santa Maria. The lure of possibly profitable discoveries caused Francisco Sanchez, commonly called Chamuscado, and a few troops to volunteer as well. With Chamuscado in charge, a party of about twenty-eight persons left Santa Barbara (a mining town near modern Parral, Mexico) on June 5, 1581, and passed down the Conchos River to the Rio Grande. Following the Rio Grande northward, they first reached pueblos in the region of present Socorro, then continued upriver to the Tiwa settlements around Bernalillo. At this point, Fray Juan de Santa Maria left the group intending to return alone to Mexico, apparently to report these discoveries to authorities there. He was killed by Indians within a few days. The main party visited the Salinas (salt lakes) east of the Manzano Mountains, and saw buffalo on the plains east of Pecos. Returning to the Rio Grande, they went west, making contact with both the Ácoma and Zuñi Pueblos. Hernando Gallegos' relation of these events is the basis for nearly all that is known about this visit and it is disappointingly brief. About the Ácomas, it says only that they lived on a high mesa, in about 500 houses three or four stories in height.[15]

The friars Lopez and Rodriguez established themselves at Puaray, near modern Bernalillo, while Chamuscado and the rest returned to Mexico. A rumor that the two friars had been killed followed the group to Mexico City and caused the Franciscan Order to arrange for another expedition northward in 1582.[16]

Fray Bernaldino Beltran, from the monastery in Durango, Mexico, volunteered to lead the expedition. Antonio de Espejo, a wealthy citizen of Mexico, offered to pay Fray Bernaldino's expenses and to equip and escort soldiers. This expedition followed the Rodriguez-Chamuscado route, and when it reached the province of the Tiwas, confirmed the deaths of friars Lopez and Rodriguez at Puaray. Despite this bad news, Espejo and Fray Bernaldino decided to explore more of the country before returning. First, they traveled for two days eastward into buffalo country. Returning to the Bernalillo area, the whole party visited Keres (Queres) Indians and then went to Zia and Jémez Pueblos.[17] Traveling southwest from Jémez, they arrived at Ácoma. Espejo wrote about their reception there:

> We set out from this province [Tiguex, Jémez, or Zia] towards the west, and after going three days, or about fifteen leagues, we found a pueblo called Ácoma, where it appeared to us there must be more than 6,000 souls. It is situated on a high rock more than fifty *estados* [*estado* is the height of a man] in height. In the very rock, stairs are built by which they ascend to and descend from the town which is very strong. They have cisterns of water at the top, and many provisions stored within the pueblo. Here they gave us many *mantas* [cotton blankets], deerskins, and strips of buffalo-hide, tanned as they tan them in Flanders, and many provisions, consisting of maize and turkeys. These people have their fields two leagues from the pueblo on a river of medium size whose water they intercept for irrigating purposes, as they water their fields with many partitions of the water near this river,

in a marsh. Near the fields we saw many bushes of the Castilian roses. We also found Castilian onions which grow in the
country, without planting or cultivation. The mountains
thereabout apparently give promise of mines and other riches,
but we did not go to see them as the people from there were
many and warlike. The mountain people came to the aid of
the settlements, who call the mountain people Querechos.°
They carry on trade with those of the settlements, taking to
them salt, game, such as deer, rabbits, and hares, tanned
deerskins, and other things, to trade for cotton *mantas,* and
other things. . . .

The Ácomas were very friendly and celebrated Espejo's arrival with
juggling acts and ceremonial dances, some performed with live
snakes.[18]

Leaving the pueblo, Espejo marched four leagues up a river which
"originates in some bad lands. We found many irrigated maize fields
with canals and dams as if Spaniards had built them. We stopped by the
said river and named this place El Río de San Martín." The following
day they marched another four leagues. "We halted at a place one
league and a half beyond the spot where the river flows into the marsh,
which we named El Salitrar." These landmarks would appear to be in
the areas around Gallo Springs.[19]

Chronicler Diego Perez de Lujan mentions what was apparently
the first real confrontation between Ácoma and Spaniard. The expedition found Ácoma people shouting at them from the surrounding hills
and they appeared to be angry. Lujan said "We decided to give them a
surprise that morning . . . we went to the *ranchería* [farming
settlement] and set fire to the shacks. We also destroyed a very fine field
of maize which they had, a thing which they felt a great deal." The
following day another field was destroyed despite defenses which the
Ácomas had set up. The fracas had been initiated by the workings of
some servants who escaped the expedition, according to Lujan, and also
by the escapades of the Keres (Queres) wife of a Portuguese soldier with
the train. The last event apparently occurred either at Ojo del Gallo or

---

°Most likely Apaches. Hodge, *Handbook of American Indians.*

at the present site of Acomita where the expedition first reported finding Ácoma fields.[20]

Evidence of extensive Ácoma settlement at springs and along streams relates to these early accounts of *rancherías,* farming sites with shacks or small settlements, which for one reason or another neither Espejo nor Lujan had bothered to mention before. The casual references which do appear in the documents indicate that numerous such settlements existed at springs and along the Rio Grande, as well as along the Jémez and San Jose rivers. Espejo did account for *rancherías* somewhat later in a report given by Baltasar de Obregon. Serving under Francisco de Ibarra, Obregon patrolled the northern frontier regions against "chichimecas,"° paying particular attention to the areas circumscribed by modern Arizona and New Mexico. He based his report on either personal participation in events or on reports received from the field. About the Province of Ácoma, Obregon was told, among other things, that their fields were at the base of the rock mesa, surrounding it. They also had other fields three leagues away which were irrigated. Each Indian had a shack on his field where he gathered his harvest.[21]

Espejo, with nine men, went northward from Zuñi in search of a reputed lake of gold. During their wanderings they visited Hopis and received 4,000 blankets. Espejo sent these back to Zuñi with five of his men, and went on with the remaining three to search for other mines which they had heard about. After traveling considerable distances, mines were discovered in western Arizona and the group gathered samples of rich ore.

When Espejo returned to Zuñi, the entire expedition set out for the Rio Grande; Father Beltran, meanwhile, set out for Mexico. After meeting with further hostility from the Tanos villages along the Pecos, Espejo descended that river, then crossed over to the Conchos River and returned to Santa Barbara, Mexico, arriving on September 20, 1583, nearly a year after starting out.[22]

These brief archeological and historical descriptions were almost all that the Land Claims Committee could find for evidence about both

---

°Term used in Mexico to identify nomadic and warlike Indians north of Mexico's central valley.

Ácoma prehistory and the period of Spanish exploration. In a land which the people have called Ácoma from time immemorial, this early record does not say as much as the myths and legends which have been passed down from generation to generation.[23]

On the other hand, the reports accomplished much by defining the Ácomas as one people who had lived for many centuries in a large area around their central, sacred city on Ácoma Mesa. Ácomas were farming when the Spaniards first came to visit their land, and had developed irrigation methods which astonished these European visitors. They built houses for their own protection, and that of their outlying fields, from marauders such as the Querechos. The Ácomas believe that Old Ácoma was once at the center of rich farming lands in the valley surrounding the mesa. Drouth apparently forced some Ácomas to move to where they could find water, as along the San Jose River, where they were when Coronado and the first Spaniards encountered them. Finally, the Ácomas were ambiguous about receiving the Spaniards as friends. Some believed that they were one with all peoples, and that the Spaniards who came from the east had perhaps come from the people of the first Ácoma sister, Nautsiti. Others thought the Spaniards were unfriendly and meant to harm them. Too soon the Spaniards came to occupy the land and to claim it all for the King of Spain, fulfilling, if only indirectly and temporarily, the expectations of the latter.

Ácoma Under Spain, 1598-1821

EARLY CONFLICT: BATTLE WITH THE ZALDIVAR BROTHERS

Spanish colonization brought about many changes in the traditional Indian ways of life. Some things changed gradually, many others were changed suddenly and violently. The peaceful aspect of the modern-day pueblo belies the fact that fierce battles were once fought on Ácoma Mesa.

Profitable gold and silver mines were being worked far north of Mexico City and the prospect of new discoveries beyond these sustained the interest in New Mexico. Undoubtedly, Espejo's report about a lake of gold and the mines of western Arizona helped to promote further exploration and, eventually, colonization. Three years after the Espejo expedition, in 1586, the Council of the Indies directed the viceroy in Mexico City to "endeavor to carry out the discovery, pacification, and settlement of the said New Mexico."[1]

In 1595, don Juan de Oñate was awarded a contract by Spanish authorities which allowed him to conquer and pacify New Mexico. Having persuaded 129 soldier-colonists, their women, children, and servants to accompany him, Oñate set out on April 20, 1598. Ten Franciscans and two lay brothers also joined the group. When they reached the area of modern Juarez and El Paso, Oñate took formal possession of New Mexico. Later, on July 11, 1598, he established headquarters at a temporary settlement near San Juan Pueblo.[2]

Word of these latest invaders traveled from pueblo to pueblo, but several months would pass before the Spanish arrived at Old Ácoma. In September, Oñate assigned one of the Franciscans, Father Andres Corchado, to minister to the pueblos of Santa Ana, to the Provinces of Zia, Zuñi, and Moqui (Hopi), and to Ácoma and surrounding and adjoining pueblos.[3]

At the end of October, Oñate and his officers assembled with all the people of Ácoma, including chieftains and leaders. Among them were three men named Coomo, Chaamo, and Ancua, who claimed they were Ácoma chiefs. The Spanish asked the people to subscribe to the Act of Obedience and Homage° and believed that they were understood when these three chiefs at once pledged the allegiance and vassalage of themselves, and in the name of their three "nations," to the Spanish Crown.[4]

Oñate's group then left Ácoma for Zuñi and Hopi villages, and to explore beyond. Shortly afterwards, Captain Juan de Zaldivar, who was following Oñate with a smaller party of about thirty men, arrived at Ácoma. At first, the people received them in a friendly fashion but, on December 4, the Ácomas suddenly attacked the Spaniards. Captains Zaldivar, Nuñez, and Escalante were among the thirteen who were killed. It is likely that the Spaniards were camped on the mesa because seven of them actually leaped over the sides and some saved themselves that way.[5]

An avenging company of seventy men was organized by Juan's brother, Vicente de Zaldivar and arrived at Ácoma on January 21, 1599. Taking care that witnesses recorded the events, the Spanish three times formally requested the Ácomas to accept them peacefully. When this produced no results, Vicente ordered his soldiers to prepare to attack on the following day. That night some of the Spaniards secretly scaled the cliffs and gained the summit to prepare the way. The battle which

---

°A formal ceremony during which the Ácomas agreed to obey the king of Spain. Such a ceremony was often accompanied by conversions and baptisms of Indians into the Christian faith.

11

followed continued for three days. Zaldivar later reported that his men set fire to the village on the third day because:

> the lieutenant governor and captain general sent for the Indian chiefs and the rest of the people to ask them why they had killed the *maese de campo* and his companions [Juan de Zaldivar and others]. He had them [the chiefs] seized and placed in *estufas* [probably kivas] where these Indians fortified themselves. They broke away through tunnels and mines concealed in the *estufas,* which opened out into adjoining houses. The Indians ran from house to house and killed each other without sparing their children, however small, or their wives. In view of this situation, the lieutenant governor ordered the battle to proceed without quarter, setting fire to all of the houses and even to the provisions. He ordered that all Indian women and children who could be found should be taken prisoners to save them from being killed by Indian warriors.

In the end, the Spanish took some five hundred Ácomas—men, women, and children—as prisoners.

There is, however, another version of this battle, according to which fighting ceased about four o'clock on the afternoon of the second day, January 23. Zaldivar invited the Ácomas to surrender. Thereupon, the Indians renewed the battle but after another hour they sued for peace. Ácoma casualties were estimated to fall between six and eight hundred. Seventy or eighty men were taken prisoner along with some 500 women and children. Captain Luis Casco de Velasco, treasurer for the expedition and one of Oñate's critics, declared three years afterwards, that the Indians surrendered after the war had lasted some time. They then offered the corn, blankets, and turkeys which had been originally demanded by Juan de Zaldivar and his companions. Vicente de Zaldivar refused their offerings and imprisoned many Ácomas in the kivas. From there, they were taken one at a time, murdered, and pitched over the cliff.[7]

One of the more amazing trials in Spanish records followed in the aftermath of these tragic events. According to custom, the Spanish conducted legal proceedings to establish responsibility. However, after they satisfied themselves as to the guilt of the Ácomas, they then carried out sentences which today seem both extreme and barbarous.

The first of two hearings took place late in December 1598. The soldiers who had escaped the attack upon Juan de Zaldivar testified. All told of meeting Indians and seeing tracks in the valley around the Ácoma Mesa. As the soldiers advanced, the Indians, friendly at first, came out to meet them. Then the Spaniards were attacked, for no discernible reason. One Spaniard described how they escaped and traveled westward about six leagues (some fifteen miles) where they were attacked again by Ácomas. Further on at a small hill, they were attacked for the last time.[8]

Most of the soldiers pointed out that the pueblo was built on a towering rock, precipitous, strong, and impregnable on all sides. They testified that unless it was destroyed so that it could not be inhabited again, and the Indians punished according to the seriousness of their crimes, any attempt to settle the land would fail, because "it is said that this is the place where the natives take refuge when they wage war on other nations. If not destroyed, the pueblo will serve as a shelter for the Indians who rebel."[9]

Vicente de Zaldivar arrived at Santo Domingo Pueblo during the first week in February 1599, bringing the Ácoma prisoners with him. Oñate then presided over a second hearing to ascertain the seriousness of their crimes. Five Ácomas gave statements and testimony. They were Caoma, Cat-ticati, Taxio, Xunusta, and Caucachi (according to the Spanish spelling). From them it was learned that the Ácomas had argued and disagreed about the way to deal with the Spaniards but chose to fight as one people rather than submit. After several more days of testimony from various soldiers, the fate of the Ácomas was sealed. The sentence, in full, follows.

> In the criminal case between the royal court and the Indians of the pueblo and fortress of Ácoma, represented by Captain Alonso Gómez Montesinos, their defender, accused of having wantonly killed don Juan de Zaldivar Oñate, Maese de Campo general of this expedition, and Captains Felipe de

Escalante and Diego Núñez, eight soldiers, and two servants, and of other crimes; and in addition to this, after Vicente de Zaldivar Mendoza, my sargento mayor, whom I sent for this purpose in my place, had repeatedly called upon them to accept peace, not only did they refuse to do so, but actually received him with hostility. Wherefore, taking into account the merits of the case and the guilt resulting therefrom, I must and do sentence all of the Indian men and women from the said pueblo under arrest, as follows:

The males who are over twenty-five years of age I sentence to have one foot cut off and to twenty years of personal servitude.

The males between the ages of twelve and twenty-five I sentence likewise to twenty years of personal servitude.

The women over twelve years of age I sentence likewise to twenty years of personal servitude.

Two Indians from the province of Moqui (Hopi) who were present at the pueblo of Ácoma and who fought and were apprehended, I sentence to have the right hand cut off and to be set free in order that they may convey to their land the news of this punishment.

All of the children under twelve years of age I declare free and innocent of the grave offense for which I punish their parents. And because of my duty to aid, support, and protect both the boys and girls under twelve years of age, I place the girls under the care of the father commissary, Fray Alonso Martínez, in order that he, as a Christian and qualified person, may distribute them in the kingdom or elsewhere in monasteries or other places where he thinks that they may attain the knowledge of God and the salvation of their souls.

The boys under twelve years of age I entrust to Vicente de Zaldivar Mendoza, my sargento mayor, in order that they may attain the same goal.

The old men and women, disabled in the war, I order freed and entrusted to the Indians of the province of

Querechos that they may support them and may not allow them to leave their pueblos.

I order that all the Indian men and women who have been sentenced to personal servitude shall be distributed among my captains and soldiers in the manner which I will prescribe and who may hold and keep them as their slaves for the said term of twenty years and no more.

This being a definite and final sentence, I so decree and order, Don Juan de Oñate.

The sentence was carried out in Santo Domingo Pueblo and other nearby towns. Beginning on February 12, hands and feet were cut off on different days. On February 15, Oñate distributed the slaves at San Juan Pueblo, where the main army was stationed.[10]

The trial made news throughout New Spain and in Europe for many years. Captain Gaspar de Villagra, a member of the Vicente de Zaldivar expedition, published a leaflet in Madrid describing how Oñate had ordered him to take sixty or seventy young Ácoma girls to Mexico. These girls were delivered to the viceroy and then were sent to different convents in Mexico.[11]

Vicente de Zaldivar and Oñate later applied to the viceroy for authority to continue their exploration on the northern frontier. In this document they told the viceroy that the Ácomas farmed many plots of land which had dams and irrigation ditches like those of the Spaniards. Furthermore, they claimed, the Ácomas now welcomed them "with festivity and rejoicing" and gave them maize and many blankets, deerskins, and turkeys.[12]

Don Pedro de Peralta was appointed governor of New Mexico in 1609. The viceroy in Mexico ordered Oñate to return within three months after Peralta's arrival in Santa Fe. What he did during the next few years in Mexico is hazy, but his *residencia* finally came to pass.* Thirty complaints were made against him and on twelve of these counts

---

*In Spanish colonial times, appointed governors and some other officials of similar rank were required to undergo an evaluation of their term in office by the audencia in Mexico City. When present, local officials conducted a *residencia* before the official being evaluated departed for Mexico, where he then faced a second and final series of hearings to answer any claims or charges against him.

15

he was held guilty. Among them were the hangings of two Indians without cause at Ácoma and the indiscriminate slaughter there when it was destroyed by Vicente de Zaldivar. For these crimes Oñate was sentenced to perpetual banishment from New Mexico, and exiled for four years from Mexico City and its environs for five leagues around. He was also fined six thousand Castilian ducats and required to pay the costs of the case. Vicente de Zaldivar, in turn, was also convicted and banished from New Mexico for eight years, from Mexico City and vicinity for two years, and fined two thousand ducats and the cost of the case.°[13]

Further exploration and colonization in New Mexico were continued by colonists there. Vicente de Zaldivar had carried the colonists' petition for exploration and colonization to Mexico City. Officials were anxious to hear more about New Mexico and questioned the returning soldiers carefully. One of them described the New Mexico of 400 years ago with these words:

> The land is level rather than craggy. [Indian] settlements are located on the banks of small rivers, although the Rio del Norte [Rio Grande] is much larger. They have fields of corn, beans, and calabashes as in New Spain [Mexico], except that the cornstalks are smaller. They have many pine forests where they gather quantities of piñons [nuts] which are as good or better than those of Castile [Spain], and they also have small prickly pears. They raise native fowl. The Pueblos are small; the largest had almost four hundred houses; the others were smaller down to thirty houses. In some years their harvest of corn is abundant and in others very poor on account of the frequent frosts; the land is very cold and it snows for long periods, as much as six months of the year, from October to the end of March, and some years even longer.[14]

Much of the same general description applied to Ácoma except that the country around Sky City was broken by mesas and valleys. During the next several years, the Ácomas remained peaceful but refused to have

---

°Ducat is more or less equivalent to $1.50 U.S. contemporary.

any dealings with Spaniards. In fact, there were few if any contacts. The thrust of settlement was directed some sixty miles to the east, toward the new Villa de Santa Fe. Communications with Mexico City ranged from there south along the Rio Grande to El Paso. The resultant isolation of Ácoma is basic to understanding the land and its people throughout their history.

EARLY ADMINISTRATION AND REBUILDING THE PUEBLO

As Spanish settlement of New Mexico progressed, quarrels between the temporal and ecclesiastical authorities in the colony often concerned treatment of the Indians. Bickering began even as Oñate conducted expeditions into western Arizona and around the Gulf of California, and it continued under subsequent governors. Basic disagreements pertained to the appropriate division of Indian tribute and labor, as well as to the supervision and use of Indian-owned lands.

The viceroy in Mexico had dealt with treatment of Indians in instructions given to Oñate, and after him, to Governor Pedro de Peralta. First of all, Indian settlements were to be consolidated to simplify their administration and defense—a policy which would require relocating some of the people.° At the same time, the governors were to see to educating the Indians so that they might understand the Franciscan instructions in Spanish. This was intended not only to eliminate the different languages among the Indians but also to ease the problem of administration. In addition, Peralta received permission to assign Indians in *encomienda;* that is, to allot groups of Indians to a specific Spanish settler who, in return for taxes or tribute, would teach the Indians Christian doctrine.

Indian complaints of abuse of power reached Mexico and prompted the 1620 viceregal orders to Governor Juan de Eulate, and to Fray Estevan de Perea, custos†. These orders appeared to have been

---

°No record has been found to indicate that resettlement was ever carried out in New Mexico. However, the question is not yet satisfactorily resolved because records of the first Spanish years in New Mexico may still be uncovered.

†Superior of a Franciscan province, or custody: in this case, the Custody of the Conversion of St. Paul.

based on works of the second audiencia°° in Mexico (1530–35), which passed a series of humanitarian ordinances to revise administration in Indian Pueblos. Traditions thereby established exist today at Ácoma.[16]

It is not known when the Ácomas began to elect their own civil officials but annual elections appear to have been the practice in the more centrally located pueblos by 1620. This tradition continues today in many pueblos, including Ácoma. The early ordinances concerning elections and other matters relating to management of the pueblos reveal much of the paternal and protective intent of the Spanish administration:

> 1. It was ordered that on the days of annual pueblo elections, when the local officials, such as the governor, fiscal, etc., were named, no representatives of the State or Church should be present in the pueblos in order to insure to the Indians complete freedom of action. Regarding this point the document stated, "the governor may give orders that each of the Pueblos of these provinces on the first day of January of every year, may carry out their elections of governor, *alcaldes, topiles, fiscales,* and other public officers without my said governor or any other Judiciary, you or any other Religious of your Custos being found present. Thus the Indians may have the freedom which is fitting. The [elections] which may be effected in this manner may be correct [reported] to the governor in order that [the elections] having been affected and by the majority [of the Indians] with the freedom indicated, he [the governor] may confirm that everything is in accord with what is customary in Spain."

> 2. Governor and custos were instructed that on feast days and Sundays friars should go to the several pueblos where there were Churches, so that the Indians would be spared the trouble of going to distant pueblos to hear Mass.

> 3. In those pueblos already subject to tribute or *encomienda,* the friars were not to impede the collection of such

---

°°Spanish ruling body in Mexico City prior to appointment of the first viceroy.

tribute. In pueblos converted in the future, no tributes were to be levied until governor, custos, and guardian of the convent made reports to the viceroy who would decide what was best. Moreover, no tributes were to be collected in the Zuni and Hopi Pueblos, as they were still unconverted.

4. The governor was instructed to see to it that the *encomenderos* provided military escort for mission supply trains coming from Mexico City and also for the friars going to administer the sacraments in frontier pueblos.

5. The governor was forbidden to graze herds of livestock for his own account.

6. To avoid damage to the growing crops of the pueblos the Spaniards were instructed not to pasture their stock within three leagues of the pueblos, except in certain circumstances.

7. Both the governor and the custos were ordered not to permit the uses of Indian labor in illegal ways, or in such amount that the Indians would suffer hardship. All levies or *repartimientos* of Indian laborers were to be limited only to the work of sowing and planting. The number of Indians to be called from each pueblo was strictly limited, and the wages duly paid. The allotment of Indian women as servants in the houses of Spaniards was forbidden, unless "they go with their husbands [and] voluntarily." The custodian was instructed that Indian labor at the missions should be used only "for things necessary for the church and the convenience of the living quarters." And then only "with the greatest moderation."

8. The practice of cutting hair of Indians guilty of minor offenses was forbidden. This order was the result of a complaint that the friars had used this form of punishment "for errors and light faults."

Some Pueblo Indians who were punished by haircuts sought refuge in the isolated and "unconverted pueblo of Ácoma, returning to idolatry."[17]

There is no record that Fray Andres Corchado ever visited Ácoma, although it was included in the mission assigned to him by Oñate on September 9, 1598.[18] It would seem that Ácoma was for some time without a resident missionary. When Oñate was recalled, the New Mexican colony began to decline, as did the missions, because of disputes between political and religious authorities. The Franciscan Province of the Holy Gospel from its headquarters in Mexico City pushed for more conversions and sent Fray Estevan de Perea as special inspector to New Mexico to help reestablish mission activities at some of the pueblos. A Fray Geronimo de Zarate Salmeron may have served at Ácoma between 1623 and 1626, but the first permanent resident priest was Fray Juan Ramirez. Father Ramirez was sent to New Mexico with Inspector Perea who, along with Governor Silva, escorted him to Ácoma in 1629. From all accounts, Fray Juan chose to serve at Ácoma and remained there for many years. Ácomas hold him in great respect and some even endow him with saintly virtues. An Ácoma legend describes Fray Juan's arrival at the pueblo. As he climbed up the mesa for the first time, one of the women in the waiting crowd dropped her child over the edge. Miraculously, he caught the infant and delivered her unharmed to the mother.[19]

Fray Juan is remembered by the Ácomas not only because he ended their isolation from Spanish settlers, but also because he built the large mission church of San Estevan. Those whom Oñate had condemned in 1598 to twenty years of servitude doubtless returned in time to join in one of Ácoma's great historic undertakings—the rebuilding of Old Ácoma. Tradition places the responsibility for this task entirely in the hands of Fray Juan. It was he who taught the Indians about woodworking and construction and how to make bricks from clay—the Spanish *adobes*.

It is estimated that Ácoma was rebuilt between 1629 and 1640 but no records of this work survive other than the buildings themselves. The main church is over a hundred feet long and stands thirty-five feet high. The towers are higher still. In places, the walls are nine feet thick at the ground level to support the weight above. The convent on the north side of the church required considerably more dirt and clay for construction. To the east, in front of the church, Fray Juan Ramirez and the Ácomas built stout retaining walls of stone along the contour of the mesa and back again to the church to form an atrium. These were filled with countless tons of earth, carried from the valley below, to create a burial site.

Under the friar's guidance, the Ácomas used the same techniques to reconstruct the village. The adobe bricks used throughout the older sections and walls of the church, convent, and houses were of the same materials and dimensions. Little of the original stone was used in reconstruction of the walls. The main plaza was placed in the middle of Old Ácoma, running lengthwise north and south. On either side, there were at least three long rows of multi-storied houses and apartments, with an east-west orientation. No one now remembers where the bricks were made, nor is there any way to estimate the tons of earth which must have been carried from the valley floor to the mesa top. Ácomas do believe that the massive support timbers came from mountains to the north, and refer specifically to Mount Taylor. One story tells how the men carried logs for construction of buildings on Ácoma Mesa from Mount Taylor without permitting them to touch the ground en route.[20]

THE SEVENTEENTH CENTURY AND THE PUEBLO REVOLT

Resident Franciscans continued to influence the Ácomas for forty years, more or less. General mission work progressed, with triennial caravans from Mexico City providing new friars and supplies as needed. Probably Ácoma joined with other pueblos to register complaints with the Spanish governors in Santa Fe about the friars' concerted efforts to rid the pueblos of ancient idols and ceremonies. Nonetheless, they maintained the mission with personal services and supplies, and rendered tributes of various kinds. The Ácomas gradually converted to the Catholic faith and adopted many Spanish ways of farming and husbandry. The Spanish names for many landmarks around Ácoma doubtless date from this early relationship with the Franciscans.[21]

The Spanish Crown regarded the Franciscans as "protectors" of the Indians in the New World. At the same time it regarded all the land (and minerals) as the Royal patrimony. The missionaries acted to

interpret Spanish policy and helped to insure the appropriate assign-
ment of lands to Ácoma and other tribes. The body of Spanish laws, as
set forth in the *Recopilación de Leyes de los Reynos de las Indias* in
1681, provided that each Indian town, whether preconquest or
postconquest, should have ample lands. The town site was to measure
at least 600 *varas* in each direction from the church. Beyond this, a
minimum of one square league (six to nine square miles) was to be set
aside for common use by members of the village. It was, however,
common practice of the viceroys, conquistadors, and adelantados to
recognize special claims for land, especially those of leading members
of any Indian tribe. There is little doubt that Spanish officials employed
the usual formula to set aside certain lands for each pueblo, as any
failure to do so would have been cause for a major complaint (among
many others) registered by Franciscans against the governors throughout the seventeenth century. The lack of extant and specific documen-
tation about Pueblo Indian lands during this period leads to a measure
of confusion concerning the exact amounts of land each pueblo
received.[22]

One outspoken critic of the Spanish practices which did exploit
the Indians was Fray Alonso de Benavides. Yet he maintains that there
were no adverse effects in the mission work. He told of successful
conversions of the New Mexico Indians and their friendly attitude
toward Spaniards in glowing reports to the King of Spain in 1630 and to
Pope Urban VIII in 1634. Benavides was appointed custos of New
Mexico on October 19, 1623, although he did not arrive on the frontier
until the spring of 1625. Before his departure in the autumn of 1629, he
visited Ácoma. He described it as follows:

> To the west of the Rio del Norte, at a distance of thirty
> leagues, lies the Peñol of Ácoma, very famous for the many
> lives that it has cost both the Spaniards and the Indians. This
> was not only because it was impregnable but also because of
> the courage and industry of its inhabitants, who are of the
> Queres nation. It is a steep cliff with only one narrow path
> hewn out by hand. On the summit there is a space of about
> half a league where the pueblo is situated. There are here

more than one thousand residents of this Queres Nation, and also of many others, delinquents and apostates, who have sought shelter and made themselves strong there. Great wars have been waged over this place.

In spite of the presence of "delinquents and apostates," he credits Fray Juan Ramirez with converting the Ácomas and encouraging them to live in peace.[23]

Benavides prompted Charles I of Spain to issue two decrees for the protection of New Mexico Indians, including the Ácomas. The first, dated January 30, 1635, exempted New Mexico Indians from being granted in *encomienda*, as well as from personal service or tributes. Subsequently Benavides petitioned the king to insure that the grants made to Spanish colonists should not infringe on Indian lands. In addition he asked that grants which bordered Indian lands have the approval of the Indians concerned. Furthermore, he suggested that the colonial governors be prevented from taking the best lands the "Indians have for their fields" and also that they not "prevent the neighboring Spaniards from helping to develop their [Indian] lands."[24]

At some of the other pueblos the Franciscans alleged interference by the governors but they were successful in establishing their mission at Ácoma. Fray Lucas de Maldonado Olasqueain, who served Ácoma from 1671 to 1680, described his "church, convent, sacristy, and cemetery, [as] one of the best there is in this kingdom."[25]

By 1680, resentments smoldering within the Indian pueblos flared into open rebellion. The story of the Pueblo Revolt begins with Tesuque and San Juan Pueblos. There some Indians apparently plotted for a number of years to rid themselves of the Spanish interlopers and finally a concerted movement came together under the leadership of a San Juan Indian known as Pope. Anyone and anything Spanish was the target, including the missions. Indeed, the opposition of the missionaries to the Indian religious leaders and their native ceremonies was a major cause of the revolt.[26]

Indian witnesses claimed that Pope divined the auspicious date to begin hostilities. A knotted cord was prepared to show it, August 11, 1680, and the cord was sent to all the pueblos so that each one might correctly account for the intervening days. The Apaches to the north and south agreed to help the pueblos. Pope's plan was a simple one—kill Governor Antonio de Otermin and all the Spanish settlers along the Rio Grande as far south as El Paso.

Governor Otermin was alerted to the plan but too late to form any effective defense. He learned the truth on August 9 from Tesuque Indians arrested for killing a Spaniard. The rebellion actually began on the morning of August 10 in Taos and Picurís Pueblos where Pope had been staying. After their tribesmen were apprehended by Spanish soldiers on August 9, the Tesuque Indians had notified all the other pueblos that the time had come to turn against the Spanish. They themselves, apparently in full battle regalia, attacked Fray Juan Pio on August 10 as he was approaching from Santa Fe to say mass at the pueblo. The other pueblos moved against any Spaniards near at hand. Reports came to Governor Otermin that all the Spaniards at Ácoma had been killed, including Fray Lucas de Maldonado.[27]

Ácoma, however, had no important role in the events of 1680 because she was too far away to cooperate effectively with the valley pueblos. These latter pueblos combined forces, besieged Santa Fe, and twice defeated the Spanish defenders before Governor Otermin decided to retreat on August 21. Otermin's central party made its way to El Paso, closely followed by various stragglers and other groups of surviving Spaniards. On September 29, the main body of refugees reached La Salineta just north of El Paso, and by October 5, Governor Otermin established his headquarters on the right bank of the Rio Grande, across from El Paso del Norte. From here, he made plans to reconquer New Mexico where most everything Spanish had been destroyed.[28]

During an unsuccessful attempt to reconquer New Mexico in 1681, Governor Otermin interviewed a number of Indians in an effort to satisfy inquiries from Spanish authorities about the reasons for the rebellion. They expressed a general desire to return to their old Indian ways and revealed that interference with Indian ceremonies and religion was widely resented. Some also told of maltreatment from Spanish civil authorities. Others testified that not all Pueblo Indians had agreed to the plan to slaughter the colonists. The colonists themselves were in a state of confusion and the governor had to order that none were to proceed any farther south than El Paso.[29]

While on an expedition to Isleta Pueblo during the following year, Governor Otermin was told that the northern pueblos suffered severe drouth. There was a plan among them, which included Ácomas, to attack the Isletas for their granaries, under the pretense that this pueblo was friendly to the Spaniards. This appears to be one of the few occasions when Ácomas joined the Rio Grande pueblos in a common cause.[30]

In 1683, Otermin was succeeded as governor of New Mexico by Domingo Jironza Petriz de Cruzate. In 1688, he led a small force of Spanish soldiers northward from El Paso to the Pueblo of Zia. When all was over, the Spanish had wrecked and burned Zia, killed some six hundred Indians, and captured seventy more who were sold as slaves. This was as close to Ácoma as Governor Petriz de Cruzate ever came but he touched the lives of the people there in another surprising way. On September 20, 1689, he executed the Spanish land grant to Ácoma, allegedly relying upon the memory of an Indian named Bartolome de Ojeda to establish the pueblo boundaries.*[31] Ojeda's landmarks were Prieto Mountain on the north and Gallo Spring on the west. Cubero Mountain formed the eastern edge, and the Peñol made the southern line. He also described other interesting things which the governor made a part of the document but some of this information is now proven to be anachronistic.[32]

THE RECONQUEST

The decade following the Pueblo Revolt was marked by several unsuccessful attempts to recover Spanish holdings in New Mexico. The authorities in Mexico City and in Spain became slightly less concerned about the religious condition of the Indians and more so with reestablishing themselves in New Mexico. They feared that the French,

---

*See Appendix 1: TEXT OF ORIGINAL GRANT, ÁCOMA, 1689.

who were known to be exploring along the Mississippi and inland as far as the Great Plains, might claim the region north of the Rio Grande and thus pose a threat to New Spain itself. Otherwise, the displaced colony which had settled along the Rio Grande near El Paso would probably have been allowed to disband and leave New Mexico to the original inhabitants. Instead, the Spanish government continued to appoint governors and to provide money and supplies for reinforcement of the northern frontier of the Spanish Empire.

On February 22, 1691, don Diego de Vargas took over as governor of New Mexico. His first expedition into New Mexico, which left El Paso in August 1692, was financed largely at his own expense. De Vargas intended to see for himself conditions there, to verify reports of quicksilver mines, and, if possible, to reduce and conquer the Pueblo Indians.

When de Vargas arrived in Santa Fe in September, the Tewas and Tanos were not only reluctant to negotiate, but also were prepared to defend the city. Matters were growing critical when the Spanish were approached by three Indians who said they were from Tesuque, Santa Clara, and San Lazaro. Shortly afterward, these men were joined by Governor Domingo of Tesuque and all four ended up acting as intermediaries. Governor de Vargas was allowed to enter Santa Fe, unarmed and unaccompanied except for Governor Domingo, the Franciscans of the expedition, and interpreters. Governor Domingo persuaded the Indians to relinquish their position and then, after many assurances and embraces, they once again pledged allegiance to the King of Spain and declared their renewed faith in Christianity. De Vargas called September 14th a day of "Exaltation of the Holy Cross."[33]

A striking political change had occurred since 1680; the Tewas had formed a league with the Tanos and Picurís. Another man named Domingo, who led the Indians assembled in Santa Fe, explained to Governor de Vargas that the Tewas, Tanos, and Picurís now rendered obedience to Picuri governor don Luis. De Vargas received don Luis on September 15, served him chocolate, and assured him that he could remain governor. During the meeting, don Luis made "three courtsies,

26

[*sic*] each time falling to one knee," and agreed to report to de Vargas on his success in influencing the people to become good Christians.[34]

De Vargas used the reception in Santa Fe as encouragement to win over the Pecos and Taos Pueblos, stopping at each place long enough to receive the Act of Obedience.[35] The same ceremonies were repeated at Cuyamungué, Nambé, Pojoaque, Jacona, San Ildefonso, Santa Clara, San Juan, San Cristóbal, and San Lázaro. De Vargas confirmed don Luis Picurí's position as governor over the thirteen reconquered pueblos, including Santa Fe, Taos, Picurís, Tewas, and Tanos.[36]

There followed an expedition in October and November against the western pueblos. When de Vargas and the troops arrived at Sky City after passing Enchanted Mesa on November 3, 1692, the Ácomas refused to let them into the village. They had even barricaded a narrow entrance along the so-called padres, or main, trail with poles and a large rock. After some entreaties, the Ácoma council decided not to give in to the Spaniards. The Indian Chief Mateo explained that "two friendly natives and several Apaches had informed them that the Spanish General would have them beheaded and hanged for their past offenses."[37] But de Vargas and nine soldiers climbed to the top of Ácoma Mesa where the Indians relinquished peacefully. Two missionaries baptized eighty-seven Indians while de Vargas and the soldiers inspected the village and church. The last he found "even larger than the Convent of San Francisco, at the court [Mexico City]," with firm walls almost a yard and a half thick. The skylights (clerestory) and windows had been broken. From here de Vargas and the Spanish company proceeded for Zuñi.[38]

During the next four months most of the former Spanish homes and churches were found in charred ruins. Although he left no colonists behind him, de Vargas reported his first expedition as a total success because twenty-three pueblos of ten Indian nations had been returned to Spain without expending a "single ounce of powder or unsheathing a sword, and without costing the royal treasury a single Maravedí."[39]

Resettlement began with de Vargas' second expedition. Some 800 settlers and an army escort left El Paso on October 13, 1693, arriving in Santa Fe on the morning of December 16th. It was reported to de

Vargas that the Tewas and Tanos received the Spaniards with rejoicing, and with gifts of food and supplies. Again, Governor Domingo of Tesuque was most active in assuring the safe arrival of the colonists. Once established in Santa Fe, the *cabildo* (town council) was reinstalled, priests were assigned, and settlers claims for the abandoned properties and ranches were recognized.[40]

All too soon they received warning that the pueblos were arming and threatening to resume the rebellion. Leaders of the unrest included Governor Domingo; Joseph, the captain and governor of Santa Fe; Naranjo, captain and governor of Santa Clara; and Luis and Antonio Bolsas of Santa Fe.[41] On the other hand, Luis Picuri and his brother, Lorenzo, remained friendly to the Spanish. The Pueblos of San Juan, San Lázaro, Nambé, San Ildefonso, and San Cristóbal continued to be friendly and reconfirmed their submission and obedience to the Spanish. These mixed reactions prevented any cohesive effort to drive the Spanish out again.[42]

Isolated instances of rebellion did occur. Such was the case with the occupation of the government quarters in Santa Fe by the Galisteo Indians in December 1693. Helped by some unfriendly Tewas and Tanos, this group resisted until the Spaniards successfully attacked the walled villa on December 29 and, early the next day, once again established dominion over Santa Fe. The Indian prisoners were enslaved and divided among the colonists.[43]

From January until the middle of March 1695, de Vargas sought to reach a peaceful settlement with the Jémez who had joined the unfriendly Tewa and Tano settlements, as well as with the Apaches and Navahos. During the same period, Apaches and Utes menaced the northern pueblos so much so that the Indians from them often sought refuge. Some of these northern Indians lived on the San Ildefonso Mesa and planted crops elsewhere to escape the Apache threat.[44]

In April 1694, de Vargas mounted a campaign against the Pueblo of Cochití. He was aided in this by the Pueblos of San Felipe, Santa Ana, and Zia, who were called "Indian Allies." These three pueblos also formed an alliance against the Jémez, Taos, Picurís, Tewas and Tanos. Yet another threat to Santa Fe caused the troops to return there in May. De Vargas then learned that people from nearly all the northern pueblos had collected at San Ildefonso Mesa and on May 24, the Spaniards set out for there. The expedition was not at all successful and, short of rations, de Vargas and the troops went on to Taos. Again they encountered resistance. Traveling into the Chama and upper Rio Grande areas in search of provisions, they encountered numerous belligerent pueblos. They did, however, reach the Utes from whom they obtained supplies.[45]

After this reconnaissance, de Vargas returned to Santa Fe and planned serious campaigns against the Indians. He attacked Jémez first, in July 1694, and by August 26 that pueblo had succumbed. They promised to support the Spaniards in the siege on San Ildefonso.

A planned attack against Tesuque did not materialize since that place proved to be empty. Other pueblos, too, appeared abandoned or nearly so. At San Ildefonso Mesa, however, a fierce battle which lasted for three or four hours occurred. Gradually, the Spaniards cut off supplies and access to the mesa and after three days the Indians sought peace. De Vargas had them reaffirm the faith and pledge allegiance to Spain. These formalities followed at all the northern pueblos. Once again they elected officials, who were duly sworn by de Vargas, and they accepted the missionaries he assigned.[46] Officially the reconquest of New Mexico ended on January 10, 1695. At least that was the date de Vargas proclaimed when he wrote the viceroy in Mexico City to ask for supplies and additional colonists to help secure his position in Santa Fe.

But peace was shortlived. To accommodate certain Spaniards, de Vargas moved some of the Indians and issued numerous grants that encroached on traditional Indian lands. This led to the last serious Pueblo uprising, which began on June 4, 1696, when the northern pueblos turned against their new missionaries. After they had killed the friars, they fled from their villages. Many of them were seen on trails leading to Ácoma, and there were reports which placed Ácomas as far north as Taos Pueblo. Tesuque and Pecos pueblos offered soldiers to aid the Spaniards who, at first, remained fortified within Santa Fe. Reports of destruction were confirmed when, on June 7, de Vargas reconnoitered the nearby pueblos and found the missions burned or destroyed.

Within a few days, de Vargas interrogated certain prisoners in order to ascertain the cause of the revolt and who had started it. The first two captives were brought to Santa Fe by the governor of Pecos. One of these was from Jémez and had little to say except that the Zuñis, Hopis, and Apaches were expected to join Jémez in the rebellion. The second was Diego Zenome, cacique of Nambé, and his testimony revealed one possible cause of this latest trouble: he had heard that the Cochitís believed that de Vargas planned to destroy all the young men of the pueblos, leaving only children. Another captive, the governor of Santo Domingo, was questioned and it was his opinion that the pueblos had rebelled because Santo Domingo heard from Cochití that the Spaniards planned to wage a campaign to claim all the pueblos. Although all these men protested their innocence and claimed to know nothing about the deaths of the Spaniards, de Vargas ordered three of them shot, including the cacique of Nambé and the governor of Santo Domingo.[47]

On August 13, 1696, de Vargas began a campaign against Sky City where, it appeared, many of the rebel Indians were staying. With his troops, he went from the Zia area to the Rio Puerco. The next day he advanced another nine leagues, aware that he was being surveilled by sentinels in the surrounding hills. At Paraje de la Laguna de Ácoma, de Vargas captured two Cochití Indians who had been living at Ácoma.[48] They reported that eighty Cochitís had found refuge at Sky City, along with five families from Jémez, and twenty-five persons from Santo Domingo. They also said that many more Tewas, Jémez, Keres (Queres), and Tanos had left Ácoma for Zuñi. The Ácomas had eighty horses and one hundred sheep, they said, and each of the visiting Indians had between two and four horses. A Jémez man had with him a "string of sheep." The Ácomas were also holding two Spanish women and a boy. One of the women had been obtained from the Navaho. At night the animals stayed on the mesa and the people drove them into the valley about sunrise. The men went down about the same time to work the fields where the Cochitís had planted corn, watermelon, gourds, and melons. Not all refugees farmed because the Ácomas made them carry wood and serve them in other ways.[49]

Governor de Vargas learned from these captives of a great council to be held by the Indians at the next full moon for the purpose of planning an attack on Zia and Bernalillo. Such news spurred the Spaniard on to Ácoma Mesa. With Indian allies de Vargas and his men approached Ácoma early in the morning on August 15. In two groups they surrounded the mesa, more or less, awaiting sunrise and the anticipated descent of animals and Indians. Very few men showed and de Vargas decided to attack. The Spaniards rounded up the sheep in the fields below the mesa and the Ácomas coming to recover them were repulsed by gunfire.

The Spaniards succeeded in capturing eight Indians, including the cacique, which appeared to give them an upper hand. De Vargas offered to return the enemy prisoners in return for rebels from other pueblos but received no answer. The following day, he returned the cacique with a message to the Ácomas repeating the demand of the previous day. He further issued an ultimatum that if he received no answer the Spaniards would destroy their fields and take the livestock. By ten o'clock on August 19, 1696, there still was no answer. De Vargas went forth in person to repeat the demands and again received no answer from the mesa. He ordered the fields destroyed. Then the Spaniards returned to Zia. De Vargas later explained that he had decided to leave because the mesa presented a formidable undertaking, and he had feared the arrival of Apache reinforcements, which could have resulted in defeat.[50]

Three more successful campaigns against other pueblos followed during which the military superiority of the Spanish colonists secured New Mexico once and for all. The last engagement took place at Taos, which pueblo surrendered on October 8. Following this, there were a number of minor skirmishes with scattered groups but by November 24, de Vargas reported to the viceroy that all the pueblos had nominally submitted. That is, all the pueblos *except* Pojoaque, Cuyamungué, Santa Clara, Cochití, Santo Domingo, Ácoma, Zuñi, and Hopi. He also mentioned that many of these pueblos were occupied by only a few people because most had retreated to the mountains, to the western pueblos, or to join the Apaches or Navaho.[51] Resistance gradually faded. During 1697, Queres Indians, originally from La Cieneguilla, Santo Domingo, and Cochití, left their refuge at Ácoma and founded Laguna Pueblo. These new settlers, as well as the Ácomas and Zuñis, began to make overtures for peace and on July 6, 1699, Governor Pedro Rodriguez Cubero performed the Act of Obedience on Ácoma Mesa.[52]

THE EIGHTEENTH CENTURY

After the reconquest, Ácoma apparently returned to the old ways. The Ácoma church records relate a steady progression of baptisms, confirmations, marriages, and deaths. Periodically there were civil or religious visitors from Santa Fe or Mexico. Their accounts of Ácoma, often too scant, describe a hard life by modern standards. Increasing drought made farming more difficult and the population dwindled as the result of disease. Navaho raiders struck at the western pueblos and at settlements along the lower Rio Grande. The governor formed a company of soldiers to pursue the raiders and, in his report to the viceroy, also asked for mission supplies since, he said, Ácoma, Laguna, Zuñi, Alameda, and others lacked everything.[53]

In 1705, Fray Juan Alvarez visited Ácoma to inspect the mission. He found the church inventory to be scant and the building being repaired by Father Fray Antonio Miranda, alone. Fray Juan suggested that since there were 760 Christians and a large number of other people at Ácoma, the mission should have two religious to carry on all the necessary work in such an isolated area.[54]

By the 1740s, this situation had changed little. There was still only one friar at the mission. According to Visitador Fray Miguel de Menchero, conversions to the Catholic faith lagged at Ácoma. He noted that the resident missionary there devoted himself to instructing only those who came in friendship. Yet, there were unaccountable numbers who never went near the place.[55] Fray Miguel decided to involve the Ácomas in a project to settle Navahos in villages.

In 1746, he visited Navahos and reported going to a place called "La Cebolleta where . . . he succeeded in calling in the lambs of the Divine Shepherd, bringing to his fold more than five hundred souls." All the children at La Cebolleta were baptized, but baptism was denied the adults, despite their alleged pleadings, until they could be prepared spiritually by missionaries.

32

Governor Tomas Velez Gachupin supported the church effort among these people, whom he referred to as "Navajo Apaches," and, by 1748, missions existed at both La Cebolleta and Encinal. Fray Juan Lezaun was serving at Encinal while Fray Manuel Vermejo was minister to La Cebolleta. The Indians at both places, said Fray Juan, had but recently been converted by a Father Delgado "who labored at catechizing these Indians about five months . . . and finally they repented. The governor ordered the Indians of Laguna to go to Cebolleta to work his [the father's] field, sow them, build a church and pueblo, and then ordered the Ácoma Indians to go to Encinal. These Indians, finding themselves oppressed, created such a schism among the Apaches that the latter resisted their intense conversions and revolted."[56]

Ácomas apparently were called upon to assist in building the mission and houses for Encinal during this period. Early in 1750, the Navahos at Encinal asked Governor Gachupin for permission to move their residences to Cubero, north of Ácoma. The Ácomas protested vigorously because if the request were granted, strangers would be planting corn in the Ácoma *milpas*. Furthermore, Ácomas said they could not depend on the slow-moving and distant presidio at Santa Fe for protection.[57] At once Governor Gachupin informed the church vice-custos that if honoring the petition meant the disagreement and ill-will of the mission at Ácoma over the use of the Ácoma fields, then the program of converting the Navahos surely would suffer.

Governor Gachupin's lieutenant general then proceeded to Encinal to try to settle the differences about possessions, territories, waters, and pastures to the mutual satisfaction of each group. The governor also instructed the vice-custos to make the same visit, enlisting the services of the missionaries at Ácoma and Laguna en route, in order "to fulfill their charges in the reduction and catechizing of these Indians in the wisest and most efficacious manner."

The vice-custos had reached Laguna by April 16, 1750, where a letter from the governor informed him that the Indians of Encinal and Cebolleta had rebelled and driven out their missionaries. The governor asked for a full investigation, and mass meetings of Navahos at Cebolleta and Encinal were attended by Lieutenant General Bernardo

Antonio de Bustamante y Tagle, the vice-custos, and other Spaniards. They showed much "affection" for the Navahos and both the lieutenant general and the vice-custos addressed them, using interpreters. They assured the Indians that if they submitted they would be rewarded by God and would hold the esteem of the friars and the governor. Also, they promised them settlements which would be located "apart in a good place, where they could plant their crops and live at ease," free from molestations. The vice-custos went so far as to offer a new resident friar in case they were displeased with the present one.

Negotiations got nowhere. The Indians insisted that they had been "raised like deer," and did not want to live in settlements like Christians. They said that they had never asked for missionaries and had told Fray Miguel Menchero as much when he visited them in 1746. They gave Father Menchero "some of their children to have water thrown upon them" and told him that the children, as believers, might build a pueblo and want a father. As for themselves (the unbaptized), they assured Fray Miguel Menchero that they would never change. Furthermore, they claimed that their minister complained when Father Menchero did not send all of the hoes and picks he promised to those who brought their children to be baptized.[58] A Christian interpreter at Encinal assured the Spaniards that although his people might be fickle, they were truly opposed to being settled.

During this period when Spanish authorities were attempting to settle nomad Navahos on Ácoma lands, Fray Andres Varo and Fray Manuel de Trigo, mission inspectors, each visited Ácoma. In 1749, Fray Andres remarked that the Ácomas had to go seven leagues from the pueblo to irrigate their fields along the river.° Five years later, Fray Manuel also mentioned that the Ácomas had to leave the mesa and go four leagues north (probably in the Cañada de la Cruz), where they had fields which depended on rain.[59]

Ácoma and Laguna probably started to squabble over rights to the waters of the San Jose River when Laguna was founded. In 1757, Spanish Governor Francisco Antonio Marin del Valle, intervened in the

---

°In those days, the San Jose was often called the Rio Cubero.

dispute and restated a decision made fifteen years before by Governor Gaspar Domingo de Mendoza. At the time the Ácomas occupied Cubero and, for the most part, were dry farming. Governor Marin del Valle ruled again in favor of Ácoma although he recognized that Lagunas should have

> the privilege of irrigating their sowings in case the running water subsides . . . this does not mean that these [Indians] of Ácoma shall cease for this reason to plant wheat, vegetable gardens and make what other use of pasturage and water, which they lack, that they have been accustomed to do, because they do dry farming only. And let them not be prevented by said Lagunas from the ancient use of their pasturage for all kinds of livestock and herds of horses.

This decision also served as one of the first records indicating that Ácomas kept livestock and horses.[60]

A few years later, Ácoma was visited by Bishop Pedro Tamaron y Romeral who was on an inspection trip for the Bishopric of Durango. He found a population of 1,502 with a resident missionary, Fray Pedro Ignacio del Pino, who kept the Indians better instructed in Christian doctrine than at the other pueblo missions. "He has to whip them and he keeps them in order." In the Bishop's view, however, there were two major problems at missions in New Mexico. The language barrier prevented the pueblos from understanding the significant and finer points of Christianity. Secondly, he was concerned about the entire frontier which appeared to be poorly defended against numerous hostile Indians.[61]

Because of its isolated position, Ácoma continued to be of special concern to the Franciscans. One of the finest descriptions of the mission and pueblo dates from 1776, the year Fray Francisco Atanasio Domínguez inspected and inventoried New Mexican missions. The location of the church and pueblo astonished the sophisticated Father Domínguez who explained the "although I have not spent so much time at the beginning of my description of other missions as I have here, it is because there is no comparison with the situation here. . . . This makes what the Indians have built here of adobes with perfection, strength, and grandeur, at the expense of their own backs, worthy of admiration."°[62]

Domínguez noted that the population had dropped by more than half since the census report in 1768, "some from natural causes in epidemics or from other diseases, others at the hands of Apaches so insolent that if this pueblo were not by nature defensible, perhaps nothing would now remain of it."[63] In 1768 there were 1,114 Ácomas but in 1776, Domínguez counted only 530 persons. As a consequence of another smallpox epidemic in 1780–81, Ácoma became a *visita* of the mission of Laguna even though the population had risen again to slightly more than 800. A mission census in 1795 reported a population of 860 for the Pueblo of Ácoma and again blamed Apache raids for depressed conditions.[64]

Fray Francisco reported that the Ácomas farmed for a living. In 1776, despite three years of severe drouth, Ácomas maintained fields on level, usable grounds in the cañadas to the south, east, north, and northwest. Ácomas at Cubero, he said, farmed by irrigating with water from the San Jose River.[65] The men had cows, horses, and numerous sheep which were driven up to the mesa each night for safekeeping.

Ácomas apparently made the finest blankets in New Mexico during this period. In 1779, Governor Juan Bautista de Anza claimed that at Ácoma "there was formerly a great deal of commerce in blankets and chamois, it being the richest of all the kingdom. Nowhere are better blankets made than in Ácoma nor have there been Indians more inclined to hunting deer and antelope."[66]

That this industry continued to be important is indicated by Fray Diego Muñoz' comments accompanying the 1795 census. He reported that the Pueblo Indians had as their principle industry the spinning and weaving of cotton and wool. From these materials they made sarapes for wear, bed blankets, *tilmas* (a mantle, smaller than a sarape), and another article shaped like a scapular which they called "cotones." Laguna, Ácoma, and Zuñi did more spinning and weaving in wool than any of the other pueblos.[67]

°See Appendix 2: FRAY FRANCISCO ATANASIO DOMÍNGUEZ' DESCRIPTION OF ÁCOMA, 1776.

Governor de Anza also wrote there was dry farming around Ácoma Mesa and along the San Jose. The plains extending in all directions from Ácoma abounded in pastures, summer and winter, and there were many canyons and other sheltered places for the herds. The Ácomas at Cubero worked some of the best fields which they irrigated but had to give them up because Gila Apache raiders killed the people and ran off their herds. The people harvested corn, or maize, only in those years when there were rains.[68] Sowing lasted from March until the middle of June; harvesting took place in October. The Ácomas also mined a very good jet from which they made crosses and many other "curiosities." They mixed black, yellow, and red earth to paint their houses and their pottery.[69]

When official expeditions against Apache and Navaho raiders were ordered by Spanish and Mexican authorities, both Ácoma and Laguna Indians participated. Sometimes this was done by a direct request for militia to the Spanish representative who lived at Laguna and bore the title variously of justice, alcalde, or alcalde mayor of Laguna and Ácoma. More often, the local Spanish official simply responded to raids with the men who were available and afterwards reported the results to the governor.

The earliest known record which includes Ácomas and Lagunas as a part of a Spanish expedition against the Navaho dates from 1774. Navaho raids upon Pueblo Indians and Spanish settlements in the jurisdiction of Albuquerque had left six Indians dead, two wounded, and numerous slaughtered or stolen cattle and horses. In reprisal, Governor Pedro Fermin de Mendinueta led two expeditions which resulted in the deaths of twenty-one Navahos and the capture of forty-six men, women, and children. The governor had four dead and thirty-one wounded.[70]

Navaho raids and Spanish reprisals grew in number and intensity over the next hundred years. Either action often ended in tragedy with some persons dead or wounded, others—both Indians and settlers—captured and placed in servitude, and valuable animals lost. For the Ácomas, Cebolleta was frequently headquarters for expeditions against the Navahos. This Spanish settlement and military outpost was located on the northeast shoulder of San Mateo (Mount Taylor) directly in the path of Navaho depredations along the San Jose River and on settlements along the middle Rio Grande from Bernalillo to Socorro. In 1786, Jose Antonio Rengel, Commandant General of the Provincias Internas (including New Mexico), directed Governor de Anza to establish a strong command at Laguna and to supply sufficient arms and munitions to the people for use against the Apaches and Navahos.[71]

By joining with the Spanish expeditions, the lines of battle were drawn between Ácoma and her Apache and Navaho neighbors. Navaho attacks decreased during the 1770s but by 1782, they had driven Lagunas from the Cebolleta area. In June 1785, Ácoma and Laguna sent ninety-four Indians and 120 horses to augment Governor de Anza's large expedition against the Gila Apaches. There were also forty-six friendly Navahos on the expedition which proceeded to Sierra Azul, described as the heart of the Gila Apache country. Here more than forty Apaches were killed and "both parties having recognized each other, [they] burst forth in reciprocal threats to destroy one another." When Navahos continued to combine with pueblos against the Apaches in similar engagements which followed, Governor de Anza began to encourage commerce and communications with them.[72]

Although Spanish authorities reported damages suffered by the Ácomas at the hands of Apaches, very few raids were recorded. In June 1792, Ácomas notified the resident Spanish justice that Gila Apaches had attacked Ácomas guarding horses and made off with the animals. The justice, probably aided by Ácomas, followed the Apaches to Ojo de Gallo where they fought. All but five of the horses—which had been stabbed—were recovered. Soon after, Governor Fernando de la Concha ordered 150 men under Ensign Antonio Guerrero and an equal number under Captain Don Miguel Cañuelas to reconnoiter the Blanca, Oscura, San Nicolás, and Organ mountains to catch and punish the raiders.[73]

Another raid was recorded when the alcalde mayor of the Jurisdiction of Ácoma and Laguna notified Governor de la Concha that fifteen Apaches had killed an Ácoma herder and stolen thirty head of cattle. The alcalde, with forty Ácomas, traveled eight leagues and caught up with the aggressors. Just as they were commencing to attack, another group of Apaches appeared from behind, shouting their "customary war cry." The Ácomas still managed to get the upper hand and the Apaches fled, abandoning the cattle and three of their dead. Governor de la Concha then formed two search parties from the Santa Fe presidial company. The governor led one group of twenty to the Ladron Mountains and dispatched the other party of forty-five, under Ensign Pablo Sandoval, to the point where the altercation had taken place. From there, they were to follow the Apaches' trail until finding the enemy.

The whole affair became overly complicated when the second group of Spaniards followed the trail on to San Mateo rather than to the Ladron Mountains where the first party was waiting. Governor de la Concha next ordered out scouts, a group of Laguna and Navaho Indians under the command of Soldier Gregorio Leiba. The governor waited two days whereupon the scouts returned, reporting that they had fallen unexpectedly upon the Apaches and killed three. Being outnumbered, they had retreated, having to abandon Soldier Leiba in the process. Governor de la Concha reinforced Sandoval's detachment at San Mateo with presidial troops, under the command of First Ensign Antonio Guerrero, and fifty Indians from Taos and the Tewa Pueblos. This group searched all over the mountainous country of San Mateo but found no signs of either the Apaches or the Soldier Leiba.[74]

Early in 1800, the Governor, then don Fernando Chacon courted serious troubles with the Navahos when he granted the land in the Cebolleta area to thirty Albuquerque residents. According to custom, all Indians who might have an expressed interest in such a grant were solicited for objections, but the Navahos raised none. In truth, certain Navahos wanted the site.[75] Navaho hostilities erupted with a series of raids along the rivers Puerco, San Jose, and the Rio Grande in April 1804, during which one boy as well as cattle, horses, and sheep were taken. Later in April, 200 Navahos burst into the plaza at Cebolleta where they wrecked three houses, and carried off twelve cows and fifty heifers. They then proceeded to a sheepherders' ranch where they killed three people, kidnapped a young boy, and stole the sheep.[76]

Governor Chacon's campaign against the Navahos lasted through the summer and involved the use of Laguna and Ácoma auxiliaries.

Navaho attacks concentrated on Cebolleta and, in August 1804, the Alcalde Mayor of Laguna (and Ácoma), Jose Manuel Aragon, petitioned to abandon Cebolleta. The governor responded by stationing a detachment of thirty men there to protect the settlers and ordered the campaign to continue.[77] Reinforcements came from Laguna and Ácoma and attacked along two fronts (west via Zuñi and north into Navaho country, and north and east through Cebolleta or Jémez). The entire effort ended in the battle at Cañon de Chelly on January 17–18, 1805, which brought the Navahos to seek peace. As part of the conditions of peace, Governor Chacon required the Navahos to agree neither to claim nor to settle Cebolleta or to use it as a pretext for a new uprising. Beyond that, the Navahos were to return two captive boys and stolen goods and also to agree not to trespass on the lands around the San Jose and the San Mateo mountains.[78] No record remains to show whether a peace treaty was actually agreed upon. In any event, Navaho depredations against Cebolleta and elsewhere resumed soon afterward.

During a few years of inactivity, some friendly Navahos planted small fields in the Cubero region, at Encinal, San Jose, and Cubero. Some Spanish settlers had petitioned for grants to these farmlands as early as 1768. A grazing permit was issued by Governor Mendinueta to one Baltazar Baca and his two sons who might have been occupying lands in the vicinity during the early 1800s. Their boundaries extended for a castilian league west from Encinal; and were marked by a mesa close to Zuñi road on the east; some white cliffs on the south; and a mountain on the north. Because the grant bordered on a ranch belonging to Ácoma, Governor Medinueta ordered the Bacas not to harm the fields of the Indians. There is no evidence to show they did otherwise.[79] In the spring of 1816, the Navahos abandoned their fields in the area and began raiding once again.

For the next five years this raiding continued. As a result the Spanish conducted an extensive retaliatory campaign lasting from October 3 through October 23, 1821.

During this period the Ácomas furnished auxiliaries for many chases. Sometimes they traveled to the slopes of San Mateo, or to the regions of Jémez or Zuñi; occasionally they performed escort duty; but most often they went to Cebolleta. In 1821, at the insistence of Captain

Bartolome Baca stationed at Cebolleta with the reinforcement troops provided by Governor Facundo Melgares, an expedition against the Navahos was dispatched. Under Juan Armijo, the militia forces traveled from Cebolleta to the Chusca Mountains and Ojo del Oso.[80]

The major part of Armijo's troops rebelled and departed on October 4, shortly after leaving the San Lucas site in the Cebolleta Mountains. "And seeing myself with only the Indians of Isleta, those of Laguna and Ácoma, with their officials and those leaders who had surrendered to me," Armijo reported, "I continued my march under these circumstances, to the place where I had determined to go if those who had surrendered confirmed their good intentions. [I] arrived at the site of Seven Springs to make camp with the people who remained with me." Other defections followed but the determined group which remained engaged and routed the Navahos near Ojo del Oso.[81]

3
Ácoma Under Mexico, 1821-1846

On September 16, 1821, Mexico won her independence from Spain, a political change of some magnitude for America in general, but one so distant that the Ácomas would not be affected by it. Over the years the pueblos' mode of living did not change perceptibly. Mexican authorities accepted the agrarian and peaceful Indians as citizens and with a few changes in the old Spanish laws, their life went on as before. They continued farming, hunting, and grazing their own lands. Likewise, there were no apparent changes in administrative procedures when the Mexicans took control of New Mexico in 1821. If there were changes which affected the Pueblo Indians, other than those of citizenship and national loyalty, they went unrecorded.[1]

Inhabited pueblos under the Mexicans included all those extant today: Jémez (Jémez-Tano), Ácoma (Keres), San Juan (Tewa), Picurís (Tiqua), San Felipe (Keres), Cochití (Keres), Santo Domingo (Keres), Taos (Tiqua), Santa Ana (Keres), Santa Clara (Tewa), Tesuque (Tewa), San Ildefonso (Tewa), Pojoaque (Tewa), Nambé (Tewa), Zia (Keres), Sandía (Tiqua), Isleta (Tiqua), Laguna (Keres), and Zuñi (Zuñi). Mexican authorities thought of the Hopi, or Moqui, pueblos as another province and by 1844, they were considered to be beyond the departmental limits of New Mexico although still within the jurisdiction of the Republic of Mexico.

Population figures (Table 1) provide a general idea of Ácoma strength through the years:

TABLE 1
Ácoma Population, 1540–1798

1540	200 fighting men; 200–500 houses	1744	Families 110
1581	500 houses	1746	Population 750
1582	Population 6000; 600 houses; 500 fighting men	1749	Population 750–960
		1750	Population 960; 247 fighting men; 300 families
1598	Population 3000; 500 families		
1599	Population 1400–2000	1760	Population 1052; 308 families
1626–29	Population 7000; 2000 houses	1768	Population 1114
1630	Population 2000	1776	Population 530; 135 families
1664	Population 600	1779	Families 272
1680	Population 1500	1793	Population 820
1706	Population 1052	1798	Population 757

For a comparison, census figures for Ácoma and the other pueblos from 1790 through 1850 are listed in Table 2.[2]

TABLE 2
Indian Population, 1790–1850

Pueblo	1790	1808	1809	1821	1850
Ácoma	820	797	816	477	350
Cochití	720	672	697	339	254
Isleta	410	471	487	511	751
Jémez	485	285	297	330	365
Laguna	668	1,007	1,022	779	749
Nambé	155	186	133	231	111
Pecos	152	132		54	
Picurís	259	309	313	320	222
Pojoaque	53	83		93	48
Sandía	304	358	364	405	241
San Felipe	532	394	405	310	411
San Ildefonso	240	272	283	527	139
San Juan	260	201	208	232	568
Santa Ana	356	535	550	471	399
Santa Clara	134	213	220	180	279
Santo Domingo	650	701	720	726	666
Taos	518	527	527	753	361
Tesuque	138	156	160	187	119
Zia	275	278	286	196	124
Zuñi	1,935	1,557	1,598	1,597	1,500

Most of the pueblos experienced some decline in population between 1821 and 1850, but San Ildefonso had the most dramatic change. Epidemics were usually the cause for fluctuations of this sort. Jémez showed a slight increase, probably because the pueblo served as a key outpost against the Navahos. Pecos had been abandoned by 1850.[3] The mission report of 1821 listed sizable Indian groups residing in Abiquiu and Belén. On the other hand, the same report showed both a large Spanish population and numerous "people of other classes" residing at Nambé, Pojoaque, Tesuque, Pecos, San Juan, Picurís, Taos, Abiquiu, Santa Clara, Cochití, and San Felipe. A few "people of other classes" lived at Santa Ana and Zia, San Ildefonso, Jémez, and Laguna; and eight at Ácoma, Isleta, Sandía, and Santo Domingo. These people outnumbered the Indians at Pojoaque, San Ildefonso, Tesuque, Pecos, San Juan, Picurís, Taos, Abiquiu, Santa Clara, Cochití, San Felipe, Jémez, Isleta, and Sandía.[4]

Mexican authorities included the pueblos in official territorial divisions for the purposes of census taking, levies, defense, and general civil administration. Ácoma Pueblo was a part of the Alcaldía of Laguna, established some time in the eighteenth century, and appearing on the Bernardo Miera y Pacheco Map of 1779. Official transactions generally took place through the office of the alcalde mayor unless, as happened on occasion, the governor in Santa Fe chose to deal directly with the governor of Ácoma. The alcalde mayor in 1815, don Jose Manuel Aragon, complained that he was "forbidden by superior orders from availing himself of the labor of the Indians for any purpose except by paying them the just value of their labor; neither can he compel them to serve on escorts for private individuals unless required by the government to trust upon subjects connected with the royal service." Aragon's office of alcalde mayor included jurisdiction over the Ácoma and Laguna Pueblos, Cebolleta, and their districts.[5]

On January 4, 1823, the government in Santa Fe divided New Mexico into four districts (*partidos*) in order to apportion a levy voted by the Mexican Congress. The division ran as follows: El Vado de Pecos, Cochití, Jémez, and Alameda were part of the District of Santa Fe; Villa de Albuquerque included Isleta, Tomé, Belen, Socorro, Laguna, and Ácoma; Villa de Santa Cruz de la Cañada had three *ayuntamientos* (municipalities) comprised of San Juan, Abiquiu, and Taos; and El Paso del Río del Norte included Isleta del Sur and San Lorenzo del Real.[6]

On May 22, 1837, the system was changed to comply with the Mexican Constitution of 1836 which had created the Department of New Mexico (as part of the departmental system being established throughout the Republic). On the same day, the New Mexican Departmental Assembly reorganized the entire area into two districts. The First District included the alcaldías of El Vado, Santa Fe, San Ildefonso, Cañada, Abiquiu, Ojo Caliente, San Juan, Chama, Trampas, and Taos. Within the Second District, the Assembly placed the alcaldías of Cochití, Jémez, Sandía, Albuquerque, Isleta, Tomé, Valencia, Belén, Sabinal, Socorro, and Laguna, the last including the pueblos of Ácoma and Zuñi. The districts were further subdivided, but in practice the incipient bureaucracy was not rigid. Alcaldes supervised civil and military matters within their respective areas, assisted by a justice of the peace who was responsible for a specific settlement or pueblo. As in the Mexican villages, each pueblo had a justice who was often a member of the pueblo. All of the officials were appointees of the governors in Santa Fe, however, and by 1844, there were indications of gross incompetence and corruption among these local officials.[7]

Civil authorities made no effort to educate the Pueblo Indians prior to 1844 since education, as well as religion, continued to be a function of the Church. In 1821, there was a priest resident in each of the pueblos with the exception of Ácoma, Santa Ana, and Zia. These were visited periodically, while the isolated Pueblo of Zuñi was neglected completely by 1844.[8]

Mail was delivered to some pueblos. In 1833, the administrator of mails in Chihuahua listed mail received in the pueblos of Sandía, San Felipe, and Santo Domingo. These along with Mexican villages and ranches along the Rio Grande to Santa Fe received mails fortnightly, more or less. The two main post offices held mails for outlying settlements, Santa Fe for the northern area and Tomé for all other settlements south of Alameda and Albuquerque. Ácoma and Laguna received mails through Tomé.[9]

Governor Mariano Martinez, an aging general from Chihuahua

who replaced Governor Manuel Armijo for a year in 1844–45, found the department badly organized. No one knew exactly which communities lay within the confines of the department or what the divisions were supposed to be. With little or no regular communication, many settlements were vulnerable to Indian depredations, foreign invasion, and all manner of crimes. Law and order could not be maintained, Martinez believed, without revamping the entire department. Accordingly, on June 17, 1844, he issued the following decree to be voted on by the departmental assembly:

Art. 1. The Department shall be divided into three Districts called Central, North, and Southwest.

Art. 2. Central District is divided into three parts called Santa Fe, Santa Ana, and San Miguel del Vado, with the Capital at Santa Fe.

Art. 3. Santa Fe shall be composed of Santa Fe, Nambé, Pojoaque, San Ildefonso, Tesuque, Cuyamungué, Río de Tesuque, Cienega, Cieneguilla, Agua Fría, Galisteo, Real del Oro, and Tuerto; the capital is Santa Fe and the population 12,500.

Art. 4. The second division is made up of Mojada, Cochití, Peña Blanca, Chile, Santo Domingo, Cubero, San Felipe, Jémez, Zia, Santa Ana, Angostura, and Algodones. Population is 12,500 inhabitants and the chief city is Algodones.

Art. 5. The third division is composed of Pecos, Gusano, Río de la Baca, Mulas, Entrañosa, San José, San Miguel del Vado, Pueblo, Puertecito, Cuesta, Cerrito, Antón Chico, Tecolote, Vegas, and Sapello; the head will be San Miguel and the population is 18,800 inhabitants.

Art. 6. District of the North is divided into two parts called Río Arriba and Taos, and the capital is at Los Luceros.

Art. 7. The first includes Santa Cruz de la Cañada, Chimayo, Quemada, Truchas, Santa Clara, Vega Chama, Cuchillo, Abiquíu, Rito Colorado, Ojo Caliente, Ranchitos, Chamita,

San Juan, Río Arriba, Joya, and Embudo. The chief center is Los Luceros and the population is 15,500 inhabitants.

Art. 8. The second division includes Taos, San Fernando, San Francisco, Arroyo Seco, Desmontes, Cieneguilla, Picurís, Santa Bárbara, Frananos, Chamizal, Llano, Peñasco, Mora, Huérfano, and Zimarrón. The center of the division is San Fernando, and the population is 30,600.

Art. 9. The Southwest District is divided into two parts: Valencia and Bernalillo.

Art. 10. The first district includes Valencia, San Hernando, Tomé, Jémez, Casa Colorada, Sebilleta, Sabino, Párida, Ladrones, Socorro, Lémitar, Polvaderos, Sábinal, Belen, Lunas, Lentes, Zuñi, Ácoma, Laguna, Rito Sebolleta; the head of the division is Valencia and the population is 20,000.

Art. 11. The second division includes Ysleta, Padilla, Pajarito, Ranchos de Atrisco, Placer, Albuquerque, Alameda, Corrales, Sandía, and Bernalillo. The population is 8,204, and the whole district has 28,204.

This constituted the major reorganization of the Department of New Mexico during the entire Mexican Period.[10]

In pursuit of reorganization and reform, Governor Martinez pushed the assembly to revise the *"Juzgados"* [judicial districts] so as to align them with the new departmental scheme. Many villages had no justice of the peace and justices were known to travel four days when called upon. The assembly acted to create new district and ward justices (*jueces de barrio*), by two decrees dated July 5 and October 17, 1844. Pueblos, including Ácoma, received ward justices by the appointment of one of their tribal members. During crowded events of that year, the governor also took time to order the destruction of the stocks used for punishment which he had noticed in some of the plazas. He declared that such punishment opposed the Mexican system of government.[11]

Governor Martinez became a protector of the Indian way of life and often called upon the pueblos to support civic projects. He invited a number of pueblos to dance at the celebrations of Mexican Independence Day, September 16, 1844, but Ácoma was too far from the capital to participate.[12] On one occasion, Justice J. Miguel Montoya complained to the governor about some Indians from Santo Domingo who were conducting scandalous pagan dances in public. Furthermore, the Justice, upon checking around, said he had found a "machine with frightful figures." Governor Martinez advised him at once that he should "respect the customs of the pueblos as they are observed, without making an issue of these dances which they frequently hold, achieving a better end through the example and good morality which they introduce into civilization and which is to be desired." Such a policy not only indicated the extent to which Martinez would protect the Indians' way of life, but also his deep respect for that way of life.[13]

Governor Martinez' concerns included the problem of formalized education in the pueblos and involved Ácoma more indirectly than directly. In 1844, Mexican authorities in Santa Fe considered Zuñi Pueblo an outpost beyond which the territory was under control of nomadic Apaches and Navahos. Yet on April 6, acting Governor Mariano Chavez ordered Felipe Ortiz, Vicar of Santa Fe, and Mauricio Arce, a school teacher, to proceed to Zuñi where they were to establish a primary school, and an office of the justice of the peace. The Vicar was to arrange for a visitation by a religious at least once a month. Mauricio Arce was to serve both as teacher and justice. The governor pointed out that the numerous inhabitants at Zuñi were neglected and because they had no local officials, "in a state of barbarism . . . lacking the obedience they owe the government."[14] Pueblo Indians furnished men, animals, and supplies along the way. On April 25, the expedition set out. From Santa Fe an escort of twenty-five men accompanied the Vicar and Arce to Jémez; there the escort was replaced by twenty-five men from the pueblo (and horses); and at Laguna, twenty-five others replaced those from Jémez.[15] What occurred while at Zuñi was apparently acceptable and positive for Mauricio Arce left Santa Fe on or about September 23 as teacher for a primary school, and as justice at Zuñi. The expedition had ten men and a corporal for escort.[16]

No one knew the northernmost Mexican frontier better than

Manuel Armijo, governor of New Mexico (on and off) from 1827 to 1846. Born in Albuquerque, he was generally popular, related to, or otherwise well-known to New Mexicans. Armijo handled Indian problems with direct action, conducting at least three extensive expeditions against them. During the last decade under Mexico, the harassments by warring Navahos were only surpassed by the raids of the Comanches which reached into Mexico as far south as Durango and Zacatecas. In 1841, Governor Armijo captured and imprisoned the members of the Texas-Santa Fe Expedition—ostensibly composed of traders, but generally acknowledged as having had more expansionistic than economic motives. Because Texas was known to covet the New Mexico territory, Armijo was made the highest national hero of all Mexico for having stopped this "invasion."

Navaho raiders continued to funnel through Cebolleta into the river bottomlands south of Albuquerque. In 1822 such raids caused Mexican troops to muster in force at Cebolleta for a Navaho campaign, which event prompted the Navahos to open negotiations for peace. Mexican officials met with the Navahos at Laguna Pueblo and Paguate, with Pueblo Indians gathered around as witnesses. The Navahos agreed to exchange captives and were persuaded to agree not to steal again, but nothing more.[17] The "peace" was temporary.

During June, July, and August 1823, a campaign against Navahos was led by Governor Jose Antonio Vizcarra. Hopes ran high that the results would "create harmony in the unhappy Province," but the raids continued to intensify in the area over the next twenty years. Various pueblos also suffered from these raids which covered the region from Cochití south to Isleta and from Santa Ana up the Jémez River to Jémez Pueblo. By 1834, the alcalde at Jémez reported that the Pueblos of Jémez, Santa Ana, and Zia were in very poor and demoralized conditions because of the raids.[18]

In 1835, Miguel Garcia, Navaho interpreter at Jémez, reported to the commandant general that the "rich Navahos have settled their rancherias in the Silver and Datil mountains for the year." As a postscript, he added that on January 13, a large party of Navahos had approached Jémez and on the following day had taken fifty animals. Eighteen of the animals were retrieved by the alcalde of Jémez and one

Navaho was killed. In one of the most devastating raids Navahos fell upon the new settlement of Lemitar: on June 7, 1835, over 2,000 sheep, and a herder, were taken. Toward evening that same day around 200 Navahos hit Socorro "taking with them horses, cattle, goats, and sheep."[19]

No fewer than twelve major retaliatory expeditions were led by the Mexicans against the Navahos. Generally the defense of a community was left to local volunteers led by commissioned members of the militia. Some of the pueblos, including Ácoma and Laguna, furnished Mexican authorities with militia lists showing the names of the volunteers, and the horses and arms, which they could furnish. Ácoma produced one such list on August 4, 1828, and another on February 11, 1838.° Navaho chases led by the alcalde or the local militia leader were doubtless more lucrative than the formal expeditions. For example, during the expedition of February-March 1835, New Mexicans killed thirty-five warriors, captured four Indians of both sexes, fourteen horses, 6,604 sheep, and 109 cattle. The expedition of December 1836, led by Governor Albino Perez, netted many thousands of sheep and other booty. Probably the largest number of sheep was recovered —over 10,000—during the expedition lasting from October 12 to December 13, 1839. In December 1843, the Mexicans reported capturing 13,000 more sheep.[20] The Ácomas may have shared in the grandest catch of all when the inspector of militia of the Third District reported taking 16,000 sheep "which they [Navahos] had stolen." On the other hand there is the possibility that the Ácomas joined in the action only rarely, and then, reluctantly. In September 1837, the justice at Albuquerque reported to the governor that the alcalde at Cebolleta was having difficulty getting support from Ácoma and Lagunas. "It is believed," the alcalde even wrote, "that these pueblos are in collusion with the Navahos; at least your Excellency well knows that with Ácoma and Zuñi there is no doubt."

Militia response had to be quick to be most effective. In 1839 Governor Armijo had yet another service in mind for the Indians. He ordered Captain Jose Francisco Chavez y Baca of the Second District

---

°Appendix 3: ÁCOMA MILITIA MUSTER ROLLS, 1838.

to "reorganize a company composed of the useful men of the pueblos of Ysleta, Laguna, and Ácoma. These troops will be used to open vacant plazas and to reoccupy any useless lands there might be." The militia survey from February 1838, probably was most helpful to the captain.[21]

Raiding further intensified from 1840 through 1846 and resulted in a series of retaliatory expeditions by the Mexicans. There is no direct evidence of Ácomas participation, but many reports mentioned Laguna involvement. Governor Armijo made extensive preparations for a large campaign in 1846, promising volunteers the booty and spoils of war taken from the Navahos as payment for services rendered. He told commanders of the volunteers: "The war with the Navahos is slowly consuming the department, reducing to very obvious misery the district of the Southwest." The need for action was inescapable. On July 8, 1846, he placed Julian Perea in command of the volunteers from Bernalillo, Corrales, Alameda, Ranchos, and Albuquerque; Colonel Ramon Luna commanded those from Padilla, Valencia, Tomé, and Laguna [Ácoma]; and Colonel Jose Chavez was in charge of the volunteers from Belen, Sabinal, and Socorro. This concerted effort to protect the settlements, from Bernalillo to Socorro, and westward to Laguna, was interrupted by the arrival of General Stephen Watts Kearny and United States troops who occupied Santa Fe on August 18. Governor Armijo fled southward to his home in Albuquerque, and ultimately to Chihuahua.[22]

4

The Old Ways Disappear

"Acoma!" He stopped his mule.

The Bishop, following with his eye the straight, pointing Indian hand, saw, far away, two great mesas. They were almost square in shape, and at this distance seemed close together, though they were really some miles apart.

"The far one"—his guide still pointed.

The Bishop's eyes were not so sharp as Jacinto's, but now, looking down upon the top of the farther mesa from the high land on which they halted, he saw a flat white outline on the grey surface—a white square made up of squares. That, his guide said, was the Pueblo of Acoma.

(Archbishop Lamy's arrival at Ácoma in
Death Comes for the Archbishop by Willa Cather)

THE UNITED STATES SURVEYOR'S REPORT

The nineteenth century brought a new breed of men to Ácoma: United States Indian Agent, trader, soldier, and homesteader. New arrivals led to specific changes in the pueblo's preferred way of life. Still, in 1846, their culture seemed so unspoiled that Lieutenant James William Abert of the United States Army Corps of Topographical Engineers, was of the opinion that there was little or no evidence of Spanish influence. As an example he noted that only one or two Ácomas could speak the language.[1]

United States military reconnaissance of the country began as soon as General Kearny had settled affairs in Santa Fe and started toward

California. Exploration of the Arkansas and Gila rivers, as well as the Rio Grande, and their tributaries was delegated to Lieutenant Colonel William Hensley Emory. His subordinate, Lieutenant Abert was leading a detachment up the Puerco and San Jose rivers when he heard that the area was being harassed by a band of fifty Navahos whose war trail led through the Puerco Valley from Cebolleta. The inhabitants warned them to travel with caution and to do without campfires at night.

Lieutenant Abert reported that they reached the valley leading to Ácoma on October 21, 1846, where they saw many flocks of sheep attended by Indians and their watchful dogs. Abert tried to buy some sheep, but was unsuccessful until a chief with eight to ten companions rode up and helped make the purchase. To Lieutenant Abert the chief appeared to be a wealthy man; his party was armed with bows and arrows and guns and they were traveling to Santa Fe. "They reminded me very much of the Comanches, except that these Indians wear long woollen stockings, of their own manufacture."

A little further on they came to Ácoma Mesa and were amazed at the position of the village, the steep stairways, and the large church. As they approached, they met and passed many Ácomas who drove burros loaded with peaches. When they entered some of the houses, the Ácomas greeted them with "great gladness," and served a wafer-thin *guayave*° made of a corn mixture baked on a special stove until crisp and easily crumbled. They brought out the *guayave*, which bore a striking resemblance to hornets' nests, on nearly flat circular baskets.

To enter a house, the visitor climbed a ladder to the second story. The next floor had the same arrangement, but to reach the roof, the partition walls separating each family extended to form steps. "Each family occupies those rooms that are situated vertically over each other; the lowest story is used as a store-room, in which they put their corn, pumpkins, melons, and other eatables. The fronts of the houses are covered with festoons of bright red peppers, and strings of pumpkins and mushmelons [*sic*] that have been cut into ropes and twisted into branches to dry for winter use." Lieutenant Abert found

---

°Similar to the Hopi piki bread.

the roof tops covered with peaches cut in half and spread to dry in the sun. In the streets below, Ácomas were unloading burros and dividing quantities of large clingstone peaches so as to carry them up the ladders. The soldiers were invited to help themselves to peaches. Indeed, the Ácomas seemed to be a quiet people, happy, generous, and well provided with all the "necessaries and luxuries that New Mexico affords." In appearance, "They generally wear the Navajoe blanket, marked with broad stripes alternately black and white.° Their pantaloons are very wide and bag like, but are confined at the knee by long woollen stockings, and sometimes buckskin leggins and moccasins. The women stuff their leggins with wool, which makes their ankles look like the legs of an elephant."[2]

That night the troops made camp at a spring about three quarters of a mile from the mesa. On reaching the valley they saw large flocks of sheep, herds of cattle, and droves of horses. There the Ácomas had dug holes which yielded a constant source of water. In the evening, "at a quarter past ten o'clock, a meteor of dazzling splendor dashed across the sky; its path was perpendicular to the horizon, and passed through the head of the constellation Draco; the brightness was such as to eclipse the light of the candle by which I was writing; five minutes afterwards I heard a report like that of a distant cannon."[3]

No other description left by other early Anglo visitors is as interesting. In 1849, another lieutenant of the Corps of Topographical Engineers marched east through the San Jose Valley. After copying inscriptions from rubbings made at El Morro (Inscription Rock), Lieutenant James H. Simpson and his party marched 28.93 miles and stopped within sight of Old Laguna Pueblo. From somewhere in the vicinity of modern Acomita and McCarty's the troops passed through a valley that was:

> gradually unfolding itself more uninterruptedly, and continuing so down to Laguna, a distance of fourteen miles, within two miles of which we are encamped. All along the valley, for this distance, the land is cultivated in corn and mellons, the

---

° Ácomas used a vertical loom and excelled at weaving long before the Navaho began to take up the craft. The interesting thing here is Lieutenant Abert's casual reference which indicates that in this point of time the Navaho blanket was a recognizable commodity.

luxurience of their growth attesting to the good quality of the
soil.

Lieutenant Simpson found a number of "circular places" where wheat
was threshed by trodding horses. The Indians along the way were
friendly and offered muskmelons to the men. "I notice that to preserve
them for winter, they peel them, take out the seeds, and hang them in
the sun to dry." The party also encountered a flock of 2,000 sheep.[4]
Pueblo farming along the San Jose River was also described by
Lieutenant A. W. Whipple, yet another member of the Corps of
Topographical Engineers, whose mission in 1853 was to find the best
railroad route between the Mississippi and the Pacific Ocean. Most of
the valley from Laguna Pueblo west was cultivated by Pueblo Indians.
"The stream, as we ascended, bore a greater volume of water, forming
lagunas, and fertilizing some very broad bottoms."[5]

ENCOUNTERS WITH UNITED STATES LAW

The peaceful overview presented by these visitors was belied by
other forces working against the pueblos during the lawless years after
1846. Sometime between that year and 1850, one Victor de la O, a
Vicente Abilucia, or Jose Ramon Sanchez, or all three together,
approached the Ácomas with what they claimed were original grant
papers. Eventually, Ácoma agreed to pay $600 or give an equitable
amount of property in exchange for the papers, but then the attorneys
representing the pueblo interests charged de la O with extortion before
the first Territorial Supreme Court Chief Justice in New Mexico, Kirby
Benedict.
There were few facts of the case that anyone could be certain of,
including the judge. Several years were spent gathering evidence and
holding hearings, during which the court uncovered a scandalous traffic
in grant titles which appeared to implicate high officials of the former
Mexican regime, including Governor Armijo. As for de la O and the
other accomplices, their testimony demonstrated many layers of artful
deception. De la O had come to Santa Fe from Chihuahua in 1833, he

said, followed in 1836 by his wife who brought the family papers, including the Ácoma grant. He claimed that the family had protected the papers since the grants were made. By contrast, the pueblo copies of the original grant were lost, although the Indians claimed another copy was deposited with the government archives in Santa Fe.

The court ordered de la O to furnish his papers for exhibits and the court recorder made faithful copies. Apparently these survived and became the documents used to patent the Ácoma grant. The first exhibit or document was the one that de la O had contracted to sell to the Ácomas. It was an abbreviated version of the second more involved paper; both purported to describe the Ácoma boundaries. The first tells briefly about the Indian Ojeda and his willingness to outline grant boundaries for the pueblos of New Mexico. Although both documents refer to Ácoma-Laguna squabbles over water, the second provides Ácoma Pueblo with rights to all the water she needs from the San Jose River. Both were signed by Governor Cruzate and Bartolome Ojeda (he of the remarkable memory for grant boundaries). The first carried the date September 28, 1689; the other, September 20 of the same year.[6]

Justice Benedict restored the documents to Ácoma with no kind words for de la O. In his opinion, de la O's act came at a time when the Indians were defenseless and liable to fall victim to extortion. With certain astuteness, Benedict warned that "Every man's titles and all documents would become prey to insecurity. The fraudulent man would riot in this species of plunder, and the extortionist revel in his iniquity."[7]

During this period the Indian Agent for the United States Territory of New Mexico was the first to describe openly the encroachments being made upon Indian farmlands. Matters were growing worse between the pueblos and Mexicans. In 1849, writing the Commissioner of Indian Affairs in Washington from Santa Fe, the agent reported that Mexican officials intentionally kept Ácoma and Laguna embroiled over boundaries. In this way, the officials were able to adjudicate the boundaries to their liking and to continue collecting fees and making "rank impositions." Hardly a day went by without complaints from Indians about the Mexican aggression.[8] Again in 1851, the same agent wrote:[9]

56

> The Pueblo Indians have caused me much anxiety during the present month. Laguna and Ácoma have had angry disputations, and the shedding of blood has been prevented so far, by my sending an Agent to their Pueblos to compromise their respective claims to certain lands. They have agreed to abide his award. There is not a Pueblo within one hundred miles of this superintendency that has not sent me delegations, during the month, to make known their grievances caused by encroachments upon their landed property around their Pueblos. This topic of great danger to the quiet of the Territory has been so frequently presented for the consideration of the Department, I deem it unnecessary to enlarge upon it.

The United States Indian Agent in Santa Fe also had to cope with the daily problems of the pueblos which went beyond encroachments. The Pueblos were unique when compared with other United States Indians, in that they were settled on their own lands, and living peaceably. In 1850, the agent recommended that each group should have their own subagents. Better communication services were necessary for their protection and general administration. They needed farming tools and blacksmiths. Better arrangements which would permit trade with other peoples were needed. And even though some United States officials recommended it, the agent argued that the Pueblos should not be removed and concentrated on reservations. Rather, a commission should be established which would determine and mark boundaries and settle all suits growing out of disputes with Mexicans over Indian lands. Finally, public schools were not considered suitable because the Pueblos had a low opinion about them, something apparently derived from the feelings of the Catholic priests who had traditionally taught the Indians in their missions.[10]

From the beginning, then, Indian agents supported the Pueblo cause in theory. But action did not always come fast enough. The Treaty of Guadalupe Hidalgo on February 2, 1848, brought New Mexico under United States jurisdiction. It assured New Mexicans of the validity of land ownership stemming from their Spanish and Mexican land grants, as well as that of any properties acquired during the two previous regimes.

As for Ácoma, and all Indians in New Mexico, however, a general assembly had met in Santa Fe during December 1847, just prior to the Treaty of Guadalupe Hidalgo. Ten acts had been passed, including a proviso incorporating the Pueblos as legal entities. This meant that the Pueblos could sue or be sued and was the reason that they were vulnerable to speculators in general and Victor de la O in particular.

Indians were considered citizens and remained citizens under the provisions of the Treaty of Guadalupe Hidalgo; an act organic to the treaty also maintained the Pueblos' incorporated status. These acts of incorporation ignored a precedent established by the Indian Intercourse Act of June 30, 1834. In this Act, by definition, Pueblo Indians would have been considered as tribes, and as such, wards of the government (as they had been under Spain, and more or less, under Mexico), and entitled to the full protection of federal courts. Under these circumstances, any unauthorized settlement upon tribal lands would have constituted a federal offense.

As a consequence of this 1847 incorporation, Indian agents were helpless to protect Indian lands against either squatters or encroachments. Despite their protests on behalf of the defenseless Pueblos, the U. S. Court of the First Judicial District ruled that these Indians were still citizens and as such their only recourse was through the courts. In 1876 the United States Supreme Court upheld this position. That decision meant that since Pueblo Indians had not been under the jurisdiction of the United States in 1834, they were not encompassed by the meaning of the Indian Intercourse Act. A series of decisions by the Supreme Court of the Territory of New Mexico allowed the Indians to dispose of their lands, inasmuch as there were no federal statutes prohibiting non-Indian settlement. The protection of the Act of 1834, however, was denied the Pueblos until after New Mexico became a state at which time the Supreme Court reversed itself. In 1913, it ruled that Pueblos were entitled to the same protection given to other Indian tribes in the United States.[11]

ÁCOMA STRUGGLES TO PROVE HER CLAIM

Paralleling the development of the official position taken by the United States in the treatment of the Pueblos was the long struggle by the Ácomas to confirm and patent their Spanish grant. As early as 1850 Indian agents recognized this as a serious problem for Ácoma, but Congress took only an initial step when the Act of 1854 established the Office of the Surveyor General for the Territory. He was to supervise and administer the provisions of the Treaty of Guadalupe Hidalgo in regard to land ownership as well as other matters. Paragraph eight of the Act further provided that he investigate and make recommendations with a view to confirming all bonafide land claims within the territory. One of his first efforts, as soon as all pertinent land records had been recovered from Spanish and Mexican archives, was to invite petitioners to bring any proof of their land ownership to his office. When the papers were found to be acceptable, boundaries established, arrangements for surveys would follow.

The Ácomas produced one Spanish document, a copy of the grant dated 1689, which was probably a copy of the exhibit then in Justice Kirby Benedict's court.* In 1856, when the Indian agent again urged the survey of Pueblo grants, Ácoma's was surveyed and the necessary paperwork on the part of the Surveyor General resulted in Congress confirming both grant and survey on December 22, 1858. The General Land Office was yet to issue the patent, the instrument by which the United States relinquished all rights and claims within the Ácoma grant area.[12]

Among the problems inherited by the United States was the old

---

*Twitchell believed there were no grants made prior to the so-called Cruzate grants to the Pueblo Indians in 1689. However, David Merriwether, Governor and Superintendent of Indian Affairs in 1854, reported to the Commissioner of Indian Affairs about his observations probably made at the time when the Surveyor General borrowed land papers from the official archives:

> The Pueblo or partially civilized Indians are a very interesting portion of the Indian population of this Territory, and richly deserve the fostering hand of government. They hold their lands under special grants from the governments of Spain and Mexico, many of which are of very ancient dates—one that I examined being dated in 1661—and they usually cover one league, or nine square miles.

See, David Merriwether to Commissioner of Indian Affairs, in *Annual Report of the Commissioner, 1854* (Washington: Printed by A. O. P. Nicholson, 1855), p. 173.

dispute between Ácoma and Laguna involving use of lands and waters along the San Jose River. The argument flared again in 1856, doubtless as a result of the Ácoma survey then in progress. Some Santa Fe officials were inclined to allow the Indians to settle their differences in the courts, the same as other "ordinary citizens" of the United States. Greatly sympathetic to the Indians, acting Governor William Watts Hart Davis, believed "their recourse to our courts of law appears to have inflamed the mind of these people against each other, to a higher degree than before." He described Ácoma as the aggressor because her concern about important irrigable lands had forced her to take possession of a portion of the planting ground supposedly belonging to Laguna and to threaten to hold the land by force.[13] "The Act of [Territorial] Assembly, giving these Indians the right to sue and be sued, is most mischievous in the tendency, and is working great wrong to this simple minded people. In my message to the Legislative Assembly which met the third of last December, I urged the repeal of this law strongly upon the attention of the two Houses, but they refused to take any action in the matter."[14]

In 1857, Ácoma brought suit against Laguna to settle the long-standing dispute over a mutual boundary. During this action, the territorial governor sided with Laguna going so far as to indicate that Laguna would be justified in resorting to force if Ácoma won the case. The courts decided in favor of the boundary lines described by Ácoma. Jose Lovato, Governor of Ácoma, claimed that the inhabitants of the pueblo were the descendents of the Pueblo of Tsiama [modern day Seama] and as such successors to and inheritors of all and singular rights to property which formerly had belonged to that ancient pueblo.[15] All parties hoped that the compromise line reached by agreement between the two pueblos would end further argument. However, subsequent surveys, including that of 1856, overlooked the compromise effort and the matter would continue to cost Ácoma and Laguna time and money in the years that followed.°

The all-important patent rights to the confirmation of the Ácoma grant were still twenty years away, more than enough time for other

---

°Appendix 4: BOUNDARY AGREEMENT BETWEEN ÁCOMA AND LAGUNA, 1857.

encroachments to modify severely the line that Ácoma understood to constitute her boundaries on the north and west. An official census for 1870 listed numerous non-Indians settlers near the site of old Fort Wingate at Ojo del Gallo, also known as Ojo Caliente. Apparently, some of the area was homesteaded as early as 1857, before the army had even constructed the Fort. Actual construction of the fort took place in 1862, at which time the land around the spring was also set aside for a military reserve. In 1868, the year of the historic Navaho roundup, the army moved Fort Wingate about fifty miles north and west to its current location. The abandoned area, however, remained a reserve occupied by a number of ex-soldiers and camp followers who stayed on as squatters. They made improvements and irrigated farmlands with the abundant spring water. Their refusal to move upon notice brought a detachment of soldiers to conduct them off the reserve. One of them, a Spanish-American, was killed when he attempted to decapitate the officer in charge. The others left without further resistance.

The army effort to keep the reserve free of squatters had nothing to do with the fact that it was within the Spanish grant to Ácoma and was perpetually used by the Indians. Within a year of the squatters' incident, the territorial government opened the area for settlement, and all who had been expelled returned along with others. When they learned that the springs were property of the Ácomas and that the area was about to be surveyed for patent rights, they met and "decided to bribe the officers and principal men of the tribe to change the boundary calls (surveyor's landmarks) by representing to the surveyor another insignificant spring about 10 miles to the east." In addition to money, the settlers proposed to get for Ácoma a part of the Laguna lands which were not surveyed as yet. The Ácomas, lured into a trap, gave testimony to the surveyor, misguiding him as agreed. In doing so Ácoma lost about one third of the original grant.[16]

Further attempts to get the survey for the Ácoma grant were classic examples of how the pueblo suffered at the hands of encroachers of all kinds because of having been denied recourse to federal protection. In August 1876, Benjamin M. Thomas, then Indian Agent in Santa Fe, urged Walter E. Marmon (government teacher at Laguna) and the Reverend John Menaul (Presbyterian missionary) at Laguna

Pueblo to supervise quietly the survey about to be made at Ácoma.[17] Apparently when the time arrived to place Ácomas in possession of the Laguna lands (according to Thomas' *Annual Report for 1877*), a "Mexican" justice of the peace supervised the proceedings. There was an armed battle among the pueblo men which forced the Ácomas back. It is not clear from the reports which land was involved here but Thomas received word of the conflict and upon arriving at the scene arrested a number of Ácoma's principal officers. While on the way to Santa Fe the story of the fraud unfolded and they returned to Ácoma. At a meeting of officers from both pueblos, Agent Thomas informed the Ácomas that the land they wanted was Laguna's by right of an earlier purchase, that of Santa Ana in 1875. However, he allowed a second survey in March 1877 to follow the perjured landmarks on the west side and again excluded valuable lands especially around El Gallo.[18]

Realizing full well that the enmity between the pueblos, already heightened as a result of the first survey, might flare up, Agent Thomas sent to both Forts Union and Wingate for ammunition. It was to be issued to the Lagunas. At the same time, Thomas urged the Lagunas to plant their fields up to the disputed boundary line.[19] He warned Ácoma that she would be compelled to respect the survey then in progress, and the east boundary, saying to the governor of Ácoma, "you have only yourselves to blame for the great trouble and uncertainty which has followed; for by your lies told either at the time of the survey, or at the investigation at San Rafael in December last, you have made a new survey necessary."[20]

Agent Thomas continued to plant the seeds of ill will by befriending the Lagunas, and Ácoma was left with an incorrect survey of her grant. While the surveyor proceeded, Thomas wrote Walter Marmon:[21]

> I have written Dr. Menaul pretty fully in regard to the Ácoma and Laguna business and that letter is intended as much for you as for him. Until the Ácomas can show a title to the land in Cañon de Cruzate, I want the Indians of Laguna to plant the land and I will undertake to protect them in it.
>
> Ponder what I say about the two boundary lines and the

1 Ácoma ca. 1900 by William H. Jackson. *Photograph courtesy Library, State Historical Society of Colorado.*

2   Ácoma No. 1. *by James Abert (1846).*

3   Ácoma No. 2. *by James Abert (1846).*

4 Ácoma Mesa and Pueblo.
*Photograph courtesy New
Mexico Department of De-
velopment.*

5 Foot Trail ca. 1899 by William
H. Jackson. *Photograph courtesy
Library, State Historical Society of
Colorado.*

6   Ácoma No. 3. *by James Abert (1846).*

7 Horse Trail, 1900, by William H. Jackson. *Photograph courtesy Library, State Historical Society of Colorado.*

8 Horse Trail, 1899, by William H. Jackson. *Photograph courtesy Library, State Historical Society of Colorado.*

9 Ácoma Pueblo ca. 1899 by William H. Jackson. *Photograph courtesy Library, State Historical Society of Colorado.*

10 Interior of Ácoma home by William H. Jackson. *Photograph courtesy Library, State Historical Society of Colorado.*

11   Ácoma Indians ca. 1899 by William H. Jackson. *Photograph courtesy Library, State Historical Society of Colorado.*

12   Father and daughter ca. 1899 by William H. Jackson. *Photograph courtesy Library, State Historical Society of Colorado.*

13 Street view with burros by William H. Jackson. *Photograph courtesy Library, State Historical Society of Colorado.*

14 Ácoma horses by William H. Jackson. *Photograph courtesy Library, State Historical Society of Colorado.*

15　Aerial view of Kowina ruins, home to Ácoma ancestral clans. *Photograph courtesy Lee Marmon.*

16　Aerial view of Kowina purchase area. *Photograph from Arthur Bibo Collection, Pueblo of Ácoma Archives.*

17   Ácoma Mesa and Pueblo by William H. Jackson. *Photograph courtesy Library, State Historical Society of Colorado.*

18   Miss Ethel E. Gregg, schoolteacher at McCarty's, 1907. *Photograph courtesy Museum of the American Indian, Heye Foundation.*

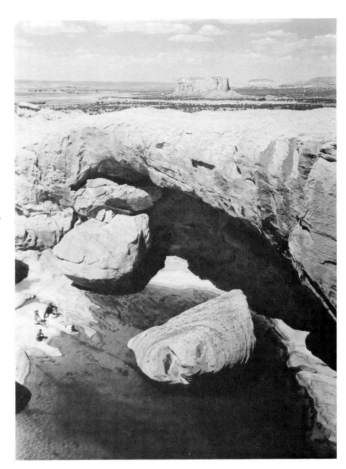

19 Natural cistern. *Photograph courtesy New Mexico Department of Development.*

20 Water pool by William H. Jackson. *Photograph courtesy Library, State Historical Society of Colorado.*

21 Ácoma church before restoration, by William H. Jackson. *Photograph courtesy Library,*
State Historical Society of Colorado.

22 Balcony end of church, 1903. *Photograph courtesy Museum of the American Indian, Heye Foundation.*

23 Procession leaving church on San Estevan feast day ca. 1915. *Photograph from Arthur Bibo Collection, Pueblo of Ácoma Archives.*

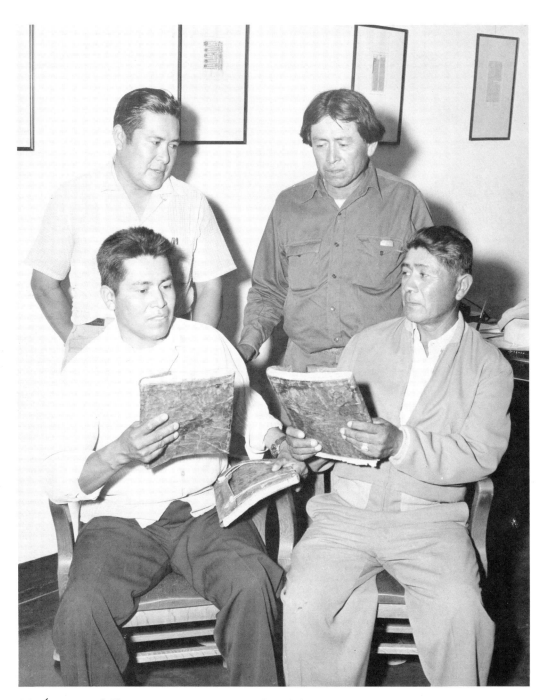

24　Ácoma Land Claims Committee, 1957. Standing, left to right, Joe Ray and Syme Sanchez. Sitting, left to right, then-Governor Castillo Vallo and Joe Chino. *Photograph courtesy Skrondahl Photo.*

25 Pottery vendors on old
Highway 66, 1936. *Photograph
courtesy National Archives.*

26 Ácoma sheep roundup, 1937. *Photograph courtesy National Archives.*

27 Ácoma runners, 1906. *Photograph from Arthur Bibo Collection, Pueblo of Ácoma Archives.*

compromise on the one that was established last summer. It might have a good effect to tell the Ácomas that they will not be crowded back clear to the dam if they will act with moderation and will be satisfied with the line that was established last summer. I will consult with [Attorney Thomas] Catron in the matter by letter if there is need of it, and will try to be ready for the Ácomas if they desire to [make trouble].

Troops were sent to place Laguna Indians in possession of the land disputed by the two pueblos and Agent Thomas made it known that the Ácomas would get the worst of it if they took the matter to the courts.[22] Because the boundary lines remained unclear, Thomas urged the governor of Laguna to persuade his people to farm up to a line drawn north and south of Cubero mountain. His contention was that the Ácomas had a clear title only as far east as the mountain and no more. In this instance, Agent Thomas not only ignored past agreements but also pretended ignorance of the Ácoma grant.[23]

Attorneys for Ácoma arranged to bring another lawsuit against Laguna over the disputed territories. Meanwhile, Anglo and Spanish encroachers continued to occupy Ácoma farmlands to the north and west, both within and without the as yet unsurveyed grant. The Ácomas refused to accept any of the proposed boundary markers.

Agent Thomas urged the Honorable Thomas B. Catron, then United States District Attorney in Albuquerque, to be partial to Laguna because they appeared to be more clearly entitled to the land in dispute than Ácoma. "I hope, therefore, that you will interest yourself in confirming the right of Laguna to the land," he wrote, "and more particularly because the trouble seems to have been instigated and prolonged until now by parties for the money the Indians may be able to scrape together."[24]

In July 1877, when the so-called second survey for Ácoma was finished, Thomas wrote the Indian Commissioner:[25]

> I have the honor to refer to my monthly report for April 1877, and to respectfully submit the following further report on the subject of the Ácoma and Laguna land contest.

The papers pertaining to the second survey of the Land Grant of the Pueblo of Ácoma have been completed by the Surveyor General of New Mexico, and are now being forwarded by that officer, with his approval, to Washington. *While I am firmly of the opinion that the Ácoma Indians would be defrauded of a valuable portion of their Grant—the Old Fort Wingate site—should a patent issue on the basis of this last survey, I nevertheless recommend that the survey be approved*° as it is and patent issued on that basis as soon as possible for the following reasons, viz:

1. The two pueblos—Ácoma and Laguna have been fighting for a great many years on account of the dividing line between the two, and the fight is certain to continue until a patent is issued for one or both of the grants.

2. The Ácomas have only themselves to blame for the loss of Old Fort Wingate district, because they falsely swore it away for a consideration.

3. A project should not be entertained to reimburse the Ácomas from the Laguna lands for that which they saw fit to bestow upon settlers by perjury.

4. There is no dissatisfaction on the part of the United States officials, who can only be interested in the equity of the cause, with the present survey in respect of its bearing upon the two pueblos interested.

I respectfully urge the importance of so representing this matter before the proper officer as to meet the anticipated representations of interested settlers at Old Fort Wingate.

As a result of his efforts and recommendations, the survey passed through channels without delay and the patent was signed by President Rutherford B. Hayes on November 19, 1877. On December 10, Agent Thomas notified the governor of Ácoma that he was to present himself in Santa Fe to receive it.[26]

Land problems dominated pueblo affairs during this period and beyond, but Indian life remained virtually unchanged until around

---

°Author's italics.

1880. In that year the Atlantic and Pacific Railroad Company entered New Mexico. The government expected to use the rails for all manner of transactions at the pueblos and news of the progress made toward laying track in New Mexico had become common exchange by 1879.

In 1880, the company began to lay track south and west of Isleta Pueblo. The agency reported that the Indians were apprehensive about the negotiations for the road to cut across Indian lands. Arrangements went slowly since railroad representatives had to reach lease agreements with each Indian whose property was involved. In the final stages of settlement, company officials, as at Ácoma, agreed to certain monetary demands from pueblo officials.[27]

Next came the hard labor of building the grades and laying tracks which took all available and willing men from Laguna, Ácoma, and Zuñi the remainder of 1880 and part of 1881. The rails entered and crossed over the northern portion of the Ácoma grant, at one point breaking an irrigation ditch which the company repaired (besides compensating the Ácomas with $500 for damages).[28] Further on, the track blocked the dirt road between McCarty's and Baca stations for a time.[29]

Economic and cultural changes were inevitable. In addition to the Indian agent, who visited Ácoma only rarely, the Indian trader was now introduced. On December 12, 1882, Solomon Bibo applied to the Indian Commissioner for a license to trade with the Indians of the Pueblo of Ácoma. His was the first trading establishment at Old Ácoma and he immediately began to exert great influence. Due in part to his engaging and shrewd personality, his influence was probably made more acceptable by the fact that Bibo's wife was an Ácoma. Although he was to be officially replaced by other licensees during 1884 and 1885, Solomon Bibo, aided by his brother Simon, who lived in nearby Grants, New Mexico, actually monopolized a great share of the Ácoma economy.[30]

The railroad itself was to bring more mobility to the Ácomas than they had ever had and it probably encouraged greater settlement along the San Jose River; McCarty's, for example, originated as a train stop. However, many Ácomas continued to live at Old Ácoma, preferring to travel to Acomita and McCarty's for spring and summer planting and harvesting. The railroad furnished transportation for the children attending school in Albuquerque and provided a convenient way to send wool to the traders. A post office opened in Acomita in 1905, closed in 1906, and opened again in 1912; at McCarty's a post office existed intermittently between 1887 and 1911.[31]

During these years the Ácomas repeatedly appealed for a resurvey to correct the grant boundary calls. Their appeals were denied even though some government officials recognized that an injustice had been committed. The first appeal was made in 1883, but after looking into the data, the Board of Indian Commissioners recommended no action. Their report not only acknowledged the claim but also stated that the Ácomas had a grievance and were in fact victims of a fraud. "But as the grant has been confirmed by the United States Government, on the basis of that survey, we advised them to be content with the land they have, enough and more than enough for their wants. It would be impracticable now to get an additional grant by Congress, especially as some portions of the land taken from them are already occupied by white settlers."[32]

The same appeal caused the commissioner of the General Land Office to request the surveyor general in Santa Fe to conduct a hearing of the appeal. This was done at Ácoma on October 15 and 16, 1884, and the surveyor general made the following observations.[33]

Personal examination of the ground exhibited undoubted evidence of current and long continuous possession by Ácoma of the land extending five to six miles south of the surveyed boundary of 1877 immediately south of Old Ácoma. There were growing crops and orchards of long-standing in that area south of Old Ácoma and the surveyed line.

The south boundary call of the pueblo, according to the Cruzate Grant, was "the peñol." According to the Ácomas this was actually located eighteen miles south of the current boundary.

The Sierra Prieta to the north, the original landmark referred to, was ignored by the survey in favor of the Cerro Prieto.

The Ojo del Gallo question could not be settled, because Pedro Sanchez, Pueblo Indian Agent, was called away on official business.

The commissioner of the General Land Office rendered the official decision to do nothing for the appeal and from January 26, 1885, the Ácomas were given thirty days within which to appeal further. No further appeal was made. An inquiry by the commissioner later revealed that the Ácomas had been given no notice of the deadline. However, the land agent for the Atlantic and Pacific Railroad Company had requested to be notified if the Ácomas decided to pursue the case.[34]

Attorneys Thomas B. Catron, William T. Thornton, and Frank W. Clancy finally filed on behalf of Ácoma on January 4, 1886. Once again, the Ácomas asked for their old boundaries but because of the procedural deadline, their plea was too late.[35] The appeal, nevertheless, was replied to by the attorney representing those non-Indian settlers whose lands would be embraced by an extension of the grant to the proper boundaries. The arguments in brief follow.[36]

The south boundary of the Ácomas had been clearly fixed by the 1877 survey. The whole matter of the boundaries at Ojo del Gallo had been investigated twice, and the survey was correct. Ácoma Pueblo had originally been on the San Jose River but because of hostility toward the Laguna Indians, was removed to the mesa which constituted the traditional south boundary of the grant, the location having been logically adopted for defensive purposes, and so forth.

Ácoma's appeal was also rebuffed by attorneys Henry S. Waldo and Ralph Emerson Twitchell, representing the Atlantic and Pacific Railroad, who pointed out (among many other things) that the Ácomas had not appealed within the thirty days allowed. They claimed that there was no fraud involved and accepted evidence which indicated that the spring near the house of Ramon Sanchez, about ten miles east of Old Fort Wingate, was the true Gallo springs. "It is a notorious fact," continued their statement, "that Ácoma Indians have not, nor can of necessity, use or occupy the whole area of the Grant as now defined, for they have leased the grazing thereof to the Ácoma Land and Cattle Company, a corporation, now, by virtue of such lease, grazing their cattle within said Ácoma Grant."[37]

On June 10, 1886, the Surveyor General reaffirmed the January 1885 decision. On the same day, the negative results were forwarded to Catron, Thornton, and Clancy with the explanation that the appeal had not been submitted in time and that conflicting evidence did not produce any more definitive information which might justify a reversal of the decision or provide cause for another survey.[38] Clearly the protestants were safe in their settlements and investments. The Ácoma attorneys were given sixty days to appeal the last decision but did not do so.[39]

On April 7, 1884, the Ácomas leased their entire grant area to Solomon Bibo. The lease agreement for the patented 95,791.66 acres was to endure for thirty years for payments of $300 for the first decade, $400 for the second, and $500 for the last ten-year period. Usage extended to grazing and water rights, although any coal mining would provide a royalty of ten cents per ton for the Ácomas. Word of the lease incensed Indian Agent Pedro Sanchez, who threatened to revoke Solomon Bibo's license to trade with the Ácomas. Then he turned for guidance and support to the United States Commissioner of Indian Affairs, claiming that such a lease opened the area to all speculators, that it had been obtained from the Ácoma governor without common consent of the people. Sanchez felt that losing use of their lands, "They will come, eventually, to beg their own bread, and probably, turn out stealing, etc."[40]

Next, Sanchez pursued a complaint he had received about the Ácomas having three cows illegally, "which you [Ácomas] have refused to deliver, giving, as an excuse, that you bought them from a Mexican." Under territorial law, anyone buying cattle was required to have a certificate of sale with the buyer's and two witnesses' signatures, as well as a description of the animal, its price, and brand. In the absence of this, Sanchez accordingly ordered immediate return of the three cows. He added that cattle stealing had become a very common practice in the area and warned that if the Ácomas were caught they might find themselves in the penitentiary.[41]

After this admonition, Pedro Sanchez held a meeting at McCarty's Station, reporting the results promptly to the Commissioner. There, within the Ácoma line on the Atlantic and Pacific Railway, he said, using a native of Laguna as interpreter, he asked some sixty Ácomas if they had agreed to the Bibo lease. Except for Governor Martin del Vallo, they all answered in the negative. In writing the Commissioner, Sanchez quoted the Ácomas as saying, "We have not agreed to any such thing and know nothing about that agreement or paper that has been read to us. . . . We would rather die than agree to it." When questioned about the transaction, Governor del Vallo said: "When Bibo spoke to be about leasing land, he spoke to me about that portion of land that we have near the Gallo Spring. [He] told me he wanted that tract to pasture the cattle that would be left him after delivering the ones that some of the Ácoma Indians had given him on shares, and under that understanding did I sign that paper." Sanchez reported that he asked the governor if he would have signed the lease if he had known it was for thirty years instead of three as the governor supposedly understood it. Governor del Vallo claimed that he would not have signed it "for all the money in the world." Thereupon Sanchez demanded that Bibo cancel the lease. Bibo refused. Sanchez ended his report to the commissioner by recommending "that measures be taken to protect this poor Pueblo."[42]

When it appeared that they might lose in Solomon Bibo a trader and a person whom they very much admired and respected, the Ácomas held a general meeting at McCarty's on July 21, 1884. They petitioned the Commissioner of Indian Affairs, asking that Bibo's license be continued. Furthermore, they declared that they sustained and protected "in every particular" the lease which Sanchez claimed had been taken from Ácoma by fraud. Their petition bore nearly a hundred Ácoma signatures and marks, including Governor del Vallo's.[43]

At the same time, Sanchez was taking the necessary steps in Santa Fe to replace Solomon Bibo. He licensed another trader, one Alexander de Armand from Cubero, New Mexico. Writing to Governor del Vallo about Bibo's intent to defraud, Sanchez warned him to "look out for that Solomon Bibo and his band." It would be the Ácoma's fault, not his, he claimed, if "you allow yourselves to be cheated by those who come among you, clad of sheep but rapacious wolves."[44] Finally, on July 30, Sanchez notified Bibo that his license to trade with the Ácomas was revoked and that he must remove all his belongings from the Indian country by August 20, 1884.[45]

Wrapping up matters, Sanchez turned to the United States District Attorney: "I have the honor to request that you take the necessary steps for and on behalf of the Pueblo of Ácoma to compel Solomon Bibo to vacate the lease and for the removal of said Bibo, his property, and employees from the lands of the said pueblo." This action was also reported to the commissioner.[46]

Solomon Bibo did not leave the Ácoma lands. On his behalf, the Ácomas and Simon Bibo, his brother and also a trader at Ácoma, contacted the United States commissioner to explain their side of the lease problem. They stated that Solomon's offer was made to counteract one the Marmon brothers of Laguna had made the preceding year. The Marmons had wanted to lease the grant for ten years—for ten cows. Solomon Bibo told the Indians that one cow a year was too little. Rather, if they wanted to rent, he proposed an alternative lease arrangement which would allow the Ácomas to retain all their own rights for grazing and cultivating. At one time, Agent Sanchez had thought the lease to Bibo was a good idea but he had obviously changed his mind. Furthermore, Marmon of Laguna wanted Solomon Bibo removed because Bibo had told the Lagunas that they must give back some lands belonging to Ácoma.

Simon Bibo's version of the meeting with Sanchez at McCarty's Station was somewhat different. According to him, about thirty Indians had gathered there. There was no interpreter, only the governor's son, who told the Agent that he perfectly understood the situation and was well pleased with the Bibo lease. "What!!!" thundered Sanchez at him, "You have no right to say so—sit down!! This man Solomon Bibo has sold you, sold your land, and sold your children's land and if you do not take that lease back immediately the government will punish you severely." The last remark was directed to old Governor del Vallo who was so intimidated that he was ready to do anything for Sanchez. The agent then produced a paper drawn up at Laguna (which apparently constituted a repudiation of the contract with Bibo) for the governor's signature (or mark).

Simon reported that the leading men of Ácoma later united to submit a petition repudiating Sanchez. They could do without him. As for removing Solomon Bibo, Simon believed that no ordinary authority could prevent Solomon from trading with Ácomas so long as they wanted him. "His intentions with these Indians are of the best nature and beneficial to them—because the men, women, and children love him as they would love a father and he is in the same manner attached to them." Since working with the Ácomas, Solomon Bibo had persuaded them to settle a pueblo "in a more comfortable location, has induced them to send their children to school, and is suggesting new ideas in methods of agriculture, simple improved machinery, etc., etc., etc."[47]

Commissioner Hiram Price apparently decided the truth was likely to lie somewhere between the two versions but, in any case, decided that the proposed lease should not be allowed. The license for Alexander de Armand was approved but Sanchez was replaced the following year. In 1885, the Ácomas elected Solomon Bibo as their governor.[48]

In 1896, the Court of Private Land Claims was established, superseding the Surveyor General. After the survey of the Cubero grant that same year, the new court found that the grant did in fact overlap the Ácoma grant by 283.23 acres. The Ácomas continued to plead for both a resurvey and boundary adjustments. They claimed that an untold amount of land was being taken from them on all sides and that the poorest lands were generally all that were left them.[49]

MORE HARVEST FROM THE LAND

Indian agents reported that Ácoma agricultural techniques and animal husbandry were primitive by contemporary standards, but before 1900 did very little to improve conditions. Periodic drouths worked incredible hardships. Such a drouth brought agent Pedro Sanchez to Old Ácoma in 1883. He reported that the extent of the work and risk involved in ascending the mesa "would move to pity even the hardest heart." He thought that the Indians appeared sickly and pale and remarked that many of them died or suffered from rheumatism as they got older. They raised cows (but could not get the milk up to the top of the mesa), horses, sheep, and donkeys. He persuaded the Ácomas to consider moving to a "rich spring on their land below about 2 miles from their actual place." Upon returning to Santa Fe, Sanchez sent a request to the Indian Commissioner for ten wagons and ten medium horses to help the Ácomas haul stones and other materials needed to build new houses.[50]

The Ácomas did receive five wagons, all of which stayed in the depot until February 1885. Then the Ácomas got them along with $300 worth of lumber and three additional new wagons. About ten adobe houses were built at the springs two miles north of the mesa. There were plans to build a village and move the entire population. The Ácomas also applied for water tanks, three large plows, and scrapers that year. According to the agent, the tribe had 550 cattle, 9,500 sheep, 400 horses, 500 burros, twenty-five hogs, eight wagons, and 250 hens.[51]

In 1888, the Santa Fe Agency recommended that Indian agricultural lands be fenced and that a system of farmers and matrons be employed for the pueblos. The farmers would show the Indians how to improve farming while the matrons were to teach home economics and child care. A farmer was suggested for Zuñi; one for Ácoma, Laguna, and Isleta; another for Jémez, Santa Ana, and Zia; one for Tesuque, Pojoaque, and Nambé; one for San Ildefonso, Santa Clara, and San Juan; and one for Picurís and Taos.[52]

The years 1890 and 1891 were depressed years for Ácoma because of both drouth and devastating smallpox and diptheria epidemics. In 1890, the census count showed 582 Ácomas; in 1894, the number was 504.[53] In 1898, the agent reported another year of smallpox with many deaths at all pueblos. The disease spread into Ácoma and Laguna and their outlying villages in August and school was closed at Ácoma from September 25 to October 10. The agent blamed these epidemics on the worthless vaccine being sent with the government physicians and took steps to replace it with good, "with perfect success, almost all cases vaccinated taking perfectly, and in a short time the disease was wiped out of the pueblos, regardless of the situation in the neighboring towns, where it raged for months after disappearing from among the Indians." The same agent recommended the appointment of five physicians for the pueblos with one resident at Zuñi; another at Laguna to care for Ácoma, Laguna, and Isleta; one in Bernalillo to serve Cochití, Jémez, Santa Ana, Santo Domingo, Sandia, San Felipe, and Zia; a fourth for Taos, and Picuris residing at "Taos City"; and a fifth resident in Santa

Fe or Española for Santa Clara, San Ildefonso, San Juan, Nambé, and Tesuque.[54]

In October 1899, Ácoma's first Indian Agency farmer arrived in the person of W. G. Deason. He was followed in 1902 by the first matron, Mabel W. Collins.[55] The farmers appeared to have an almost immediate impact upon crop variety and increased production. Among the few statistics available for early times are those from 1864. Then the Ácoma population numbered 490 and owned twenty-four horses, four mules, eighty-six asses, a hundred cows, fifty oxen, and twenty swine.[56] Sometime during the following years, the Ácomas began to raise wheat in addition to the corn, alfalfa, fruit, and vegetables generally reported by the Indian agents. The method for threshing was probably learned from Spanish neighbors. The grain was placed on the ground and after animals trampled it out of the husks, it was sorted by hand into baskets. These were used to toss the grain in the air so that the chaff blew away.[57] The Indians then washed the grain in water for a final cleansing. At one time during the period, an Anastacio Garcia wanted to build a flour mill near McCarty's Station.*[58] Other statistics found in the agent's report for 1885, and the farmers' reports of 1900 and 1904, show the general increase in produce and animals. (See Table 3.)

TABLE 3

Ácoma Agriculture and Livestock, 1885–1904

	1885	1900	1904
Wheat (bushels)		1,178	2,925
Corn (bushels)		1,710	1,000
Onions (bushels)		—	50
Vegetables (bushels)		—	15
Hay (tons)		—	125
Wood (cords)		—	385
Horses	400	441	1,000
Mules		17	50
Burros	500	212	150
Cattle	550	616	700
Hogs	25	77	50
Sheep	950	3,317	10,000
Goats		323	200
Fowl	250	76	500

*Thus far, only the application to build this mill has been found but ruins of an old mill are known to Ácomas.

In 1900, income from wool amounted to $1,901. In 1904, the total income for produce of all kinds was $5,000 plus $185 in labor sold to the government. Unless otherwise counted with cattle, oxen disappeared from the pueblo sometime between 1900 and 1915.[59]

In a carefully composed document, Governor Lorenzo Concho and all the pueblo officers summarized all the irrigation and farmed acreage in 1911. There were, they declared, five ditches and "beyond the memory of any living man they have existed . . . and each of them [is] of the age of two hundred years." The first two—Juan Sarracino and Hunt's ditches—were less than a mile long. McCarty's ditch ran for three miles, the North Puncho ditch extended five and a half, and the South Candelario ditch, the longest, was six and three quarters miles. The farmer reported that the Ácomas were farming 342.5 acres in 1900. By 1911, the Ácoma officers indicated that they were farming around 700 acres.*

OUR CHILDREN LEARN THE WHITE MAN'S WAY

Prior to 1900, one major social problem in all the pueblos, according to Indian agents, was education. Ácoma was no exception, and education, probably more than any other modern institution, caused a rift in the pueblo. Some of the people saw all change as a threat to old ways and traditions, while others in these early days viewed education as a way to improve their condition in life. Some tended to blame the whites and outsiders for bringing problems, but older Ácomas saw the difficulties as more profoundly human. Fortunately, they encouraged the people to express themselves and to talk about these matters in council meetings.

Advanced educational theories and practices known to modern man have touched the Pueblo Indians in New Mexico only in recent generations. The Spanish had assigned all such matters to the Franciscans who were expected to tend each mission and its flock. Education was considered a function of the Church. At Ácoma any formal training

---

*See Appendix 5: ÁCOMA DITCHES AND FARM LANDS IN 1911.

74

was sporadic at best after the 1770s when the Ácoma mission became a *visita* of Laguna. The United States Indian Agents early enjoined the Indian Commissioners to construct school buildings and assign teachers to each pueblo, an idea which met with strong resistance from pueblo leaders. In 1864, the Indian agent reported from Santa Fe, "It is a fact to be regretted that the number of these worthy and industrious people who can read and write is so small, and that the number of such is decreasing. When under the care of the Spanish and Mexican governments more attention was paid to education, hence the number of those who can read has been decreasing since our occupation of the country."[60]

A central school for the pueblos was first suggested to the Indian agency in 1858 by the Reverend Gorman who had started a Baptist missionary school at Laguna.[61] From this time forward almost every annual report carried recommendations for schools and schoolteachers. The agent in 1868 reported that not a single school, mechanical shop of any kind, teacher, or mechanic, was to be found in any of the pueblos. "The parish priests, who in former times used to reside among them, and from whom they used to receive some instructions, have long since given up the idea, mostly for the want of encouragement on the part of the Indians, the government, and the citizens in general."[62] By 1875, however, the Santa Fe agency reported that six day schools and one industrial school for girls had been started in the pueblos. The school at Laguna added to its buildings in 1878 when the teacher purchased a large printing press to replace a small one which was broken. Jémez Pueblo opened a school on March 1, 1878. At the same time the Zuñi school closed, mainly for want of teachers. Several religious denominations had a hand in opening and operating these early pueblo schools and in furnishing teachers.[63]

About this time, Agent Benjamin M. Thomas solicited the pueblos for children to attend the Carlisle Indian Training School in Pennsylvania.° In 1880, Zuñi sent two boys and two girls, Laguna sent two boys

---

°Established by the United States government at Carlisle Barracks, the Indian Service began in 1879 to take a more direct hand in education for Indians. This school stressed general education but became more successful in the manual arts. Over the years it was popular with New Mexico's Pueblo Indians but finally closed in 1918.

and a girl, and San Felipe sent three boys. As the agent observed, it appeared to be a small contribution from nineteen communities with over 10,000 inhabitants, but it was a start. The Department of the Interior authorized an industrial school for the pueblos to be built on public domain, but this was scheduled for the future. Ácoma still had no easy access to schools. Agent Thomas overheard some Indian officers remark that if they were to stop struggling to improve their condition and begin to murder and steal they would perhaps then receive as much consideration from the "great father" as other tribes did.[64]

On January 1, 1881, the Presbyterian church opened a boarding and industrial school for the pueblos at Albuquerque. Under contract to the Church Board of Home Missions it operated out of a private adobe home. It could hold fifty pupils and had forty in attendance. A few days later, ten additional pueblo children left for school at Carlisle Barracks. This time there were two boys and two girls from Ácoma although one of the boys had to return to Ácoma because of illness. One Zuñi child died of consumption while at the school.[65]

By now, the Indians had three classes of schools available, including the day schools in the pueblos, and the boarding and industrial schools in Pennsylvania and Albuquerque.

In June 1881, Albuquerque purchased 65.82 acres of land at a cost of $4,500 and donated the area to the United States for the industrial school complex. The school was to be relocated near Albuquerque on land where the Indians could be trained in animal husbandry and agriculture.

In January 1882, there were eighteen pueblo children attending the Carlisle school. Agent Thomas persuaded six pueblo men to accompany him for a visit.

> We took with us two little girls from the Pueblo of Laguna, and brought home from the school two little girls, one belonging at Zuñi and the other at Ácoma. We escorted to Hampton, Va., the old chief Antonio, of the Pima tribe, who also went to visit his children. The Pueblos enjoyed the visit very much indeed, and were highly gratified by the improvement in the appearance of their children. I myself was

astonished at the development which had taken place in the case of nearly every one of the children. They went there dull and listless and unaccustomed to thought; I found them sharp, alert, and reasoning on all subjects about them. The school as a whole aroused my admiration and enthusiasm. The children were orderly, obedient, and attractive, and were clearly on the way of making good men and women.

Although Thomas believed that the Carlisle school was "the very best place for the education of Indians," he expected that the industrial school at Albuquerque would probably accomplish the greatest good for the greatest number.[66] In 1882, Indian children from the north began to travel into Albuquerque on the Atchison, Topeka, and Santa Fe Railroad to attend school.[67]

In 1883, the Ácomas had about thirty boys attending school either at Carlisle or in Albuquerque. At the latter school, new buildings were completed during the summer of 1884. The move from the original adobe home was delayed, however, because the new school lacked plumbing of any kind and nearly all the furniture. By 1885, however, there were six day schools at various pueblos:

Pueblo	No. Students	Teacher (and Assistant)
Zuñi	20	James H. Wilson
Isleta	12	J. R. Hawley (and Helen M. Hawley)
Santa Clara	10	William Craig
San Juan	6	T. Marcellus Marcus
Laguna	7	John Menaul (and Floretta Shields)
Jémez	7	Richard V. Leach

At this point, Ácoma asked the agency for a teacher at the pueblo, a request which was echoed by San Felipe, Santo Domingo, Cochití, and Taos.[68]

Responding to the Ácoma request, apparently in December 1885, the agency appointed Edward Walsh as the first schoolteacher at Ácoma. He received instructions to get supplies from the Laguna school. Governor Bibo at Ácoma was advised to supervise the installation. For some yet unknown reason, on March 31, 1886, the agency replaced Walsh with Lizzie Clark. Walsh was to turn the property over to her and the school was to be moved to McCarty's.[69]

Meanwhile, the agency in Santa Fe wrote Washington that there was no schoolhouse; neither were there furniture, seats, or desks at Ácoma, or authority to purchase them. The commissioner in return wanted to know how Ácoma was doing without all these things—especially since they were reporting twenty-five students in school. He asked for a detailed estimate of what was needed. The agency responded by recommending four schools, one each at Ácoma, San Felipe, Cochití, and Santa Clara. A school building consisting of one classroom, and a living room and kitchen for the teacher, officials estimated would cost about $800.[70] No money was forthcoming, either for the buildings and furnishings or for the teachers' salaries. Lizzie Clark stayed on for a while at Ácoma, but the teacher at San Felipe Pueblo resigned "because he cannot live without pay."[71]

Faced with governmental recommendations instead of the material support they needed, the Ácomas became discouraged. Enrollment began to drop. Reports showed the number of students to be down to ten; then five. Miss Clark was succeeded by a H. C. Carsen who remained only a short while. He was replaced by Page Trotter on February 3, 1887. Mr. Trotter wrote the Commissioner of Indian Affairs that the school at Ácoma was a "miserable adobe house occupied by eight or ten Indian and two Mexican children." The house belonged to Solomon Bibo who did not want it used for a school any longer. Trotter was granted a leave of absence due to illness whereupon he recommended that the Ácoma school be closed and a new government school established at Laguna. At length, the Commissioner of Indian Affairs transferred Trotter. He also authorized the agency to expend $500 on a school at Ácoma but would produce no money for a teacher until there was a school house.[72]

The Indian Agency in Santa Fe next tried establishing a Catholic school at Acomita, contracting with the Bureau of Catholic Indian Missions for a teacher and a building. The Acomita school operated for several years, taught by Miss Cora A. Taylor. In August 1887, the agent also invited Solomon Bibo to build a new school house at McCarty's Station. The Indian Commissioner, however, reviewing the agent's pessimistic report of the year before, directed him to consider closing the school if it was not attended by twenty-five students.[73]

Starting in March 1888, a serious epidemic of smallpox, lasting several months, scourged the Ácomas. It seemed to be the harbinger of bad times.[74] During that year, the Indian Commissioner dictated a policy of anglicizing the government schools, permitting nothing Indian to be spoken or taught there except the Bible "when English is not understood by the pupils."[75] In the opinion of some Ácomas, their children who attended the various schools were beginning to change radically. They wanted to get rid of the old traditions. Furthermore, Ácoma children began to refuse to return to Ácoma. According to school officials, those who did return were made to don Indian clothes and join in dances and ceremonies. Captain R. H. Pratt, the Superintendent of the Indian Industrial School at Carlisle, Pennsylvania, returned some of the Ácoma children in July 1889: "I found a great aversion to returning to their homes on the part of the girls. There were six boys from the same village [Ácoma] entitled to return but they all positively and emphatically expressed a determination to remain here for some time longer."[76]

Solomon Bibo, one of the "progressive" leaders of Ácoma at this time, corresponded with Captain Pratt about the students. Bibo accused the incumbent governor and "a little gang of his tribe" of tying up Ácoma men and boys and giving them a general horsewhipping and "hanging up" during the September 2 feast day, the annual celebration of the pueblo patron St. Estevan. This was their punishment for not staying out of school, having cut off their hair, and refusing to wear Indian dress.

Relying on these reports from Bibo, Captain Pratt recommended that the commissioner take immediate steps to "break the power of this Governor, and from the information I have in regard to it, I believe that the people would, as a mass, rejoice at any substantial action against him. The brutalities which Mr. Bibo reports are, I think, not overstated." Armed with this information, the Indian Commissioner directed the governor's arrest and the sheriff in Albuquerque held him in jail to await hearings in the district courts. Meanwhile, the agency appointed Juan Rey "a young and progressive man" as interim governor until elections were held on January 1, 1890.[77]

By late 1889, when the agent visited the Acomita contract day school, there were no pupils. The teacher was a "Mexican whose English is exceedingly poor and whose teaching is done mostly in Spanish. The school is almost worthless."[78] The commissioner ordered that the Acomita school be continued until July 31, 1890, when the government school, in a building owned by Bibo, would open at McCarty's Station. In September, while these preparations were underway, the agency received complaints about further whippings by the Ácoma governor and officials of people who put on "citizens clothes and cut off their hair." The agent visited Ácoma and recommended to the Indian commissioner that this year's governor be brought before a grand jury even though last year's offending governor returned and was reinstated to his former position to replace Rey. "I know of no other way than the one suggested," reported the agent. "A part of the people of Ácoma are disposed to get rid of their old customs and habits, but if they are to be treated as these parties have been it will be bad on all the people; the better class will be discouraged."[79]

At the beginning of 1891, Ácoma had two schools: the Acomita day school under the Bureau of Catholic Indian Missions and the government day school at McCarty's Station. Early in the year Bibo agreed to build a new school so the students and teacher could move from the primitive quarters Bibo had been renting the government. However, when attendance at McCarty's dropped to only several students, the Indian Commissioner ordered the school closed once again. Miss Agnes J. J. Davenport, the teacher who had been at the McCarty's school since the summer before, transferred to the school at Santa Clara Pueblo.[80]

The rigid positions of both the United States government and the Ácoma traditionalists were exaggerated by still another problem. The agents noted that many returning students who had learned a trade found it impossible to practice that trade. Many of them had learned tailoring, printing, painting, or other occupations of little or no use to the pueblo. Those who had learned to be carpenters, blacksmiths, or harness makers were in great demand, but were too poor to purchase suitable tools. In some cases the agency could help them but "It was well known that the returned students are exposed to very considerable ridicule from the older members of the pueblos, on account of their wearing civilian dress. It is difficult for any of them to withstand the pressure brought to bear upon them to return to their former mode of life; but I find that the females are more apt to succumb and go back to the old customs than are the males."[81]

The Ácomas continued to boycott the schools. Finally, the Bureau of Catholic Indian Missions closed the school at Acomita, turning the building over to the agency. For the first year or so under this arrangement, a Miss Turner served as government teacher but attendance was often zero. The building was of stone but had no modern facilities, no water except from a ditch, and no toilets. Then, in 1897, Miss Cora A. Taylor returned and attendance appeared to improve. In the following year, the Ácomas suffered another smallpox epidemic. Her efforts to prevent the spread of the disease and her countless visits to Ácoma homes to aid the stricken endeared Cora Taylor to the community once more.[82] For the time being, the school remained at Acomita in the old building rented by the government from the church. In 1906, the agency reopened the day school at McCarty's but attendance at both continued to be generally poor and unpredictable. One old tradition tended to prevent children from attending the day schools at Acomita and McCarty's with any regularity. This was the ancient migration from the river area to Old Ácoma for feast days, ceremonies, and the seasonal celebrations. Despite the difficulties inherent in isolation, during this same period Ácoma continued to send a remarkable number of students to training schools in Carlisle, Albuquerque, and the newly established one in Santa Fe.

The Ácomas entered the twentieth century resisting changes which the youngsters would eventually bring about. They continued to select a governor each year, who took office on January 1, and who operated with the approval and support of an existing council of elders. Also elected annually were a war chief, a secretary, and an interpreter. On state occasions, the governor appeared with a Spanish cane and the famous Lincoln cane, symbols of his office and authority. The latter had been a gift from President Lincoln in 1863. An ebony, silver-crowned cane, it was given in recognition of the peacefulness of the Pueblos, and inscribed with the year and "A. Lincoln, Pres. U.S.A."[83] The governor or the council tried pueblo cases of misdemeanor or any violation of laws and decided on punishment. They possessed few modern agricultural implements and crops were still planted, cultivated, and harvested in traditional ways. The wheat, for example, was cut with sickles and trampled out by horses. After 1880, the Ácomas began to introduce cook stoves and improved household utensils, purchased from traders. A more prosperous few had freight wagons and buggies.[84]

5
Modern Ácoma

Ácoma's isolated location continued to keep her people out of the mainstream of the twentieth century. More conservative tribal members perpetuated religious and traditional customs in the old villages. Progressives began to move to Acomita, to McCarty's, and beyond, as population growth made it necessary to find work outside the reservation. In 1913, by the Sandoval decision, the United States Supreme Court reversed its previous ruling and made the Pueblo Indians wards of the government, due all the federal protection afforded other Indians. Among other things, the decision legalized Indian agent activities in the pueblos and thus made them more influential in the affairs of modern Ácoma.

MAKING A LIVING

Agriculture furnished the greatest resources for individual Ácomas into modern times, with the major emphasis gradually shifting from sheep to cattle raising. As the governmental representative for agricultural and stock-raising activities, the resident government farmer was expected to improve techniques by providing training and farm implements, and upgrading the health standard of the animals. Yet at least one Indian agent questioned the need for these services:[1]

Having nearly five centuries in which to improve under the highest of civilized nations [Spain], to say nothing of what they knew prior thereto (and they had the greatest teachers —stern necessity with famine on her heels) it would seem to me rather idle to increase the great knowledge of these ancient people. Just as I view the Hopi Indians, I view the Pueblo Indians. They know 10,000 times more today about agriculture than any Indian Service Farmer may expect to learn in his entire lifetime, especially if he is the usual uneducated individual who comes out of the east.

At times the position appeared to be vacant, but when the government farmer was on duty, he composed weekly reports covering daily activities. Only a few of these "diaries," one of the more intimate contacts with the pueblos, survive. Between 1932 and 1933, the title was changed to "Government Stockman" and by 1940, the position became that of the "Field Workers" from the Extension Service of the Bureau of Indian Affairs.

The government farmer in 1915 worried about Ácoma's lack of water—particularly vital to improve agriculture and the grade of cattle and sheep. Pointing out that Laguna had twenty-seven wells while Ácoma had only five, he wrote the superintendent in Albuquerque asking for "a few good wells; a series of dams on the San Jose River; or at least a good storage dam. Some of these people are very poor and have no chance, unless we can help them some. I do not know how they can become self supporting."[2] The farmer's own supplies had increased over those allotted during previous years but still were barely enough to maintain a household. He did loan five bulls to the Ácomas, but had little else in quantity enough to be useful.[3] During World War I the situation worsened. The agency had trouble keeping good men in the position of farmer and cattle and sheep appeared to suffer because of neglect.[4]

Transportation to and communication with Ácoma remained substandard. In 1920 the Superintendent for the Southern Pueblos Agency reported that Isleta was the only pueblo which could be reached by telephone from his Albuquerque office. Few pueblos had telephones and a messenger service had to be used. Laguna and Ácoma were connected by a local telephone line but neither could be reached from Albuquerque.[5]

After the Sandoval decision, in an effort to increase Indian profits and break the hold local traders had gained on the wool business, the Indian agency tried to take a direct hand in the pueblo wool industry. The local traders had avoided any possible government supervision by locating their trading posts within the railroad right–of–way, rather than on reservation land, and they were operating on the various reservations without licenses.

Beginning in 1914, the agency superintendent encouraged the Indians to pool their wool and to invite bidders whose offers could be accepted or rejected by the unanimous decision of the growers. In practice, the buyer offered an advance on the wool gathered for sale. The cost of handling, defatting, and cleaning the wool added to a buyer's overhead, but after the wool was sold on eastern markets or in Europe, the growers received supplementary checks representing their share of the profits.

The superintendent was able to gain support for this only in Laguna where a pool was formed in June or July. Even though pooling always seemed to bring in more money than individual sales, the Indians were suspicious of the procedure. For one thing, they doubted that they would receive a fair share of the grand profits they were sure eastern business concerns enjoyed. For another, the Indians knew the local traders and very often were indebted to them for items purchased in their stores during the year. The traders would appear on auction day and tempt individuals from the pool with offers a fraction higher than those under consideration by the pool. However, as the government farmers knew and tried to point out, the price proposed by the trader was likely to be the only payment received by the Indian for his wool.[6] There was no question of future profit sharing. Ácoma eventually joined the Laguna pool, although the sellers resented having to transport their wool to the other pueblo.

In 1920, the wool market had been falling to such an extent that the Indian agency wondered if any sales would occur. Finally, the entire lot of Ácoma and Laguna wool was consigned to an Albuquerque broker, W. E. Mauger, representing Mauger and Avery of Boston. Laguna received an advance of fifteen cents a pound for an improved quality of wool, while Ácoma got ten cents. In June 1921, the Indians received an additional sum from Mauger and Avery which increased the total price for the 1920 wool clip to $.17841 per pound for Laguna and to $.164 for Ácoma. Total earnings for both pueblos was $16,979.56.[7]

During 1921, the wool market dropped even lower. The local traders began to take an aggressive part in breaking up the practice of pooling. The biggest troublemaker, according to the agency superintendent, was Sidney Gottlieb. Gottlieb managed the Cubero Trading Company, a subsidiary of the Bernalillo Mercantile Company in Grants. The mother company was owned by Carl Seligman, who also had affiliated stores in Bernalillo and at Santo Domingo Pueblo. Confident of Seligman's backing, Gottlieb used his familiarity with the Indians to secure the Laguna pool with a bid only a fraction higher than the advance offer made by Avery and Mauger of Boston. This so exasperated the government farmer at Laguna that he denounced Gottlieb's motives in front of the Indians. The confrontation prompted Seligman to write Superintendent Leo Crane for an explanation. Crane answered that the United States government, represented by the Indian service or its agents in dealings with the Indians, was not bound to accept either the highest or lowest bid but would "always make such terms and conditions as in their best judgment they see fit."[8]

Superintendent Crane was actually bluffing his way through a situation which was already undermining his policies. The government farmer at Laguna had informed him that Gottlieb and Emil Bibo (Solomon's brother) had bought up the 1921 clip from Ácoma and some Lagunas for seven cents a pound. The market continued to be low and the ready offers from the Bernalillo Mercantile Company were tempting no matter how low they really were. Crane was not confident that there would be another pool.[9]

Despite the gloomy indications, some Lagunas elected to pool their 1921 clip and Mauger and Avery advanced nine cents per pound on July 14. At the same time, Gottlieb appeared to change his previous offer of eight and a half cents to nine and a half cents a pound, but without success. Later, Mauger and Avery supplemented the advance with an additional payment of six and a half cents per pound, raising the total revenue for the Lagunas to $10,897.13. The interference from the local traders, however, infuriated Crane as their influence tended to discredit him and the government policy.[10]

Seligman, Gottlieb, and Bibo somehow got their grievances into political channels and Superintendent Crane received a visit from a traveling auditor in September. A special investigator followed in January 1922. The first had a look at the government's handling of the monies being paid to Ácomas and Lagunas for their wool; the inspector was more directly concerned with the government's relations with the Indian trader.

Meanwhile, Crane blamed Congress for not clearly defining the responsibilities of the agency. He maintained that the Pueblos continued to receive treatment unlike that accorded other reservation Indians. For that reason, he thought it better to allow Mauger and Avery to pay the Ácomas and Lagunas directly by check. Making such payments a matter of government record, he feared, only made the Indians distrust governmental interest in these matters.[11]

To the inspector, Superintendent Crane made serious and somewhat emotional allegations about the Indian traders. These traders had married Indian girls from Ácoma and Laguna, he reported, as a means of worming their way into Indian confidence. At Laguna, such a person became a "squawman" and henceforth his grafts were winked at and accepted. For years such traders had been operating without licenses and had made "quite vigorous fight against recognizing any authority of the Indian agent." The major difficulty grew out of the liaison formed by the trader with the individual Indians who sold him their wool either because they were friends or because they were indebted to him. This practice concerned agency officials because they believed that it constituted less profitable sales. Furthermore, Superintendent Crane stated that every year the traders attempted to prevent the Indians from pooling. He believed, but could not prove, that they even tried to bribe the governors to achieve this end.[12]

Superintendent Crane could not guess how the sales would go in 1922. The wool market appeared favorable though, and he was determined to protect Ácoma and Laguna from the "small-priced local buyer." Governor Frank Paisano of Laguna gave the first indication of the Lagunas' desire to pool. At the same time, Ácoma Governor Juan Pablo Garcia invited the local traders to Acomita for a meeting. Gottlieb appeared and led everyone to believe that he was handling the Ácoma wool that summer. However, Ácoma postponed making any deals: it was still too early to sell and the market seemed to be going up. Crane was convinced that the Ácomas, after having watched the Lagunas earn about twice as much as anybody else in 1921, would pool.[13]

By June, ten prospective bidders had expressed an interest in the wool sales. The government farmers began collecting and storing the 1922 clip. The Ácoma governor indicated a desire to pool, but preferred to store the Ácoma wool at Acomita.[14]

On June 12 the advertisement went out for the auction to be held on June 20. About this time a rumor spread in Albuquerque that local traders had already purchased most of the wool. In apparent contradiction, a local trader (not Gottlieb) in Grants reached the New Mexico Congressional delegation and accused the Indian Agency of forcing the Indians to pool even though they had made previous contracts to sell locally.[15]

In a mass meeting, the Indians turned down offers of twenty-eight and twenty-four cents, voting unanimously to sell on consignment to Charles Chadwick and Company of Albuquerque, for an advance of twenty-two cents per pound. There was a total of 114,074 pounds (uncleaned), with 22,452 pounds from Ácoma and 91,622 pounds from Laguna. Chadwick represented Jeremiah Williams and Company of Boston which sold the wool and remanded additional payments directly to the Indian sellers.[16] The final payment added another ten cents per pound making 1922 one of the more prosperous years in wool sales to date.[17] In spite of this, in 1923 the Ácomas chose not to pool their wool. The Indian Agency, frustrated though it may have been by the decision, held to the policy that it should advise only and in no way force the Indians to pool against their wishes.[18]

Roscoe Rice, serving as goverment farmer in 1923, compiled a report on stockraising and agricultural production which showed that

88

along with wool sales, Ácomas relied mainly on farming for their livelihood. (See Table 4.)

TABLE 4

Ácoma Agriculture and Livestock, 1923

Kind	Number	Value
Sheep	2,094	
Goats	9	$ 22.50
Cattle	112	1,344.00
Horses	55	825.00
Chickens	283	141.50
Turkeys	25	15.00
Chili	685 strings	1,027.50
Corn	149,336 pounds	2,986.72
Mutton	584 head	2,044.00
Eggs	3,528	102.00
Wool	24,776 pounds	8,299.96
Beans	1,300 pounds	91.00
Alfalfa	517,000 pounds	5,170.00

The Routzen family raised the largest flock of sheep and reported the largest clipping. Francisco Barela and Estevan Antonio harvested the most corn and alfalfa (the latter selling for one cent a pound) in 1923. The Ácomas said they were farming about 415 acres.[19]

During 1922–23, Ácoma suffered a severe drouth but in 1924 the livestock holdings appeared to increase. There were some 8,000 breeding sheep and lambs, 1,000 horses, and 800 cattle. Total earnings amounted to $100,136 that year and Laguna earned almost twice that. Together the two pueblos earned considerably more than all other pueblos, although Santo Domingo came close to Ácoma with reported earnings of $88,507.47.[20]

For several years Ácoma and agency officials tried unsuccessfully to break the control of the wool growers by the Cubero Trading Company. Individual Indians continued to owe money to the Company which was happy to accept wool as payment. But in 1928, the Ácomas formed their first pool apart from the Lagunas. Their clip brought a final total of thirty-five cents per pound, the highest price paid for wool in the southwest. At this point Ácoma understandably expressed a desire to continue this practice annually.[21]

The effect of the national economic depression was driven home in 1930 when the bottom dropped out of the wool market. Prices fell from between thirty and thirty-five cents a pound to fifteen cents. To make matters worse there were no prospects for buyers. Given this state of affairs, the Ácomas began to think of the cattle market as more promising. Nevertheless, the wool industry continued to grow during the next decade, accompanied by a marked increase in cattle raising.[22] The Great Drouth during the 1930s also effected stockraising. In 1938, the United Pueblo Agency claimed that the Ácoma range, with a carrying capacity of 2,122 cattle, was being "badly overgrazed."[23] To save all ranges, the Secretary of the Interior directed that steps be taken to reduce the excessive number of animals. Thus, in June 1939, the Ácomas agreed to reduce their herds by marketing the culls. As a result, the number of cattle, horses, and burros dropped from 1,840 to 1,719, while sheep went from 15,985 to 15,511.[24]

At the same time, the United Pueblos Agency decided that the herds should be upgraded. Dr. Sophie D. Aberle, general superintendent of the agency, was placed in charge of the improvement program. By 1940, Ácoma had reduced the number of its livestock to meet the "carrying capacity" for the range. The pueblo had also purchased new rams. Dr. Aberle, on the advice of a Soil Conservation Service agent, determined that the Ácomas required forty more bulls for their herds.[25] The governor and the council met on May 7, 1940, and agreed to borrow $1,600 from the federal government to purchase sixteen Hereford bulls.[26]

This was the beginning of the Ácoma community herd. In 1941, the Ácomas bought sixteen more bulls, all registered Herefords. After clearing up some misunderstandings among individual cattle growers, the governor and council passed an ordinance which defined the community herd. This ordinance stated that Ácomas might keep their own bulls only if they were of a quality equal to those being purchased by the tribe. Cattle growers had access to the bulls but had to pay service fees to a community fund designated the "Pueblo of Ácoma Bull Fund." Payment could be guaranteed by the growers' execution of a lien upon the cows for which the bull services supplied. The plan was to pay off the loans used for purchasing the bulls within five years.[27]

The increase in stockraising—to the detriment of agricultural production—which resulted from the improvement program and the establishment of the Ácoma community herd, is graphically illustrated in Table 5, which follows. The Ácomas have never returned to farming on a scale comparable to that before World War II, when nearly fifty percent of Ácoma's income came from agriculture and about seventeen per cent from other employment. By 1944, labor produced over half the income while stockraising and agriculture contributed only one fourth to the total, with stockraising leading over agriculture. In recent years only nine per cent of the Ácomas have been farming.[28]

TABLE 5

Ácoma Agriculture and Livestock, 1941–45

Commodity	1941	1943	1945
Cattle	1,020	1,060	1,072
Sheep	10,780	13,362	18,895
Goats	20	21	40
Swine	45	56	70
Horses	710	653	515
Chickens	1,000	3,140	3,240
Turkeys	50	128	79
Alfalfa	1,050 tons	600 tons	289 tons
Corn	9,135 bushels	6,500 bushels	2,100 bushels
Beans	329 bushels	375 bushels	150 bushels
Chili	15,400 pounds	15,000 pounds	6,800 pounds
Melons	29 tons	3 tons	2 tons
Apples	585 bushels		
Peaches	700 bushels		
Pears	280 bushels		
Apricots	85 bushels		
Cherries	36 bushels		
Plums	185 bushels		
Grapes	100 bushels		

When the railroad came through the Ácoma grant, Acomita and McCarty's Station became outlets for the sale of pottery, a secondary industry with which Ácoma women supplemented the family income. This had been going on for some years before 1918 when an Indian Agency survey listed Ácoma women who sold pottery.[29] (See Table 6.)

TABLE 6
Pottery Sales

Name of potter	Sales at Acomita	Sales at Acomita and McCarty's Station
Mrs. Juana Dolores Sanchez	$ 6.00	
Mrs. Anna Pino	16.00	
Mrs. Loreta Watchempino	3.00	
Mrs. Concepción Ray	1.75	
Mrs. Loreta Victorina	20.00	
Mrs. Louisa Victorina	21.25	
Mrs. José Peconta	14.25	
Mrs. J. R. Sarracino		$30.00
Mrs. Victoria Lupe		15.00
Mrs. Maria Simirrón [sometimes Cimerone]		50.00
Mrs. Faustino Vallo		40.00
Mrs. Lola Ortíz		40.00
Mrs. Lupe Pasquale		5.00
Mrs. Lupe Chávez		50.00
Mrs. Juana García		15.00
Mrs. Maria Chino		18.75
Mrs. Lupita Simirrón [sometimes Cimerone]		5.00
Mrs. Juana Simirrón [sometimes Cimerone]		13.75
Mrs. María Vallo		45.00
Mrs. Lupe Lucario		12.00
Mrs. Juana Poncho		35.00
Mrs. María García		45.00
Mrs. María Estevan		1.50
Mrs. Dolores Abeita		35.00
Mrs. Santana Sánchez		5.00
Mrs. Juana Sánchez		5.00
Mrs. Jofera Antonio		25.00
Mrs. San Pablo Corn		20.00
Mrs. Cecilia García		1.00
Mrs. María Sarracino		79.00

During the 1920s, when tourists began to arrive in automobiles, pottery sales increased. "The Ácoma people are stockmen and agriculturists," wrote the superintendent in 1924, "and the women excel in pottery but their weaving for which they were once so favorably known is a lost art."[30] By 1939, Ácoma potters reported an income of $4,825. This dropped to about $4,410 in 1940.°[31]

°See Appendix 6: ÁCOMA ARTISTS AND TRAINEES.

In addition to stockraising, agriculture, and arts and crafts, Ácomas supplemented their income in other ways. In 1928, Governor Juan Luis Huskay formalized pueblo fees charged to tourists who visited Old Ácoma. These included a twenty-dollar charge to take motion pictures.[32] The railroad and automobile brought even more non-Indian traders and in 1924 the governor and councilmen began requiring outsiders to obtain tribal approval and permits to carry on trade. The Ácomas encountered something new in one outside trader: a Home Supply Company was retailing goods from a "commissary car" which traveled from place to place on the reservation.[33] Permits to traders increased tribal income only slightly.[34]

During the decade preceding World War II, the population of Ácoma exceeded 1,000. After nearly 400 years, the pueblo began to regain the numbers first reported by the white man. Larger population, however, meant that more income was necessary. The community herds did not benefit the entire community, only those who were members and paid dues. The same principles applied to sheep raising. Supplemental income was obtained from the sale of piñon nuts, firewood, wild horses, and hides. A few Ácomas continued craft work, supplementing potting with silverwork and ceremonial drum making. In 1940, income from pelts was $50; piñon nuts, $150; silverwork, $40; leather and beadwork, $970; drums, $275; and pottery, $4,410.[35]

Ácomas' income remains deplorably low. In thirty years it has not improved commensurate with the cost of living. A recent survey revealed that one third of the working-age population was without income of any kind and specified:[36]

> Another 18.3 per cent received less than $500 during 1967. Still another 18 per cent of the population reported incomes ranging from $500-999. Only 9 per cent were able to attain incomes in the $1,000-1,999 category, and 8.5 per cent were in the $2,000-2,999 bracket. In total, 86 per cent of the working-age population receive incomes under $3,000 per year.

More and more Ácomas look toward better education and training for their children as a means to help resolve the reservation's many problems. Meanwhile, Ácomas work at wholesale and retail trade, mining, some construction, manufacturing, and transportation. Home gardening, hunting, and bartering also contribute to family incomes. In addition, there are Ácoma women who work for wages, generally as domestics, off the reservation. The growing tourist trade provides some employment on the reservation and the promise of more if the potential can be developed.°37

IS EDUCATION SERVING OUR IDEALS?

Today Ácomas have a more direct role in deciding what should comprise the educational experience for their young. Heretofore, the Bureau of Indian Affairs not only shouldered the administrative burden of education, but also directed what Indian children should be taught. Agency superintendents, who approved local programs, have always insisted that Indian children learn English, then some of the white man's "civilized ways," and finally, if possible, a trade. This is not a condemnation of these efforts, simply a statement of their one-sidedness. The Queres (Keres) language is rapidly disappearing among the young.

The older people of the pueblo often openly resisted the school system, but children did attend the day schools at Acomita and McCarty's. As they grew older, some were able to leave the reservation to attend federally operated or church-run secondary schools.[38] Public schools, colleges, and universities were available after 1913 but generally beyond the financial reach of Indians. The new status of governmental wardship offered many advantages to the Pueblo Indians but did not help to prepare their children for higher learning.

For years, the subjects taught in the day schools remained the same but teachers were of uneven quality. Each morning was given over to reading, writing, and speaking the English language. After lunch, there were drills in elementary arithmetic and on the days of the week and

---

°Ácomas reported over 10,000 tourists visited Old Ácoma in 1965 and gross sales connected with this enterprise totalled $59,825.

1   Overview of Ácoma Valley. Sky City in distance, causeway on left. *Photograph courtesy Lee Marmon.*

2   Sky City with Enchanted Mesa in the distance. *Photograph courtesy Lee Marmon.*

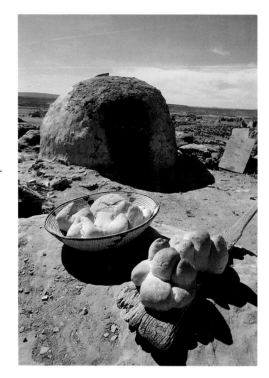

3 Ácoma bread and horno. *Photograph courtesy Lee Marmon.*

4 Sky City street leading to San Estevan Mission. *Photograph courtesy Lee Marmon.*

5, 6, and 7   Ancestral Ácoma pottery. *Photographs courtesy Lee Marmon.*

8, 9, and 10   Contemporary Ácoma pottery. *Photographs courtesy Lee Marmon.*

11   Ácoma-Canoncito-Laguna Hospital. *Photograph courtesy Calvin Aragon.*

12   Medicine man's curing room at hospital. *Photograph courtesy Calvin Aragon.*

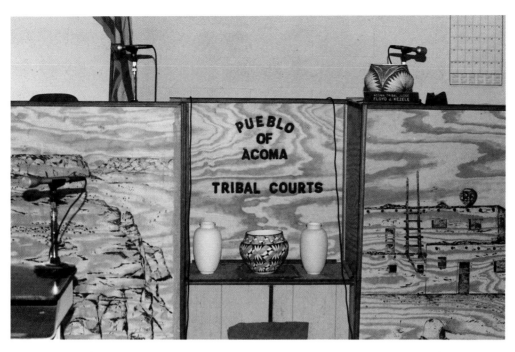

13   Pueblo of Ácoma Tribal Courts judge's bench. *Photograph courtesy Pueblo of Ácoma Tribal Courts.*

14   Pueblo of Ácoma Tribal Courts, portion of jury box. *Photograph courtesy Pueblo of Ácoma Tribal Courts.*

15　Wilson Ranch/Bar-15 purchase area, main buildings. *Photograph courtesy Land Office, Pueblo of Ácoma.*

16　Wilson Ranch/Bar-15 purchase area, cattle drive in 1988. *Photograph courtesy courtesy Land Office, Pueblo of Ácoma.*

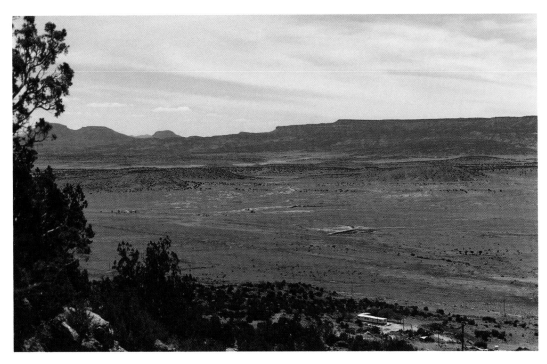

17   Red Lake Ranch purchase area. *Photograph courtesy Land Office, Pueblo of Ácoma.*

18   Well on Red Lake Ranch. *Photograph courtesy Land Office, Pueblo of Ácoma.*

19   Cisterns after a storm and mission of San Estevan from the south. *Photograph courtesy Lee Marmon.*

20   Padre's or Horse Trail to Sky City. *Photograph courtesy Lee Marmon.*

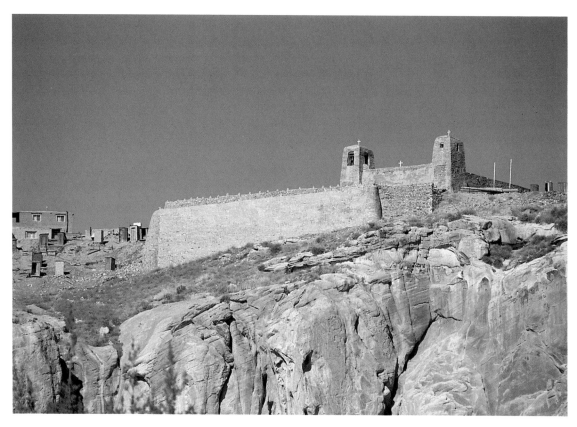

21 Cemetery wall after repairs. *Photograph courtesy Lee Marmon.*

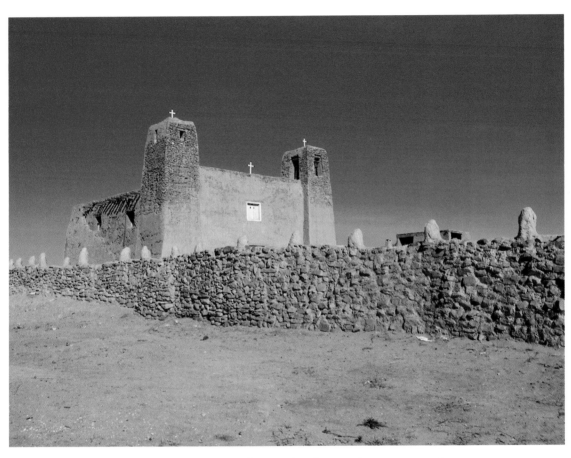

22   Church facade and cemetery wall with mud sentinels. *Photograph courtesy Lee Marmon.*

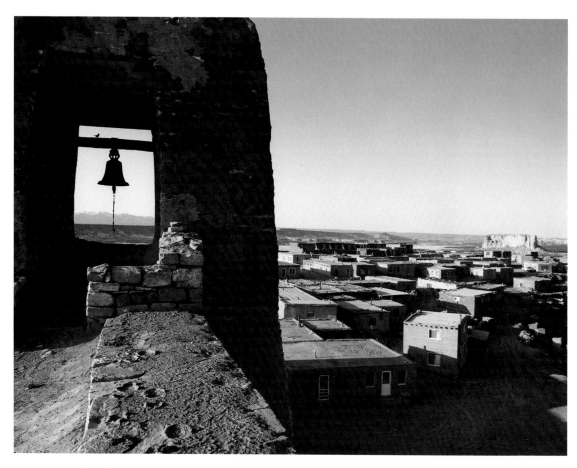

23   Tower and bell donated by Spanish king. *Photograph courtesy Lee Marmon.*

24   Convent courtyard. *Photograph courtesy Lee Marmon.*

25 Christmas Eve at San Estevan. *Photograph courtesy Lee Marmon.*

names of months. Late in the afternoon came training in industrial work and housekeeping. Teachers celebrated national holidays, especially Thanksgiving, Christmas, Lincoln's and Washington's birthdays, with programs and games which often included the parents. Such occasions usually featured a talk by the government farmer or by the visiting doctor who would hold forth on tuberculosis or some other threat to health. In 1919, the superintendent of the pueblo day schools, including those at Acomita and McCarty's, proudly reported that headway was being made vis-a-vis the utilitarian subjects taught in the nineteen schools.[39] (See Table 7.)

TABLE 7

Subjects Taught In Day Schools, 1919

Girls

Beadwork	1 school
Cooking	7 schools
Crocheting	3 schools
Embroidery	2 schools
General elementary housekeeping	15 schools
Sewing	18 schools
Washing and ironing	7 schools

Boys

Basketry	11 schools
Beadwork	2 schools
Care of school grounds, etc.	19 schools
Clay modeling	3 schools
Gardening	16 schools
Woodworking	2 schools

The wonder was that there was any enrollment at all. Although compulsory school attendance was required under a Congressional Act of July 13, 1892, superintendents appeared powerless to enforce it except by gentle persuasion. The day schools remained small and primitive. At Acomita, school was held in the church building which the government rented. There was room for only thirty pupils although facilities were needed for at least 120 youngsters. The McCarty's school was a government building, but again facilities were almost entirely lacking. Over a three-year period, the attendance at Acomita was less than half what it should have been. In 1916, the Department of Interior ruled that all Indians had to complete third grade before attending boarding school; and it was only at boarding school that the youngsters could finally learn a trade.[40]

For several years the Indian Agency tried to enlarge the Acomita Day School to accommodate 120 pupils. By 1920 the agency had land, but still no money. The Ácoma schools were not the only ones neglected. Superintendent Leo Crane requested four new schools, one each at Acomita, Santa Ana, Seama, and Encinal. At the last two places he described the rented buildings as "decided National disgraces of which the Indian Service should be heartily ashamed." Neither did he forsee a brighter future. After allotment of the school funds for 1921, he was left with "four large round dollars with which to keep life in the day schools and from which to pay all the routine expenses incident to office, travel, etc. etc."[41]

As for the accomplishments of the day schools, the same superintendent reported in exasperation:

> It is believed that the text books authorized for our schools are fairly good—as good as likely we will ever have—unless some teacher of mentality recognizes the necessity for producing a series of texts designed specifically for Indian Schools. Most teachers are unimaginative, and they say that this "can't be done." The criticism will be answered some day by some person of imagination, experience, and vision, DOING IT. Even the books prepared for use in teaching other aliens are not adaptable to our work. We attempt to teach Indian children, having alien home conditions, training, etc., and being familiar with field, forest or desert environment of a narrow horizon (having practically no comparison), through books prepared for white and largely city children. Most of the illustrations, lessons, and problems are foreign to Indian children, and therefore for a long time incomprehensible. The child is confused and muddled before a real beginning is made. Everyone of the text-books may be paraphrased into words, phrases, sketches, stories and

problems common to his daily life, and therefore made easy to
understand and interesting from the beginning. I have found
but one teacher who sensed this opportunity to aid the child
and at the same time lift himself from the commonplace rut in
which most teachers must be classed. Two books would be
required. The best teacher, in my opinion is the one who
depends the least on books.

Even so, a schoolteacher's influence seldom passed beyond the
classroom to older Indians. Unless conditions changed, Crane feared
that "the schools will be inefficiently wrestling with the problem of
education for a long time, probably several generations."[42]

Even after a new day school was established at Acomita in 1925,
conditions changed little. Enrollment increased to as many as seventy-
five students for a while. A few always stayed away, either because
parents forbade attendance in the belief that such instruction was
destroying their culture, or because the students were needed to help at
home.[43]

It was during this period, when the Ácoma population was
approaching the 1,000 mark, that there were only between 150 and 175
children in school. About a sixth of these attended the Albuquerque
Indian School, a third were in boarding school in Santa Fe, and half
were enrolled at the two day schools on the reservation, the school at
Acomita always having about twice as many students as that at
McCarty's. Another few students attended St. Catherine's in Santa Fe
or public schools in California. A handful of parents refused to send
their children to school at all. Several youngsters were married or
worked outside the reservation, and there were a number of young
people unaccounted for.[44]

Educational policies were as limited in scope as ever. In 1930,
however, some measure of success was reported.[45]

Industrial work has been carried out largely along the
lines described by the General Supervisor of Education for the
district. Some of our schools where the children are of the
proper age have enrolled for 4-H club work. We have sewing
clubs for girls, rabbit clubs and handicraft clubs for boys, and

in one or two places cooking clubs have been established. Home gardens have been encouraged, but where teachers are going away for summer school and for their annual leave these things have not proven to be a very great success. . . . Our day schools have been able to bring to the people of the villages a better knowledge of the English language and English customs. Our teachers have done excellent community work among the pueblos and, generally speaking, the people of the pueblos have cooperated fully with the schools. Probably the most outstanding accomplishments during the past year has been greater uniformity in the character of the work being done in the day schools. More English has been used in the pueblos than at any time in the past, in our opinion. . . . Every Indian child between the ages of 6 and 18 has been placed in schools or accounted for. The children are not incorrigible and there has been no problem of discipline in this district which the teachers have been unable to handle. Returned students offer no problem among the pueblos at this time. The home conditions are such that if these young people upon graduating from our schools do not secure positions where they can work and earn their own living they can return to their homes and take up the life of the pueblo. They build better homes and keep their homes in a manner that is a credit to the educational institutions from which they have graduated. These young people are having a decided beneficial effect upon the pueblo life.

At other times, however, the Southern Pueblos Agency could identify as many as a hundred youngsters who were not in school. Authorities were never certain but what the actual figure might be higher. Superintendents placed the blame for absenteeism squarely on those parents, not only in Ácoma but in all the pueblos, who seemed agreeable to the benefits of education but who still felt that sheepherding or housework was of greater practical benefit to the people. The agency was deprived of its legal clout when the Courts for Indian

Offenses ceased to exist in 1924. After that, superintendents noted an increase in absenteeism.

> They [the pueblos] quickly relieved themselves of the school burden by taking the position that as long as these were government schools it was up to the government to see that the children attended them, with the result that we have received practically no assistance from the Governors, the only authority apparently having the power to enforce attendance. We have absolutely no authority to arbitrarily take a child away from its parents and send it to school, and we could not do it every day, as would be necessary in the day schools, without a considerable part of all of the Indian Service personnel assigned to this Agency.

In 1929, Congress passed an act which permitted individual states to enforce compulsory education within Indian reservations but New Mexico failed to respond, probably because the federal government retained all other prerogatives connected with the education of Indian children.[46]

Acomita Day School still furnishes local elementary education. The Bureau of Indian Affairs moved two buildings for classrooms onto the grounds three years ago and there are now eight classrooms. The Bureau had funded educational projects beside the day school, including a new beginners school which opened three years ago on the road between Ácoma and McCarty's. The McCarty's Day School, used as a head-start project for five year olds, is being funded with Office of Equal Opportunity funds. From local grade schools, Ácoma children may go on to attend the Ácoma-Laguna High School, opened in 1952, or public and parochial schools.

In 1970, Ácomas were encouraged by the Bureau to select their own school board. Since then the board has interviewed and recommended the hiring of a principal and six teachers (all professionals), eight aides, and three bus drivers. Aides and bus drivers are all Ácomas. Although the board has attempted to hire Ácomas as teachers, it has had little or no response. In 1973, the Ácomas instituted a Parent-Child Development Program which funds mothers to use their homes for day care centers, and for the training of expectant mothers. Bilingualism is being encouraged at these centers.

LAW AND ORDER

Until recently, Ácoma had no law enforcement agencies which would have fulfilled the white man's idea of such institutions. Agency superintendents pointed out that the Sandoval decision in 1913 not only made the Pueblo Indians wards of the government, entitled to the protection afforded reservation Indians, but also provided them rights as citizens who could vote, pay taxes and own property. But the Pueblo Indian retained a peculiar legal status which was not only ill–defined, but also represented a kind of double standard. For example, it was thought that penal codes should apply equally to Indians and whites but New Mexico state laws did not apply on the reservation. Applicable federal statutes were often either inadequate or unequal in application. The superintendents claimed that this state of affairs inhibited their efforts to install a police force in the pueblos.[47]

Even if the Indian Agency could have found funds to organize a formal police force, Ácoma traditionalists regarded any attempt to do so as a threat to an existing ritualized institution as old as the tribe. This institution, the office of war chief, has always been vested with the authority to supervise tribal ceremonies. There are three war chiefs, assisted by three cooks and ten "little chiefs" all of whom are chosen annually. In the 1920s, ethnologist Leslie A. White described the war chiefs as the most important officers of the entire pueblo since they were the men who actually came into contact with the people and directed their affairs.

> They do their utmost to preserve the old traditions intact; they oppose any initiation of white or Mexican customs and deplore lack of interest in the old ways. The war chiefs constitute one of the most vital forces in the Pueblo.

Their position remains much the same today. The *fiscales*, or sheriffs, also elected annually, continue to deal with outsiders and to help the governor preserve law and order.[48]

In 1920, the Indian Agency had seven of its own policemen stationed throughout the Southern Pueblos Agency jurisdiction. However, only one was considered "worth his salt as a policeman. The others were messengers and would not have nerve enough to arrest any men under any circumstances unless the superintendent were behind them with a prod." During some of these years at least, the resident farmer was assisted by an Indian policeman and either he or the farmer sometimes arbitrated minor disputes and domestic quarrels. The farmer's helper was entrusted with rounding up truants for the day schools. Until 1924, the Court for Indian Offenses was usually held by the agency superintendent who traveled from place to place with the so-called chief of police. Any prisoners were kept at Isleta Pueblo in the only reservation jail available for Pueblo Indians during this time.[49]

In 1916, Jose Leon Chino served as Ácoma's first judge. Judge Chino heard his first case on January 25, 1916, at Acomita, but referred it to the agency superintendent for final decision.[50] In 1922, five pueblo judges were appointed and given jurisdiction over the entire Southern Pueblos Agency. These included Bruce Vallo at Ácoma, Pablo Abeita at Isleta, William Paisano at Laguna, John Dixon at Cochití, and Jesus Baca at Jémez Pueblo.[51] The Secretary of the Interior defined the powers of their courts to include local disputes and minor crimes. Since there were only five judges to serve ten pueblos, the Indian agent was given authority to act as a trial judge when necessary. The biggest problem, however, was confinement for prisoners who were kept in "a very small concrete box" at Isleta. And, according to one agent, the four pueblos of Ácoma, Sandía, San Felipe, and Santo Domingo did not wish to have Indian judges, police, or an Indian agent, let alone any interference from New Mexico officials because, "They cling to ancient customs, that are by no means clean in ceremonial rites, and stubbornly resent Governmental measures."[52] After a year or two, the practice of appointing an Indian judge was discontinued and most of his responsibilities were transferred to the pueblo governor. Indian agents recommended that the Indian pueblos be provided with a criminal law code similar to the state codes.

Young people observed the state's marriage and divorce laws without conflict. The liquor question, however, was serious. The agency reported that there were not enough law enforcement officers to protect Indians from bootleggers. Although there were no signs that the Indians made their own liquor, neighbors near the reservation bootlegged intoxicants with little or no interference from state authorities.[53]

Leslie A. White, who wrote with such detail about the social order of things at Ácoma in 1930, described the government as "theocratic," as it is today. The cacique, medicine men, and war chiefs exercise religious authority and serve as the foundation of the political structure as well. Dealing more directly with pueblo administration is the governor, the council, and elected officials: two lieutenant governors, three sheriffs, and a water boss. In recent years, the pueblo has added a treasurer, a secretary, and interpreter.[54]

Annual elections are held during the Christmas week and results are announced during a special tribal gathering of all the men on December 28. The governor and slate of officers traditionally serve for one year but because the changeover comes too soon for the modern pace, governors often are reelected, serving two years or more.° In recent years, the tribe has considered allowing the election of the governor for a two-year term. Another innovation provided salaries for tribal officials, which frees them from other time-consuming employment.

After 1850, the old Mexican political divisions were ignored and gradually replaced by counties, sections, and townships. Ácoma was considered a corporate political entity within Valencia County.[55] After the Sandoval decision granted wardship to Pueblo Indians, Ácoma was grouped with other pueblos under one federal Indian Agency whose headquarters were in Albuquerque. On September 1, 1919, the Department of the Interior approved dividing the Agency, and Ácoma, along with nine other pueblos, became the responsibility of the Southern Pueblos Agency. Seven pueblos north of Santa Fe comprised the Northern Pueblos Agency.[56]

Also in 1919, the Neblett decision in the *Lonergan habeas corpus* case went a long way toward defining the jurisdiction of government

---

°Appendix 7: INCOMPLETE LIST OF GOVERNORS FOR ÁCOMA PUEBLO.

officials. In part the decision stated: "The jurisdiction of the United States over the Indian affairs is exclusive and the state government in which the Pueblo is located is not authorized and would not be justified in interfering with the internal affairs of the Indian Pueblo." The full effect was noted immediately within the pueblos: federal agents moved freely to evict interlopers without any further interference from civil authorities.[57]

By 1922, the Indian agent directed the work of eighty or more employees. These included an office administrative force, a field force of seven stockmen and farmers, a health field corps of five physicians, five matrons, and the staff at the Laguna Sanatorium for the treatment of tuberculosis. There were nine Indian policemen and for a time, the five Indian judges for the Courts for Indian Offenses. The Indians usually learned about agency policies and the superintendent's plans through the government farmers or stockmen.[58]

Ácoma did not have a police department in the modern sense until 1972 when the pueblos were included in revenue sharing. Since then, the reservation has added such a department headed by a chief, and including a sergeant, two helpers, and two patrol cars. The last replaced the community car which was available to the sheriffs when not being used by the governor or other Ácoma officials.

OF SOUND MIND AND BODY

When the first two sisters appeared in the world and the Ácomas began to multiply, a powerful evil—illness—arrived. Very early in tribal existence, the medicine man and the medicine societies gained great importance in everyday life. They commanded respect because they combated the forces of sickness. Today, the medicine man holds a position of paramount importance in Ácoma, although Ácomas do, of course, seek medical help off the reservation, and use hospitals in Grants or Albuquerque. The choice of healing methods depends upon whether there is money or insurance, or the ability to travel long distances.[59]

The Spanish conquerors and others who followed brought communicable diseases against which Native Americans had little or no resistance. Ácoma, whose population probably exceeded 5,000, and may have approached 10,000, during the sixteenth century, counted only 492 persons in the 1900 census.[60] The fact that Ácoma's population has grown to nearly 3,000 in the years since then can be attributed almost exclusively to improved living conditions and medical care.

Until recently, health statistics were never actually maintained for Ácoma. In the absence of a resident physician, the superintendent relied on the government field matron, whenever one was assigned at Ácoma, for what little information he received. The scarcity of experienced medical personnel plagued the agency and worked a hardship not only on Ácomas, but on other Pueblo Indians who had difficulty getting to medical help. During the winter of 1918–19, the agency reported that influenza took many lives, as much as ten percent in some of the pueblos. During this period all pueblo tribes shared the services of five physicians and five field matrons.[61]

Agency reorganization in the fall of 1919 expanded the field medical service somewhat. Even so, in 1920, the agency superintendent reported that "Physicians do not make great headway with the Pueblo Indians of San Felipe, Santo Domingo, Jémez, Zia, and Ácoma."[62] At this time, the field physicians for the southern pueblos were still widely distributed, as demonstrated in Table 8.

TABLE 8
Field Physicians, 1920

Contract physician at Bernalillo	serving Jémez, Zia, Sandía, and Santa Ana	988 Indians
Regular physician at Domingo	serving Cochití, Santo Domingo, and San Felipe	1,687 Indians
Regular physician at Laguna Sanatorium	serving Old Laguna, Mesita, and Paguate	1,129 Indians
Regular physician at Seama	serving Seama, Paraje, Encinal, Casa Blanca, Ácoma, and McCarty's	1,733 Indians
Regular physician at Albuquerque	(Dr. A. M. Wigglesworth of the Albuquerque Boarding School), serving Isleta and Navajo population	1,500 Indians

104

Field matrons, who served the immediate community to which they were assigned, were generally to be found at Jémez, Cochití, San Felipe, Bernalillo (for surrounding pueblos), and Isleta. Superintendents recommended additional field matrons for Santo Domingo and Ácoma.[63] A good field matron was supposed to inform physicians of any medical needs and, unfortunately, was equipped to do little else. In other ways, however, she reached every Indian home, organizing clubs for food preparation and preservation, and teaching sewing. For many years the matron at Santa Ana and Sandía Pueblos conducted a well-received "Save the Baby" program.

In 1922, the entire Southern Pueblos Agency had only one hospital, the tuberculosis sanatorium at Laguna. The sanatorium did accept other patients, but was too far from most pueblos to be used much. This was a major reason that the agency recommended an Indian hospital for Albuquerque.[64]

In 1928 the large Indian hospital in Albuquerque began taking patients from neighboring pueblos. With the nearest hospital service available for Ácoma in Grants or Albuquerque, except for the out-patient clinic at Laguna, illnesses and their cures continued to be dealt with largely by medicine men and medicine societies in the traditional manner. It is likely that the lack of medical facilities added to their importance in the Ácoma way of life. Pueblo health programs remained under the control of the agency until 1955 when the Public Health Service assumed the responsibility for Pueblo health care.[65]

In 1969, Ácoma officials petitioned the U. S. Congress, through New Mexico Senator Joseph M. Montoya, for a new twenty-bed hospital. The proposal had been coordinated with interested parties and approved by the Public Health Service. The tribal resolution stated that the Pueblo was willing to share the hospital facility with non-Ácomas and to make a site available without cost to the federal government. The Ácomas also said that they hoped the hospital would help alleviate their poverty. They cited Office of Economic Opportunity data which, in 1964, listed Ácoma as one of the sixteen poverty–stricken tribes in the nation, the average annual per capita income running under $750. The existing health station at Acomita was inadequate and offered no dental services. By comparison, the Laguna health center, opened in 1966, provided general medical and emergency care, minor surgery, and laboratory, electrocardiographic, and x-ray services. This center, and the hospitals in Grants and Albuquerque, were the nearest medical facilities to Ácoma. Older Ácomas resisted going long distances to hospitals; they not only had a fear of dying far from home, but also of not being able to communicate since many spoke no English. Finally, most Ácomas found it difficult and expensive to travel to any of these hospitals for a series of appointments or specialized treatments.[67]

In June 1970, Congress approved funds for planning the hospital as well as for a new school complex, the latter to be located between Acomita and McCarty's. No location was specified for the hospital. Laguna Pueblo lost no time in applying to the Public Health Service for the same hospital—to be placed on the Laguna Reservation at the I-40 highway interchange at Casa Blanca. The Ácomas, in a second resolution, offered a site on reservation lands immediately south of I-40 at the Acomita interchange.[68]

Public Health Service officials received additional resolutions from sites off reservations. Cubero, San Fidel, and the Cañoncito Navahos, all supported the Ácoma location. The Ácomas reaffirmed the location, agreeing to improve the entranceway and outlining the advantages they offered: space for housing, ample water, recreational facilities, sewage disposal, and public utilities. They argued that it would cost less to build the hospital on the Ácoma reservation and that the eighty to one hundred new jobs it would provide were very badly needed. Ácoma Governor Lorenzo Toribio reminded the Public Health Service that on at least two previous occasions, Laguna Pueblo had received major construction projects with Ácoma support; namely, the Ácoma-Laguna High School and the Laguna-Ácoma Public Health Service Clinic. The Public Health Service conducted a review of the two sites and notified the Indians on May 28, 1971, that the Albuquerque Area Indian Health Service had chosen the Ácoma location.[69]

The Public Health Service selected Ácoma because, economically speaking, the Ácomas had a greater need for the hospital, which represented their first significant reservation-based industry. In fact, the Public Health Service proposed a fifty-bed hospital to serve the entire community instead of the twenty-bed facility originally requested. There were other considerations involved in recommending Ácoma; for one thing, Laguna's proposed site was only one and a half to two miles from the existing clinic. A new hospital there would not only have constituted a duplication of services, it would also have preempted the clinic itself, which was considered one of the finest. Furthermore, it would have broken the earlier commitment to Ácoma for an out-patient facility. Lastly, the Laguna site would have required construction of a railway overpass.[70]

On July 14, 1971, the Indian Health Service concurred with these recommendations. Laguna appealed the decision on August 3.[71] In response, the Indian Health Service conducted a second site survey. This time there were three proposals: Laguna, Ácoma, and Interstate 40 at Highway 23. On February 7, 1972, the Indian Health Service announced—again—that Ácoma was the site chosen for the hospital. The planning stage was completed during the spring of 1974, but actual construction awaits appropriations from Congress.[72]

OUR LANDS

The modern world has forced the Ácomas to deal with boundaries, a concept first introduced to them by the Spanish. The natural tendency since time immemorial was to use the lands in all directions from the Ácoma Mesa as needed for farming, herding, gathering, hunting, or religious purposes. Delimiting conditions were imposed only by enemies or geography.

One of the first and most urgent boundary problems arose when Ácoma became a barrier to the railroad on its way west. On December 28, 1880, after a year or so of negotiating, the Ácomas agreed to provide a strip of land "one hundred feet wide included between lines fifty (50) feet each side of and parallel to the center line of the Atlantic and Pacific Railroad." Ácoma relinquished title "forever" to an area containing McCarty's Ranch.° In return for this right of way, the

---

°The rail stop at this point gave rise to the modern settlement of McCarty's.

railroad company paid Ácoma $1,078.85, a goodly sum for the times.°°[73]

It was soon discovered that boundaries served a positive purpose. Undesirable people could be forbidden to cross them, either to enter or use lands within the reserve. The case of former Ácoma Governor Solomon Bibo was a classic example.

Bibo's actions as a "progressive" during his years at Ácoma had brought him enemies as well as friends. For several years prior to 1920, the Bibo family had lived off the reservation, calling San Rafael, New Mexico, their home. By 1920, they were in San Francisco, California, where some of the children attended school.° Son Leo showed up in January carrying a letter from the Ácoma Governor Frank Ortiz, who claimed that Solomon was no longer a resident of the Ácoma community and no longer entitled to grazing or other privileges on the Ácoma grant.[74]

Some Ácomas insisted that Bibo should have a permit to graze sheep. Solomon himself based an appeal of his exclusion from the reservation to Governor Ortiz, as well as to the superintendent of Southern Pueblos Agency, upon the fact that his wife was Ácoma. Surely, Bibo said, she and their children had the right to own sheep on Ácoma land. He pointed out that he had a house and some farmlands on the reservation, and that he had served four separate terms as governor. He had tried to help the Ácomas in every way including paying his own expenses while doing pueblo work.[75]

Governor Garcia took the matter to the pueblo attorney, asking for a legal opinion. Since Solomon Bibo had left Ácoma, he had not assisted the people in any way; now could his children graze their sheep on the Ácoma grant? The attorney responded by saying that the governor and council had the right to exclude, in this case, the son Leo Bibo, "if he has severed his relations with the Pueblo."[76] Next a general meeting was called to consider Solomon's requests. The officers, the principal men, and all the people decided that "they will not let him come back

---

°°The centerline entered the grant in Township Number 10, North Range, 7 West, at a point 37 feet south of Mile Corner Number one of the east boundary line and at Station 3336.20 of the railroad line. The centerline left the west boundary on Section 23, Township 10, North Range, 9 West, at Station 3983.

°The children were Rose (age 30), Clara (26), Celia (24), Isima (23), Leo (20), and Carl (9).

to the Ácoma grant," and that furthermore, he had no right to come back. The Solomon Bibo family relations with Ácoma remain uncertain to this day and may never be clarified unless a new Indian census now underway accords some degree of legal status to Bibo descendents.[77] There is, however, precedent for excluding them from Ácoma land. Regarding land tenure, ethnologist Leslie A. White stated that:[78]

> All the land at Acoma 'belongs to the cacique.' Land for farming is allotted by the cacique to men who ask for it, the cacique goes to the land and marks off its boundaries.
>
> When land has been allotted to a man it 'belongs' to him and his family. At his death his widows and daughters inherit it. . . . Although in theory the 'title' to all land remained permanently in the cacique's hands, custom would not permit him to deprive a family of farmland that they were using; it was theirs as long as they continued to use it. But should a family discontinue to use a field or garden, the cacique could reassign it to someone else.

Such control ended at the reservation boundaries. Outside, Ácomas can and do purchase property, and pay taxes, just as any other United States citizen.

When Ácomas became wards of the United States government in 1913, there appeared to be an official attitude of callous indifference toward her lands and her problems which lasted for more than two decades. The Pueblo Lands Board, created by Congress in 1924 to settle land problems, found that the Ácomas as a community, by purchase or otherwise, held no lands other than those previously recognized in the grant. Agency officials insisted that this could not be, that Ácoma had access to much more land for farming and grazing. They cited Executive Orders of 1910 and 1917 which withdrew 175,000 acres of land from the public domain "for use of the Lagunas and such other Indians as the Secretary of the Interior may see fit to settle thereon."[79]

Unfortunately, the Executive Orders made no mention of Ácoma. The withdrawal of 1910 included about 25,000 acres lying between the Ácoma and Laguna grants; then the Order of March 2, 1917, withdrew some 150,000 acres south and east of the Ácoma grant. The Board had on hand complaints from Ácoma Governor Leo Garcia about Laguna having received thousands of these acres south of Ácoma grant. To the Commissioner of Indian Affairs, Governor Garcia claimed that "he had made a trip to Santa Fe where he was shown the original Ácoma Spanish patent which extended the boundary north to Mount Taylor." The Ácomas wanted all the land that was being "stolen." "We are all surrounded as taking up a homestead every American and Mexican Lagunas on our grant."[80]

The commissioner refused Ácoma appeals for land in 1917, and again in 1925, repeating that the Executive Orders were meant to apply to the Ácomas as well as "such other Indians as the Secretary of the Interior may see fit to settle thereon."[81] As to the western boundary, which the Ácomas claimed had not been settled correctly in the last century, it appeared doubtful that the area contained sufficiently large areas to be of any benefit because "of the presence of White and Mexican settlers." The Indian Commissioner cautioned the superintendent about the Ácoma requests, directing his attention to the Congressional Act of June 30, 1919 (41 Stat. 3-34), which prohibited the permanent withdrawal of public lands for Indian reservations. For this reason, the Commissioner said that it would be necessary to obtain a temporary withdrawal from the president before presenting the matter to Congress.[82]

The apparent favoritism shown by the government to the Lagunas over many years fostered suspicion and great misgivings among Ácomas. The Lagunas always got help from the Washington agents, Ácoma Governor James H. Miller pointed out in 1924. He desired to know why the Executive Order lands had been given to Laguna and speculated that it may have been because "they are better educated than my people, because they are richer, and that our former governor did not know how to explain our troubles to Washington."[83]

While Pueblo Lands Board investigations continued, the Lagunas began fencing all lands comprised in Executive Order of 1917, except that part immediately south of Old Ácoma Pueblo. This strip, about three miles long and a mile and a half wide, the Lagunas said they would concede unconditionally. On the other hand, Ácoma was claiming all these lands as part of her original grant. The Lagunas did

110

offer to assist Ácoma in recovering lands beyond her northern and western boundaries. In any case, they believed Ácomas were being incited by non-Indians residing along the railroad north of Ácoma. These non-Indians, said the Lagunas, would resist giving lands to Ácoma which would cut into their own grazing areas, particularly those around Cubero and McCarty's.[84]

The situation eventually resulted in a special investigation by the Pueblo Lands Board. A comparative analysis of Ácoma and Laguna lands plainly indicated the dire straits of both pueblos, and of Ácoma in particular. Taking the matter to the Commissioner, the Special Supervisor in Charge of the Southern Pueblos pointed out that the lands defined by the Executive Orders should not be divided without careful and due evaluation of water supply and carrying capacity of the ranges involved. "The Executive Orders set apart areas of semi-arid land and there has been beneficial use made of that acreage and of additional areas under lease by the Indian people—of a truth, largely by the Laguna people." The Ácomas made no use of this land, he believed, because of their suspicions and dislike of the Lagunas. He found Lagunas using at least 40,000 acres. If the Ácomas would only follow the example of the Lagunas whom they say are better educated, richer, and in greater favor, he explained to the Commissioner, they would perhaps make some advancement.[85]

The carrying capacity of the Executive Order lands according to the same report was exeedingly low. Sheep required not less than ten acres per head, cattle and horses needed forty to fifty acres per head during years with normal rainfall. Examination showed that Lagunas herds needed twice as much range; so did those of Ácoma. Local agency officials were of the opinion that "Ácomas were very much more in need of additional area and less able to take care of themselves."[86]

The Pueblo Lands Board, however, did settle two long-standing disputes: the Cubero grant matter and that of the Rancho of Santa Ana. In 1896, the Court of Private Land Claims found that the newly surveyed Cubero grant overlapped the Ácoma grant by 283.23 acres. Notwithstanding, the district court of Valencia County held that the Cubero grant was valid. In reviewing the case, the Board determined "that the title of the Indians to 283.24 acres in conflict has not been extinguished." The Board refused to allow the case to remain unsettled. On March 27, 1930, the attorney general filed suit in the federal District Court of New Mexico against the Cubero heirs and others. A new decision, delivered on May 14, 1937, ruled in favor of Ácoma.

On a similar overlap with some Laguna lands, known as the Rancho of Santa Ana, the Board found there were 208.67 acres belonging to Ácomas without clear title. Arrangements to obtain a deed from Lagunas proceeded on the basis of a suit settled in Ácoma's favor in 1858. However, no records could be found showing judgment in the case and there were no Laguna claimants to the land in question.[87]

The Board further sought to extinguish titles or negotiate agreements to cover easements for the Mountain States Telephone and Telegraph Company, the Postal Telegraph Cable Company, the Western Union Telegraph Company, the main highway, and the interests of the Atlantic and Pacific Railroad Company. The last included the use of stone and water, along with the right "to lay, build, and construct such pipes, drains, flumes, ditches, dams, or reservoirs as may be required to conduct the water from the points on said Grant where it may be found to the line of said railroad, etc."[88]

Finally, by an Act of Congress, on May 23, 1928, the Board ascertained there were no claims or encroachments on lands set aside for Ácoma use. This Act also formally created the Ácoma reservation. The lands included the area to the south of the Ácoma grant and amounted to 55,800.98 acres. The Board's investigations showed at this time (1929) that no other pueblo lands, other than the grant and reserved lands, had been acquired by Ácomas as a community by purchase or otherwise. At the same time, the Board felt there was not "sufficient evidence for them to consider the claims to the west under the limitations of the law under which they were working, and as far as they were concerned these claims will not be considered further."[89]

Beginning in 1934, a representative program adopted by the Office of Indian Affairs would more than double Ácoma's holdings by setting aside public lands by purchase. The program was instituted to deal with the drouth problems and to supply Ácoma's growing population with adequate farming and grazing lands. The Ácoma claims that the survey and patent did not cover the old grant boundary calls were reexamined but a resurvey was not ordered.[90]

In 1944, the United Pueblos Agency described the total of Ácoma's lands as follows: Indian land totalled 153,844.28 acres; lands included in the Federal Purchase Area administered by the Indian Service, 88,197.33 acres; and leased lands, 13,241.84 acres. All of this, used by Ácomas, totalled 255,283.45 acres.

TABLE 9
Ácoma Landholdings

Ácoma Lands	Acreage	Date Acquired	Authority
Pueblo Grant	94,158.87°	September 20, 1689	Original Spanish Grant
		December 22, 1858	Confirmed by Congress
		November 19, 1876	Patented
Santa Ana Grant	208.67		Portion used by unwritten agreenment with Laguna Pueblo
Five sections in Cibola National Forest	3,195.76	December 31, 1939	Acquired by deed from A.T.&S.F. Railway in exchange for land within Pueblo granted for railway right-of-way
Indian homesteads in Ácoma Purchase Area	480.00		
Reservation°°	55,800.98	May 23, 1928	45 Stat. 717
		March 21, 1917	Executive Order
Total	153,844.28		

°Acreage of original grant by official survey (94,169 acres) less 10.13 acres for government school site.

°°Net Indian area of both Congressional Act and Executive Order Reservation.

TABLE 10

Government Lands in Ácoma Purchase Area
(Lands within Government Purchase Areas administered by Indian Service)

Land	Acreage	Date Acquired	Authority
Resettlement Purchased lands in Ácoma Purchase Area	54,268.30	January 18, 1938	Executive Order 7792.
Public Domain in Ácoma Purchase Area (Indian Service Administration)	33,721.03	December 31, 1938	Secretarial Order.
Rehabilitation purchase within exterior boundaries of Ácoma Purchase Area	208.00	January 2, 1942	Indian Office letter of July 18, 1941.
Total Government Land	88,197.33		

The report described the maximum carrying capacity of the total acreage as 3,462 cattle and estimated that 855 acres of range was required to produce enough food for a family of five. Ácoma had about fifty acres under dry farming, 1,391 acres of irrigated farmlands, 7,386 acres of commercial timber, and 179,412 acres of non-commercial woodland.[91]

Under the Act of August 18, 1949, part of the Reservation Program, another large amount of land passed to Ácoma as trust lands. In the Eleven Township area the Ácomas received trust to 48,880.74 acres of lands formerly purchased by the government and 31,199.81 acres of former public domain.[92]

About this time, the United States heeded Ácoma's plea for recognition of the injustices suffered in the past from encroachers. The Indian Claims Commission Act of August 13, 1946, invited Indians of the United States to settle old grievances before an Indian Claims

114

Commission established in Washington, D. C. The Ácomas began working on their land claim in 1948. On December 27 they hired claims attorneys Sam and Nicholas C. Dazzo, and appointed a Land Claims Committee consisting of Jose Ulario Garcia, Syme Sanchez, Joe A. Chino, and Joe C. Ray. They presented Ácoma's petition to the Indian Claims Commission on August 9, 1951.[93]

The petition asked payment for land losses suffered by Ácoma Pueblo. Count I alleged that the United States had failed to protect the Pueblo's right, title, and interest to and in the lands occupied by the Ácomas since time immemorial, excepting therefrom certain lands. Count II alleged that the Pueblo of Ácoma, from time immemorial had had the right and lawful authority to use water for irrigation and domestic purposes. The United States by permitting construction of Bluewater Dam was depriving the Pueblo of its water rights. Count III alleged that the United States had the duty and obligation because of the fiduciary relationship to protect the aboriginal right, title, and interest of the Pueblo in the lands and waters. Lands excluded from Count I were the pueblo grant, including the Santa Ana grant of 95,500 acres; the Ácoma Indian Executive Order Reservation of 147,800 acres; and certain small overlaps in the Cebolleta grant and the Paguate Purchase, a Pueblo of Laguna grant, which totaled 9,260 acres.

For twenty years a great deal of effort went into proving the Ácoma case. The claim proceeded to hearings in 1952, 1953, 1954, and 1957, in Albuquerque, Santa Fe, and Washington, D. C. On September 19, 1957, the Pueblo completed its case. But several barriers now loomed to prevent a settlement.

For one thing, the Pueblo of Laguna, whose case was then before the Commission, contested title to some of the land. The Commission ordered the dockets of both pueblos consolidated for hearing. Then the Navaho Indians laid claim to all Ácoma and Laguna lands, except those within the patented grants. On February 23, 1961, the Commission ordered that the Laguna, Ácoma, and Navaho dockets be consolidated to the extent that the areas did overlap. During the subsequent hearing, which took place in Washington, during two weeks in September, witnesses succeeded in averting the Navaho claims, which were not subsequently appealed.

Prior to this in 1959, the historians for Ácoma and Laguna had produced United States Territorial Court judgments of July 1857 and April 22, 1858, in a suit between the Pueblos of Ácoma and Laguna. These cut off the eastern one third of the Ácoma claim and described a north and south dividing line.* This was acceptable as the common boundary between Ácoma and Laguna *for purposes of the land claim suit only.* All attorneys for the United States, the Pueblos of Ácoma and Laguna, and the Ácoma Land Claims Committee agreed to accept it with the understanding that the agreement in no way changed the present land boundaries between Ácoma and Laguna.

The Ácomas won their case by showing that they had used and occupied the lands from time immemorial. Ácoma witnesses testified about traditional land uses.[94] They described, in fact, an area which comprised 1,507,940 acres.

On March 31, 1967, the Indian Claims Commission handed down its opinion declaring that the Ácomas had aboriginal title to the lands, water, and minerals described.

> With his information at hand, the Land Committee and your attorneys sat down and determined it would be to the advantage of the Pueblo to settle this case. We determined that any value in the neighborhood of $6,000,000.00 would be very reasonable. We have Syme Sanchez' book, prepared by the BIA, which shows that the United States Government in 1934, 1935 and 1936 purchased over 500,000 acres of land for approximately $1.85 per acre. A proposal, dated March 3, 1970, was made to the United States Government to settle. By telephone, the United States Attorney, Mr. Bernard Newburg, refused that proposal. Thereafter, on March 19, 1970, a letter to Mr. Newburg was mailed wherein the Pueblo de Ácoma was willing to accept what we proposed to you today. On April 10, 1970, the Department of Justice, through Mr. Kashiwa, Assistant Attorney General, accepted that proposal and offer.
>
> This figure was the combined effort of your attorneys, the

---

*See Appendix 4: BOUNDARY AGREEMENT BETWEEN ÁCOMA AND LAGUNA, 1857.

Land Committee, and the Tribal Council of the Pueblo de
Ácoma who sat and discussed and determined it was to the
best interest of the Pueblo to settle for this amount.

The compensation finally agreed to was $6,107,157. The governing
body of the Pueblo passed resolutions to approve the settlement on
April 19 and May 9, 1970, and the stipulation and final judgment of the
Department of Justice followed on May 16. No land exchanged hands
with the settlement.[95]

The land claim satisfied, an even more critical need remains. The
"findings" placed before the Indian Claims Commission included a
plea for compensation for the loss of irrigation waters "occasioned by
the enlargement of the dam at Bluewater on the upper San Jose River
in 1927." Permanent water and good farmland had attracted settlers in
the early 1870's. Considerable local irrigation and an earth dam
constructed at Bluewater in 1894 diverted or used up water which
normally flowed through Ácoma and Laguna lands. The first dam
washed out around 1900, but it was rebuilt in 1907. This in turn was
replaced by a concrete dam in 1925, creating Bluewater Lake one mile
wide and 7.5 miles long. During the 1940s, vegetable growing was
begun on a large scale and water from the dam was supplemented with
sixteen irrigation wells.[96]

As their lands have dried up, Ácoma's population has relied more
and more on the San José River. This water is becoming brackish and
unusable as settlements, such as Grants and Bluewater, exhaust the
fresh water supplies. Drinking water must be carried to Old Ácoma
since the natural cisterns are no longer replenished by enough
rainwater. The residents at McCarty's and Acomita have several wells,
but people are worried that the water from one communal well at
McCarty's is being spoiled by impure seepage. It is becoming
increasingly clear that Ácoma cannot develop her lands and support a
greater population without more water.

Ácoma entered the bicentennial decade preparing for a better
future and desirous of identifying more closely with the outside world.
In a speech before an Air Force audience in 1971, Governor Lorenzo
Toribio, himself a veteran of World War II declared that the Indian

117

people face many of the same problems of the white man. "To better our image as leaders, particularly for our young people, we look forward to greater cooperation and facing these problems together as human beings."[97] And as evident in the next chapter, desired improvements, despite setbacks, are taking place rapidly at Ácoma.

6

Epilogue: Toward Self-Determination

Ácoma citizens fought in World War II, Korea, and Vietnam, witnessing significant changes not only to the world scene but within themselves, their families, and friends. Returning veterans saw the reservation, with its immense age and timeless traditions, in greater contrast to the insecurities and challenges they found on the outside. The objectives of preserving traditions while making a living came into sharp focus for tribal leaders who began tackling problems head on, understanding full well the reservation was beginning to lose young members to the outside world through marriages and career opportunities. Discussing these issues in view of Ácoma's natural resources, the Tribal Council formally recorded on June 11, 1981: "Among the most critical priorities are land, water, education, housing, and health."[1]

Two events played into the hands of new governors and a changing Tribal Council after 1970.[2] During meetings on May 9 of that year, Ácoma voted to accept the land-claims settlement, as noted in the prior chapter, for over $6 million. Though held in trust, the interest from those funds represented more buying power than the Tribe had ever had. No one could foresee its impact at the time.[3]

A second event also significantly modified relationships between Ácoma and the United States. A new federal law, dated January 4, 1975, replaced the paternalistic wardship established by Congress in 1934

119

and promoted self-determination and education for all Indian tribes. With the Bureau of Indian Affairs serving as monitor, the Ácomas began developing programs and services normally conducted by the federal government. Such programs included upgrading Indian education as the law insisted the Indians control their own educational activities. Further commitments on the part of Congress were made through amendments to the Act in 1988 to "permit an orderly transition from the federal domination of programs for and services to Indians to effective and meaningful participation by the Indian people in the planning, conduct, and administration of these programs and services." Henceforth, the United States was committed to the Ácomas (and all Indians) in their development of strong and stable tribal governments to carry on and administer their own programs, and, further, to develop the economies of their own communities. The impact on tribal affairs of this new arrangment was not fully understood by 1990, nor could anyone foresee changes beyond that. But on the reservation, tribal officials accepted the two phenomena with mixed reactions, seized opportunities, and began transforming Ácoma in many ways.[4]

THE RESERVATION AS A PLACE TO LIVE

Entering the last decade of the twentieth century, Ácoma continued to be for all the "place that always was"—for many centuries home to living and dead, young and old, rich and poor. Visitors to Sky City were no longer directed past Enchanted Mesa; rather they left Interstate 40 at the Acomita turnoff and drove through the village past geological outcroppings where ancient stone dwellings were barely distinguishable from the land and hills along the San José River. Recently paved roads provided access to most centers on the reservations, but the real mecca for Indians and non-Indians remained Sky City.

The road rolled and curved past the tribal offices, a new school, several businesses, housing, and over low-timbered grazing lands on a high plateau until, all of a sudden, the ground broke away steeply for hundreds of feet where an elevated road pointed to Sky City. Always

120

a thrilling sight, the Indian citadel was poised in its timeless natural beauty against a valley of legendary rock monuments next to the sacred Enchanted Mesa.

After an easy descent, visitors drove over a causeway to the new Visitor's Center and Museum. Some have compared the experience to what the great causeways must have been like on Lake Texcoco when Cortez met the Aztec emperor Montezuma in 1519. At Christmas, the Ácomas lined both sides of the roadway, from crest to Sky City, with *luminarias,* and families united for four days starting Christmas Eve. During summer months, however, the Visitor's Center was besieged with tourists who browsed through its museum or wandered outdoors under the picturesque ramadas where pottery vendors display wares. The tourists also waited their turn on the bus to ascend the steep trail into ancient Ácoma, a city still governed by the caciques and patrolled by war chiefs. By the 1980s, visitors were a major source of tribal income—the gross income from tourists in 1989 was over $1 million.[5]

After the Christmas holidays and continuing an ageless tradition, the Cacique Clan announced new tribal officer appointments for the coming year. In 1990, the ancient theocratic governmental system was still in force with clan members holding authority over land allocations and governmental appointments, including the selection of governors, first and second lieutenant governors, sheriff with two deputies, interpreter, secretary, and councilmen. These officials and the Ácoma Tribal Council directed all civil affairs for the tribe. Caciques appointed twelve councilmen to serve indefinite terms while the Council appointed a bonded treasurer for an indefinite term.[6]

Along with changes brought to the tribe by the land-claims settlement and the self-determination laws, the governors, their staff, and the Council faced increasingly complex responsibilities. Some of these were reflected in the following list of "rights and powers" enumerated by the Tribal Council:

1. To employ legal counsel. The choice of counsel and fixing of fees to be subject to the approval of the Secretary of Interior.

2. To veto the sale, disposition, lease, or encumbrance of tribal lands.

3. To execute leases, contracts, and permits, that where leasing or encumbering of the tribal land is involved, [required] the approval of the Secretary of Interior.

4. To negotiate with the federal, state, and local governments and governing authorities of their Indian tribes.

5. Power to enact ordinances to cover the following:
   a. To establish and govern the procedures of a Pueblo court.
   b. To provide for the maintenance of law and order within the Pueblo governing personal conduct.
   c. To govern the civil rights and domestic relations of the Pueblo members and their families within the Pueblo.
   d. To levy and collect membership dues and to raise revenue.
   e. To regulate trade, inheritance, and land holdings and private dealings in land among members within the Pueblo.
   f. To set up procedure for the determination of membership.
   g. To establish and operate business or civil enterprises on behalf of the Pueblo and to provide for the management of any such enterprise.
   h. To provide equally for the welfare of all the members of the Pueblo.

6. To fix salaries of the Pueblo officials and employees; to appropriate and expend available funds of the Pueblo; to regulate tourist fees; to provide procedure for the collection of local revenue; and to prescribe methods of recording the income and expenditures of the Pueblo funds and for the safeguarding of such funds.

Ácoma, unlike many New Mexico pueblos, had not adopted a constitution by 1990, and even though the Tribal Council appointed a constitution committee, there appeared no likelihood that a constitution would be adopted in the near future.[7]

An increasing number of boards and special offices created by the Council also reflected influences from the claims settlement and self-determination projects. These organizations reported to the Tribal Council and tribal officers and touched the lives of the people in various ways. On the scene in 1990 were the Tribal Court and a judge, Health and Social Services Office, Ácoma-Laguna-Canoncito Hospital Board, Title VII Bilingual Programs Office, the Ácoma School Board, Housing Improvement Program Office, Land Office, Planning Office, Records Office, an Enrollment Office, and more.[8] Also, the Pueblo annually contracted for grants from the Bureau of Indian Affairs to help pay for the activities of the Enrollment Office, for example. While the arrangement alleviated unemployment, tribal officers anticipated problems raising sufficient funds to operate these programs independently of the Bureau.[9]

Individual and family incomes continued to be a tribal priority. In 1977, Governor Stanley Paytiamo estimated unemployment was 66 percent. Population rose to an estimated 4,305 in January 1990 after an all-time low in 1900 of just under 500. Anaconda Uranium and Kerr-McGee mining companies in the Grants area, meanwhile, continued closing down and laying off workers. Those not involved in self-employment or reservation work, particularly younger people, sought careers in Albuquerque and elsewhere; some of these moved off the reservation rather than commute. In short, unemployment was a continuing problem at Ácoma.

For many years the old people tried to find some sort of cottage industry for Ácoma households and were inspired by successes in jewelry making at the neighboring Pueblo of Zuñi. However, attempts to revive textile weaving at Ácoma met with no success.[10] But some families launched their own businesses on the reservation, particularly in response to the growing tourist trade, and scattered along the highway were bread making and curio stores, pottery vendors, and a feed store. Home employment otherwise consisted of traditional dry and irrigation farming, stock raising, and pottery. Indeed, pottery making and vending increased enormously in recent years as tourists arrived in greater

123

numbers. In 1990, well over a hundred potters, men, women, and children, earned money from their wares.

For Ácoma traditionalists, the growing popularity of the industry threatened the old ways of making pottery. Too many potters took shortcuts around getting the proper clay and the hard work of preparing it with crushed shards, decorating the pieces traditionally with vegetal and earth colors, and following correct firing procedures. The late Santana Sánchez said, "We always use cow shits." Nowadays, too many potters were producing experimental forms with modern kilns, pre-fabricated ceramics, and commercial mixes and paints. One company on the reservation sold a ready mixed clay that included the necessary crushed shards. And one potter said that some used felt-tipped pens for applying designs rather than the traditional, finely made yucca-fiber brushes.[11]

For food, clothes, and automobiles, the Ácoma frequently traveled to Grants and Albuquerque. Local Mexican-American communities had gasoline service stations, grocery stores, trading posts, restaurants, and liquor. After 1977, Ácoma had its own United States Post Office in the tribal office complex. And although Ácoma did not yet have its own fire department, it was working on getting one while relying on the Pueblo of Laguna Fire Department.[12]

Most Ácomas preferred to collect drinking water from nearby springs. Wells drilled into the San José River basin filled the reserve tanks that had been placed strategically for family use and for watering livestock. The latter also got water from springs and natural cisterns during the rainy season. Government reports from the 1970s show that of 145,000 acres of irrigable lands available, the Ácomas were using only 17,000 acres of dry farmlands and 2,000 acres of irrigated farmlands. This is because an uncontrolled effluent from Grants's sewage-treatment plant began to cause crusting and soil hardness, water-logging on the surface, salinity, and a host of pollution problems.[13] From 1932 to 1966, there were twenty-six years during which irrigated lands averaged 1,030 acres per year. Crops from the fields and orchards included: alfalfa, chili, barley, garden vegetables, melons, beans, corn, oats, potatoes, wheat, apples, peaches, apricots, pears, cherries, plums, grapes, and prunes. But between 1966 and 1983, irrigated land decreased to a mere 342 acres. So in 1983, Ácoma tribal officials and the Pueblo of Laguna moved against the City of Grants "to stop the pollution of our water and [asked] for compensatory and exemplary damages."[14]

Attorneys for Grants denied that the town was at fault and said pollution fell under the purview of the federal Environmental Protection Agency and the New Mexico Water Quality Control Commission. They, not Grants, failed to enforce existing clean water and quality control acts. All these agencies eventually denied responsibility but agreed, in the end, that the problem had been overlooked. The impasse ended peacefully with a settlement in U.S. District Court on February 20, 1987. All agencies readily assured Ácoma and Laguna that the operation of the treatment plant would soon comply with existing laws and that pollution of the river would stop.[15]

The United States District Court rendered a final judgment in favor of the Indians on May 14, 1990:

1. That the defendant, City of Grants, shall pay Acoma $96,300 in five annual installments of $19,226 damages.

2. Federal defendants shall pay Acoma and Laguna the respective sums of $327,641.23 and $97,250.25 in attorneys fees.

3. The federal defendant shall pay plaintiff, Pueblo of Acoma, the sum of $9,280.77 in taxable costs.[16]

The federal defendants appealed the district court action, hoping to avert paying attorney fees and costs. By the time of the judgment, Ácoma had already received installments from Grants for damages and town officials had been directed to remove the sewage effluent from the San José River. In February 1990, Grants city officials proceeded with a new treatment plant and began to set aside money and raise $8.9 million for a proposed plant. Governor Stanley Paytiamo had stated after the 1987 settlement that the pueblo "was entitled to the good, clean water arising at Horace Springs without it being polluted by Grants sewage and the Pueblo would continue to fight to protect that water because it is very important to his people."[17]

ÁCOMA EDUCATES HERSELF

Still preeminently concerned with education, the Tribal Council created Ácoma's first school board on April 19, 1978. The people living on the reservation had access to the Headstart program through grade 6, Sky City Community School, Laguna-Ácoma High School, and grade schools and high schools in Grants and Albuquerque. The Council also enacted programs to encourage Ácoma youth to attend college. Initial school board members, all Ácoma, were Ray A. Histia, Christine P. Sims, Juan Steven Juanico, Velma Vallo, Joe Salvador, and Elizabeth Paisano. Adopted by-laws enabled the Board to serve as governing body of the Ácoma school system; make policy by creating rules and regulations for control, management, and operation of the system; and carry out and negotiate terms for all education grants and contracts from the Bureau of Indian Affairs and other agencies.[18]

The Board became a guiding force and fostered enlightened school programs. For example, a bilingual project in the reservation schools was potentially preserving Ácoma traditions and the Ácoma-Keresan language. The program especially targeted students in kindergarten through the third grade. Initial funding came from the Bureau of Indian Affairs, then directly from the United States Department of Education, and more recently from the federal Office of Bilingual Education and Minority Language Affairs.[19] Christine P. Sims was the initial bilingual project director, and with drive and vision she translated the new Title VII three-years extension grant into a "systematic and logical approach" to bilingual education. Reporting to the Department of Education in 1987, Director Sims stated, "We have made good progress thus far in all curriculum areas." Her work had brought about (a) the development of curriculum guides that listed essential skills, contents, and competence for each grade; (b) incorporation of the Ácoma bilingual approach into the regular social studies and language arts programs; (c) development of classroom materials based on Ácoma culture, history, and language; and (d) appropriate revision of all materials, as needed. From the begining, all students in the program were Ácoma Indians from homes in which Ácoma-Keres was being used for everyday pursuits as well as for communicating within the Pueblo community.[20]

In 1987, Juan Steven Juanico succeeded Christine Sims as director of the bilingual program. Director Juanico immediately became aware of the vast responsibilities of the position and the needs of the program. He expressed deep concerns that more had not been done to formalize training programs at all levels of reservation schooling. Some linguists were being successfully integrated into classes at the Sky City Community School, but to prevent gradual if not total loss of the language, special staffing, supplies, and funds were needed. However, funds were not forthcoming. Nonetheless, thanks to Christine Sims's and Steven Juanico's special talents, the efforts of a dedicated staff, and the cooperation of the older generation, bilingualism inspired some exciting results.[21]

Ácoma created its first Ácoma-Keresan dictionary as a result of the bilingual program in 1982. In an immense first step toward recording its native language, the tribe collected the most common words by topics or subject and grouped them with simple conversations, first in Ácoma-Keresan and then in English. The dictionary included borrowed Spanish words as well as several common phrases in Zuñi and Navaho. The attractive format had Ácoma designs on the cover, and all words, phonetics, and their explanations could be easily understood by Indians who had little or no knowledge of the language.[22]

The bilingual program also produced a comprehensive guide or resource book to use with the dictionary. The book included learning activities, games, and various subjects "successfully used by bilingual teachers and aides at Sky City Community School to introduce and reinforce elements of the Ácoma languages." For primary and intermediate level students, the source book was totally oriented to the experiences one has living on the reservation.[23]

Christine Sims also collected Ácoma stories into book form, another first for Ácoma. Primarily for classroom use, the stories were collected from the old people, transcribed from tapes, and liberally illustrated by David Garcia, Jr. The illustrations depict experiences, special events, and familiar surroundings the elders alluded to in their stories about the Pueblo of Ácoma. English translations were included toward the end of the book.[24]

Since becoming program director, Juanico has placed much of the language and many of the stories on computer tapes. In this process, the elders told stories and pronounced the Ácoma-Keresan words as they should properly sound. These taped sessions were then transcribed into printed and illustrated booklets. Computer printouts proved to be faster and more economical than printing. Particularly imaginative were the animated computer graphics being readied for use by students.

As for post-high-school education, Ácoma received Bureau of Indian Affairs funds specifically to encourage Indian students to continue their education. The intention was to develop leadership and increase employment opportunities in professional and vocational areas. Only lately, however, have students been taking advantage of the Ácoma Higher Education Program generated by this money. Perhaps through the influence of parents, peer pressure, and role models, Ácoma graduates were attending colleges in larger number.[25]

The Tribal Council managed the program in 1990 and hired Lloyd Tortalita to direct all higher education efforts on the reservation. The Bureau set aside $100,000 annually and students were encouraged to apply for grants and loans for which they had to compete with other students, Indian and non-Indian. Applicants number twenty-five to fifty each year and most chose to attend New Mexico colleges, with a few traveling to Fort Lewis College, Durango, Colorado, the University of Utah, or the Haskell Institute, Lawrence, Kansas. Although the policy may change, these opportunities did not apply to students interested in trade school. The Bureau suggested that these students seek help through its employment assistance program.

Since the Higher Education Program began, tribal offices have received a number of talented and highly motivated college graduates who came back to fill leadership positions. However, graduates expressed ambivalence about returning to the reservation because salaries were low.[26]

Aside from higher education, Lloyd Tortalita's responsibilities included the reservation's Adult Education Program. When local mines began closing in 1984, forcing an estimated 70 percent unemployment rate at Ácoma, Pueblo Governor Merle L. Garcia and the Council hoped to revive the Adult Education Program in an effort to increase skills and self-sufficiency among adults who needed jobs. Toward that end, the tribe created an adult learning center that featured individualized instruction and the means to issue General Education Degrees. Even though participants were transported to the center and received reimbursements for going, attendance was never very high. The program had three students in fiscal year 1984 and eighteen in fiscal year 1985. The number gradually declined even more.[27]

TRIBAL HEALTH AND WELFARE

Ácoma Social Services reflected the Tribal Council's concerns with health and welfare. The reservation population was not immune to personal problems found in any society and some Ácoma people said that these problems were amplified by isolation, unemployment, alcohol and drug abuse, and the stresses of contemporary life. Social Services, for a number of years under the able direction of Flo Hazen, lent a helpful hand through such programs as individual and family counseling and child welfare and protective services. Overall, the office sought to help individuals get services "necessary to alleviate dependency and improve self-image and strengthen personal functions of Ácoma community members."

Having always been a large, well-funded program, Ácoma Social Services was so severely affected by U.S. budget cuts in the 1980s that the Tribal Council was forced to ask for help from governmental health services. Of concern was the tribe's ability to deliver quality health care, especially in remote areas, and to deal with alcoholism and related problems. Plans for mental health services had to be abandoned.[28]

A meal service at the Ácoma Senior Center was also threatened by budget cuts. The tribe purchased the building in 1980 and established a nutrition site near the Sky City Community School and across the road east of the tribal office complex. Here seniors had a meeting place where meals were served Mondays, Tuesdays, Thursdays, and Fridays. On Wednesdays, staff delivered sixty to sixty-five meals to the elderly and incapacitated in outlying areas, and performed needed household chores.

Center Director Caroline Torres felt severely burdened because the Gramm-Rudman balanced budget act eliminated $20,000 of the Center's funds. In fact, the director had to drive the Center's vehicle because of staff shortages. Additionally, Director Torres and the staff operated a popular Senior Olympics Fitness Program and the scheduled Public Health Service Volunteer instructor failed to show. Nevertheless, senior athletes attended the regional meet and won a lot of medals in 1990 while Director Torres was optimistic about raising state funds or other unnamed resources to support the Center and her small staff. At first she said they had problems getting the elders to accept the cooking and the Center, but now many feel at home.[29]

A TRIBAL COURT AND THE POLICE FORCE

The 1968 Indian Civil Rights Act encouraged Ácoma to produce its first Law and Order Code. It was enacted by the Tribal Council on April 13, 1971, and established Ácoma's first permanent court system. The court was to have jurisdiction over all domestic relations and civil cases within the boundaries of the reservation.

While enacting the Code and the Court, the Tribal Council retained the authority to appoint a judge and one alternate, and the authority to serve as the court of appeals. All people appearing before the judge had the right to representation by a member of the tribe and could request a trial by jury. Otherwise they would face the mercy of the court. Professional attorneys were permitted only when the charges fell within offenses listed in Chapters V and VI of the Code (see list below). For civil actions, the judge could order restitution for damages, service for the benefit of the injured party, and payment of court costs. First offenders frequently received probation while those sentenced to jail terms became eligible for parole after serving half the sentence.

The Code stipulated that tribal members would recognize marriages performed by tribal custom or according to the laws of the state in which the couple resided. The court would have no authority to grant a divorce or an annulment. A judge had to hear paternity suits, determine support and custody of minors, and approve and probate wills. Heirs could claim all properties except trust property, which is assigned by the cacique in sacred trust. An adult over twenty-one could petition the court to adopt an Indian child, and a case gained more favor if the petition were made by a married couple.[30]

Chapter V listed offenses for which a member of the Ácoma tribe could be arrested, while Chapter VI enumerated common motor vehicle violations. In Chapter V appear:

1. Assault
2. Assault and Battery
3. Carrying concealed weapons without a permit from the Governor
4. Abduction
5. Theft
6. Receiving or concealing stolen property
7. Embezzlement
8. Fraud
9. Misbranding
10. Extortion
11. Disorderely conduct
12. Trespass
13. Malicious mischief
14. Injury to public property
15. Maintaining a public nuisance
16. Cruelty to animals (subject to fifteen days confinement and a $25 fine)
17. Illicit cohabitation
18. Adultery
19. Game violations
20. Liquor violations: Any Indians who shall possess, sell, trade, transport, or manufacture any beer, ale, wine, whiskey, or any article whatsoever which produces alcoholic intoxication within the confines and limits of the Ácoma Pueblo Indian Reservation
21. Prostitution
22. Failure to support dependent persons
23. Failure to send children to school
24. Curfew violations (any Indian child under the age of eighteen observed the following:
     Those under sixteen be off the streets by 9 P.M. during school terms unless accompanied by parents or guardian. Those sixteen and seventeen would be off the streets by 10 P.M. during school terms unless accompanied by parents or guardian. During school vacations all minors could remain out until 10 P.M.
25. Forgery
26. Gambling
27. Fornication
28. Giving venereal disease to another
29. Contributing to the delinquency of a minor
30. Bribery
31. Perjury

32. False arrest
33. Resisting lawful arrest
34. Escape
35. Disobedience to lawful orders of the Court
36. Refusing to brand and mark livestock

Drug offenses did not appear in the Code largely because they, unlike alcohol offenses, posed few problems. Arrests could only be made if the arresting officer witnessed the crime or had "reasonable evidence" that the person had committed the act. Otherwise, police officers were to have warrants for arrest or apprehension and could only conduct searches and seizures of property with warrants signed by the judge.

For non-Ácomas facing prosecution, the Code said no offender could be turned over to federal, state, or local officials, or any other tribe or reservation unless the Ácoma judge had warrants from the proper authorities. Also, no arrest of any Indian on the Ácoma reservation could be made without such warrant. On February 25, 1981, ten years after the initial Code, the Ácoma Tribal Council agreed to a major revision that extended court jurisdiction over all persons, Indian and non-Indian.[31]

During the first decade of the Code, the Tribal Court and the Ácoma Police Department were adequately manned. The Police Department began acquiring much needed equipment, such as autos and, eventually, communications and emergency vehicles. In accordance with a budget, the court enjoyed the services of a judge 80 percent of the time, an alternate judge 50 percent of the time, a clerk full time, and one full-time and one half-time probation officer. The Ácoma Police Department grew from a chief, sergeant, and two helpers in 1972, to nine officers in 1990. Reserve officers and two range officers patrolled outlying areas with horses and four-wheel-drive vehicles. Chief William Johnson served throughout most of the department's nearly twenty years of growth and struggle.[32]

Ácoma's first judge and first court sessions occurred back in 1916; however, the office held briefly by Judge Jose Leon Chino was vacant until the Ácoma Tribal Council created the Code in 1971. Since then, the judges have been: Tribal Judge Dwain Clark, 1971–1981; Tribal Judge Gabriel Paisano, 1981–1982; Tribal Judge Angelo Skelares, 1982–1983 (temporary); Tribal Judge Floyd J. Kezele, 1983–present. Up to

Tribal Judge Kezele's terms, applicants needed only a high school diploma and, perhaps, some experience in law. The Council's Selection Committee members favored candidates with reservation experience or Indian backgrounds. In 1983, government specialists recommended that Ácoma upgrade qualifications and hire a judge with a law degree and then pay him enough for full-time services.[33] As more Ácoma people attended law school, the qualifications were now being revised to include "additional course work at a college or equivalent level in law or related area. Law degree or advancd legal training preferred."[34]

Tribal judges with varying talents have coped with a variety of situations. For instance, Tribal Judge Clark's caseload increased yearly at the same time that budgets were being cut so eventually he was paid to serve only two days a week. Over the years misdemeanor arrests have exceeded 100 during some months, and drunk driving and liquor violations began to outnumber other crimes.[35] Under the unrevised Code some offenders tried to dodge prosecution by claiming not to have a sufficient percentage of Ácoma blood.[36] And after the first jury trial in 1984, Tribal Judge Kezele reported to the Council, "the trial was historic, the result was not." The jury had difficulty determining a verdict in the case, and the judge recommended training sessions for the general public and members of the Tribal Council.[37]

Tribal Judge Kezele introduced reforms to improve the whole system. During 1983–84, processed adult criminal cases increased 100 percent and juvenile cases were up 25 percent. Governor Merle L. Garcia attributed the improvement to stabilization of the Ácoma Tribal Court and the Police Department. Tribal Judge Kezele, with help of Police Chief Johnson, preferred to rely on existing resources and referred probationary cases to Ácoma Social Services, Alcoholism Program, Job Corps, ranch work, and to various schools or work programs in Grants. In these programs, the convicted were able to receive treatment, work off the sentence by performing a public service, or finish school. Probationary referrals might include the Ácoma-Canoncito-Laguna Hospital for mental health, Ácoma Food Distribution for community service, Headstart, or Laguna-Ácoma School.[38] The Police Department was especially supportive by monitoring prisoners who were working off referral sentences.[39]

Juvenile alcoholism caused tribal officials the greatest concern over the years. The entire court staff, with help from the Police Department, worked to help young alcoholics finish their education and find employment. Liquor was available at five establishments along five miles of old Highway 66 near the reservation, but tribal attempts to prohibit the sale of intoxicating beverages to Indian minors were continuing. Convicted juveniles frequently received assignments to perform community services, help the war chiefs at Sky City, or do chores and chop wood for seniors. Seven of these youths were known to be finishing their education, a number had successfully thrown off alcohol and drug habits, and several agreed to serve sentences by talking to grade school students about the adverse effects of alcohol and drugs.[40]

Tribal Judge Kezele also attempted to improve the jail system and cut its costs. In the past, Ácoma relied on facilities at the Pueblo of Laguna and the towns of Grants and Gallup. Ácoma paid too much for these arrangements and needed to build its own jail. Judge Kezele renegotiated agreements to lower the costs of using off-reservation facilities and implemented sentencing procedures to reduce the costs yet further. These methods included the probationary referrals, more home arrests and detentions, modified home arrests and detentions, and deferred sentences. In another innovative program, prisoners fulfilled their sentences by breaking rocks that would be used in the construction of the new jail or holding facility for Ácoma.[41]

The most visible evidence of all this activity at Ácoma was the handsome new courtroom, completed in 1989. Before, judicial offices had been moved about the fringes of the tribal complex, always to make room for other business. Now in addition to a courtroom, the Tribal Court had temporary quarters as plans moved ahead for permanent offices. Meanwhile, Tribal Judge Kezele, court employees, and community service workers designed and furnished the courtroom, judge's chambers, and law library. Emil Chino, performing community-service work, covered the jury box and the bench with wood-burnt murals depicting scenes and Ácoma symbols. Tribal officials held the work of the Tribal Court in high esteem and hoped that soon all law enforcement would move into more convenient facilities like the much admired courtroom.[42]

ÁCOMA'S FIRST HOSPITAL

A momentous occasion for Ácoma was the ground-breaking ceremony for the new hospital on June 26, 1976. Governor Merle Garcia welcomed a largely Indian crowd who heard Governor Roland Johnson from Laguna as a guest speaker and President Joe Sandoval from the Canoncito Navaho Chapter. All three tribes would be primary benefactors as well as beneficiaries of the hospital. To celebrate the occasion the three tribes furnished dancers. At noon, all visitors were treated to luncheon at the Laguna-Ácoma High School, not far from the site.[43]

The Ácoma Tribal Council had initiated efforts to get a hospital on the reservation in 1971, but debate over the location and delayed funding from the Indian Health Service held up the effort for almost five years (see previous chapter).[44] Ácoma had proposed that the hospital would serve the Pueblo of Ácoma and Laguna and the Navaho community at Canoncito. There were no in-patient facilities available at the time and the out-patient clinic at Laguna was only open on a part-time basis. Patients had to travel more than fifty miles to Albuquerque or twenty-five miles over bad roads to the Crownpoint Hospital for extensive care. The planned hospital was to feature a total health program and at least forty beds.[45] Ácoma wanted the hospital to be built at Interstate 40 and old Highway 23. But geologists finally reported in 1974 to the Indian Health Service that bedrock at the Ácoma site offered the more propitious foundation for the envisioned complex. Tribal officials, the Council, and the Cacique approved and assigned 37.9 acres for the hospital.[46]

Indian Health Service funds paid for the hospital complex—some $10 million. However, these funds were long in coming because Congress delayed approval, and when the funds became available, they proved insufficient.[47] Gradually, plans evolved for a hospital occupying 65,000 square feet and having forty-five beds. Also, the main building was to be covered with an enormous solar-heating system. Because of critical needs in this isolated location, Indian members successfully added services not normally found in similar hospitals. Fulfilling dreams for a total health care center, the hospital included optometrical services, dental care, a complete pharmacy, laboratory services, com-

135

munity health nursing, mental health care, environmental health services, and nutritional and social services. The main hospital would also house a ritual-curing room. Designs for this room incorporated Pueblo and Navaho architecture with an open doorway facing east, a domed ceiling to admit natural light, and a fireplace and stone benches around circular walls.[48] (See color plate no. 12.) Such plans took shape through advice and coordination with a hospital planning board comprised of three members from each tribe. Contracts went to Stevens, Mallory, Pearl, and Campbell, Albuquerque architects; Allison Engineering of Albuquerque for solar and mechanical engineering; and to Henry C. Beck Company, Dallas, Tex., for construction.[49]

On February 28, 1978, the hospital opened to the first patients; formal dedication followed on May 20, 1978. In February, the Indian Health Service turned over the institution to Ácoma. A limited staff and largely inexperienced board faced a variety of problems. On the first day, with only brief pauses for taking photographs to document the comprehensive services of the hospital, the staff went about treating patients. Elsewhere throughout the hospital, many company representatives made final adjustments on the radiographic and other equipment, maintenance people tested service systems, and large tractor-trailer rigs disgorged a myriad of hospital supplies.[50]

Despite careful planning, insufficient funds created near havoc. For example, in October Acting Clinical Director Michael H. Trujillo, M.D., described staffing for all clinical and allied health departments as "grossly inadequate" for providing optimum medical care and service at the hospital twenty-four hours a day, seven days a week.[51] At this time there were three general doctors and two physician's assistants on board. Lack of housing for staff and their families (many of them non-Indian) required construction of fifty dwellings, which was completed in June 1980 at an additional $2.6 million.[52]

The Ácoma-Canoncito-Laguna Hospital Board became a formal body on January 26, 1979, and with recommendations from the Indian Health Service it began to oversee management and use of the hospital.[53] Nicholas T. Redeye served for a brief period as service unit director. He was followed by James Toya of Laguna. The first employee hired to manage and coordinate hospital affairs was Ácoma Calvin J.

136

Aragon, who not only became health system administrator but assistant director of the hospital. His work resolved many serious conditions such as radio communications with Gallup, Grants, and Albuquerque; helicopter facilities for rescue units from Albuquerque and Kirtland Air Force Base; and ambulance services. Hospital officials also arranged for a kidney dialysis service operated by Rehobeth Christian Hospital, Gallup. Ácoma-Canoncito-Laguna Hospital furnished space while Rehobeth provided equipment and staffing. Benefits of this arrangement were immediate for patients and families who otherwise spent entire days traveling to Albuquerque. All six machines were regularly occupied because of the prevalence of diabetes and related complications among the Indians.[54]

Indian reservations were becoming vulnerable to alcohol and drug problems. The hospital board, at the instigation of James Toya and Calvin J. Aragon, responded by constructing a treatment center. Named "Sunrise," the center was dedicated on May 20, 1988, as part of the complex, which by that time included a parental visitor residence to facilitate family therapy.[55]

In 1990, the hospital was impressive and in full operation. A receptionist directed visitors to follow colored tapes along gleaming corridor floors to their destinations. The offices, with up-to-date furnishings and the latest equipment, appeared almost entirely manned by Indians. There were six permanent physicians and two temporary; of the total, two were Indians. Of the entire staff, 71 percent were Indian and their numbers corresponded in direct proportion to populations of the reservations serviced—Acoma, Canoncito, and Laguna. Visits to the hospital had numbered 40,000 to 50,000 annually, including dialysis patients, and of the forty-five beds only twenty-five were being used because of staff shortages.

While Assistant Director Calvin Aragon became the hospital's first employee, Nicholas Redeye served as the first official director, followed by James Toya, Laguna, the most recent director. These optimistic leaders and the hospital board looked to future additions and improvements that would provide such conveniences as solar-powered back-up emergency generators and an improved helicopter port just north of the complex. But they became most enthusiastic over plans for a nursing home next to the hospital. The facility would be open to Indians and non-Indians as a way to garner added funds for the project. No doubt the vision would grow to include day care for the elderly and children and family housing units for elderly. The Ácoma Council agreed to the proposal and the Cacique approved of the land for the purpose.

NEW TERRITORIES: REACQUIRING ABORIGINAL LANDS

Major changes to the reservation almost always come from outside and provoke conflicting views among Indians of the non-Indian world. Arrival of formal education over a century ago, for example, caused bitterness and contributed to the expulsion of Solomon Bibo from the tribe. Today some traditionalists still believe education to be unnecessary to the Ácoma life-style.[56] In another example, dissident Ácomas likely joined with other Pueblo Indians to settle the Pueblo of Laguna, formally recognized by the Spaniards in 1699, after unresolved arguments over accepting the Spanish during and after the Pueblo Revolt. And, for a number of years now, traditional pottery makers have charged nontraditional potters with catering to tourists' tastes and therefore threatening to destroy the art. The list of arguments has been very long and any public opinion directly affected deliberations by the governors and Tribal Council.

Since the 1970s, the tribe's decision to reacquire stolen lands immediately north, west, and south of the reservation has aroused deep emotions. At one time, the Ácoma nation spread over several million acres and in 1540 the first Spaniards called it the Ácoma kingdom. They were referring to Ácoma's aboriginal holdings, which were clearly understood by the Indians and delineated by major landmarks. As recently as 1972, the United States Congress agreed that most of these lands were taken from Ácoma by fraud and deception, and sought to relieve any grievances with money. But even though the Ácoma had turned to the outside world for help, most did not ultimately think the payment was proper—the land was simply too sacred. Much of Ácoma's salvation and sacred trust were inextricably bound to the ranches and wilderness areas in question. In Ácoma's view, these lands had been stolen; after 1972 they sought to get them back.

The decision, then, on the part of the people and the Tribal Council to use the money from the government to repurchase "stolen" lands caused controversy on the reservation. Some believed the tribe was paying too much for the lands. Some could not abide the thought of buying back the same land that "we owned long before the time of memory." The Tribal Council, however, resolved to restore these lands to the tribe's permanently protected land base for various economic and religious uses for the Pueblo of Ácoma.

Ácoma purchases after 1972 more than doubled the size of the reservation. Official land holdings up to that year had gone as follows:

94,169.00 Spanish grant to Acoma, September 20, 1689.

4,384.04 Executive Order of 1917, after settlement of boundaries with the Pueblo of Laguna in 1933.

51,856.97 Congressional Reservation Act of 1928.

80,080.55 Ácoma purchase area in Eleven Township authorized by Congress (63 Stat. 604), August 13, 1949.

11,715.84 Land in the purchase area formerly held by New Mexico and exchanged with the Bureau of Land Management in 1962.

320.00 Indian trust allotment in the purchase area.

3,195.76 Land on Horace Mesa, which Ácoma exchanged with the Atchison, Topeka and Santa Fe Railroad in 1968.

The acreage amounted to over 245,000.[57]

The first important purchase was in 1977. A well-known local rancher, Adrian Berryhill, died in an automobile accident and his widow, Gladdus, offered Ácoma the Berryhill Ranch, also known as the Bibo Ranch. The Tribal Council quickly authorized its purchase, stating that the land offered potential for agricultural development, homesites, and grazing. "There have been tribal members who express their desires to enter into the livestock business and feel the purchase of the Berry-hill Ranch will give them this opportunity."[58] The ranch entailed 13,860 acres, parts of which were owned by the state and by the Bureau of Land Management. These required leases would be carried by Ácoma. The purchase included water rights, especially those to Cebollita Springs, and some mineral rights. Interest among tribal officials also derived from the land's proximity to the Kowina ruins, a prehistoric Ácoma village with religious significance.

The Pueblo of Ácoma paid $300,000 and the Bureau of Indian Affairs helped to clear title and right-of-way easements and to have the ranch placed in trust as part of the Ácoma reservation on May 1, 1981.[59] Fortunately, owners of the Kowina ruins offered the property to Ácoma at about the same time.

Henry H. and Sue M. Elkins, the owners of the Kowina lands, gave the Pueblo first chance at the property before the Bureau of Land Management, who was also interested in acquiring the ruins, most likely for the El Malpais monument and wilderness areas being contemplated at the time. The Tribal Council authorized purchase on May 30, 1979, stating again that these measures strengthened Ácoma's economic opportunities while safeguarding aboriginal lands for tribal members. "The Pueblo of Acoma has taken the initial steps to forward re-acquiring areas of land which have been identified through the land claims board as aboriginal Acoma lands."[60]

Invaluable cultural artifacts returned to Ácoma with the finalized $250,000 Kowina purchase on July 5, 1979. Included were 83.80 acres, a 2,477-square-foot museum building with contents, plus the ruins. The building had restrooms, space for a twelve-space trailer park, well and well house, and an accessible road from the ruins to State Road 117. The Kowina Foundation purchase land became part of the Ácoma reservation under the same authority as the Berryhill Ranch on May 1, 1981.[61]

During the above transactions, the Ácoma were also offered the historic Wilson Ranch, known locally as Bar-15. This created consternation and excitement among tribal officials because of the ranch's excellent reputation.[62] With this property, Ácoma could add to its list of grazing and range lands that up to this point had included the reservation itself, Major Pasture, Brushy Mountain, Indian Lake, Putney Mesa, Red Rock, Horace Mesa, Largo Canyon, and the Berryhill.[63] The Wilson family had operated the ranch for sixty-five years.

Ácoma Tribal Council members authorized the Wilson Ranch purchase on July 19, 1978, stating that the tribe not only wanted the property for livestock, but because it was aboriginal land.[64] Total purchase price finally amounted to $1,050,000, plus $273,000 for cattle located there and $22,780 for horses and ranch equipment.[65] The ranch, however, was encumbered with Navaho leases, New Mexico state holdings, Bureau of Land Management holdings, and by private ownerships. Through swaps and agreements most of the acreage was eventually cleared, except for some Bureau of Land Management lands. Ácoma also purchased land from two private owners for the remainder (see below). The ranch came with a large inventory that included but was not limited to the houses, outbuildings, barns, corrals, fences, tanks, water wells, windmills, electric-generating equipment and machinery, all water rights, all leases and grazing permits, and livestock, which Ácoma agreed to purchase as listed.[66] Ácoma completed the deal on November 1, 1978, but to operate the ranch properly the Tribal Council authorized cashing the tribe's securities "to attain economic self-sufficiency in certain aspects of tribal operations."[67]

The purchase agreement described the Wilson Ranch as lying within a large, open valley enclosed on three sides by mesas. The land also produced excellent stands of native grasses and browse. These factors and the availability of expensive facilities encouraged Ácoma cattle growers to start a tribal livestock enterprise with range and soil-conservation management as goals. Tribal members could join and use the ranges at Wilson Ranch and the Berryhill. The Ácoma Livestock Enterprise had a board elected by the membership and the board hired a ranch manager.[68]

Ownership of all the lands in the Wilson deal were finally settled when the Navaho leases were exchanged by the Bureau of Land Management and the Tribal Council purchased two of the private holdings leased from Mabel and Frank Analla and from Eunice Gunn. The Analla purchase transpired on October 3, 1986, for a sum of $22,549.98, and

141

incorporated all mineral and water rights, real estate, and improvements.[69] Eunice Gunn of the Pueblo of Laguna had 160 acres in the center of the Wilson Ranch purchase that Ácoma assumed as a lease. Tribal officials moved to purchase the land in 1988 and Mrs. Gunn agreed to convey all water rights and half the mineral rights for $13,600. A warranty deed transferred the property to Ácoma on December 5, 1988.[70] The Tribal Council applied to the Secretary of the Interior for reservation status and officials planned to incorporate the Gunn land into general operations of the Wilson Ranch. Governor Ray A. Histia explained to the Bureau of Indian Affairs that the 160 acres would be opened to grazing of livestock. Trust status was pending with no foreseeable problems.[71]

Acquisition of aboriginal lands continued when in 1982 the Tribal Council authorized purchase of the Pete Baca, Jr., lands adjacent to the western side of the reservation. The old farm had two tracts for a total of 291.84 acres and all mineral rights, water rights, a submersible water pump with capacity for 30 gallons per minute, a concrete water storage tank, well, boundary fences, and more. Dated December 6, 1982, the warranty deed for the Baca purchase showed a price of $320,000—over $11,000 an acre. The Tribal Council then applied to the Secretary of the Interior for reservaton trust status.[72]

In another deal, the Los Cerritos property, which had much coveted business potential for the tribe, created considerable dispute among the Ácomas because of its complexity and costs. When the business location became available at the interchange of Interstate 40 and Acomita road, Governor Merle L. Garcia advocated buying everything available because "the Pueblo views Los Cerritos property as the cornerstone of its economic development efforts."[73]

The property was being offered by Marie S. Bibo, from a family well known to the Ácomas and a person who stood, some thought, to make a great deal of money off the tribe. There were in the offer 236.4 acres with active businesses; Governor Garcia hoped to parlay these businesses into cures for unemployment and economic depression. First and foremost in value was Los Cerritos Trading Post—it was fully equipped and furnished with an adjoining warehouse. The site also had an equipped and operating restaurant. Off to the side was a twenty-

142

five-unit mobile home and RV park with critical water wells. And the Gunderson Oil Company, Gallup, leased and operated the large and busy Chevron service station. The total asking price was $1,646,050, but Ácoma completed negotiations on December 22, 1983, for $1,250,000.[74]

No sooner had ownership transferred when expenses mounted. Governor Garcia hoped to develop Los Cerritos into a "multiple-attraction" site with an industrial park for Ácoma businesses and a tourist spot with a motel. Within a year, expenditures on the improvements ran over $2 million and the Pueblo had to withdraw trust funds. The Governor sought help from many places, starting with the Bureau of Indian Affairs Economic Development. "As you are well aware," he explained, "the Pueblo has taken an aggressive stance in enhancing its self-sufficiency. To that end, the Pueblo has spent considerable time, money, and effort in its initial planning efforts for the property."[75] Governor Garcia also launched a multimillion dollar development campaign bolstered by Governor Toney Anaya, who agreed to include a request for 60 percent of initial construction costs in the state's Capital Improvements Bill. This was to be "a dream that is finally being realized," in Governor Garcia's plan for total self-sufficiency on the reservation. The opening of an Ácoma bingo parlor on October 30, 1983, seemed to promise greater success in raising funds for the Los Cerritos project. As reported in the newspaper, Governor Garcia was "floating in the clouds."[76] He also appealed to New Mexican state agencies for market studies and site planning. With the local Economic Development offices, the Governor sought to upgrade sewage facilities, to install natural gas lines to replace butane tanks, and to complete construction on a superette (to merchandise foodstuffs and housewares) and a laundromat. While the tribe owned these businesses as a speculative "first step" in the overall economic program, the tribe also hired a manager to oversee the businesses. The tribe had hoped to add a motel to the complex, but money was slow materializing and the idea had little or no support. This aspect of Governor Garcia's vision was put on hold momentarily.[77] On September 26, 1988, Los Cerritos tracts became part of the reservation.

Probably not since the Pueblo Revolt were tribal affairs interrupted quite as much as when Governor Stanley Paytiamo sought Ácoma aboriginal lands in El Malpais. El Malpais, a Spanish term describing "badlands" to the west of the Ácoma reservation, is dominated by an enormous lava flow in a broad valley. Sections of the flow were nearly impassable, but Ácoma people frequently used ancient trails to reach prehistoric farms, pastures, and religious shrines abundantly scattered throughout the area. The Ácoma reservation not only bordered but also extended into El Malpais in places because of the aforementioned land purchases. So it was with every concern that the Tribal Council opposed a Bureau of Land Management study of the entire valley for the purpose of creating a wilderness area. Fundamentally, it appeared the United States government would remove those aboriginal lands further from possible Ácoma ownership, potentially restricting the tribe's daily economic and religious activities. The Council's formal objection included the following:

1. The mutual boundaries between Ácoma and El Malpais need clarifying.

2. The question of Ácoma's aboriginal rights to sacred areas within the area exists.

3. Mineral rights were not clear for conflicting areas.

4. Wilderness area designation opens unintended, unselective encroachments by visitors rather than creating safeguards.

5. The proposal impacted both social and economic benefits that otherwise should be reserved for local residents.

6. The Bureau of Land Management had insufficient personnel to protect the proposed area.

7. The United States Government would be better off giving the proposed wilderness a reservation status with the tribe, which would preserve the characteristic wilderness land in turn.

The Council soon learned during local hearings that the proposed wilderness area was large, around 373,000 acres. Opposition stiffened as Ácoma again faced possible encroachment by non-Indians.

> Many times through the motions of the political world, we as the first inhabitants of this area are neglected by the greater society. We do not feel that the designation of wilderness can aid us as Acoma people in any beneficial manner now or in the future. We urge that this position [be] not accepted as one comment; but rather giving due consideration to the government to government relationship and the number of people that the tribal government is representative of. This information has been presented to our tribal members at various community meetings through the past three years and rest assured that they support our position.[78]

In 1986, Congressman Bill Richardson introduced House Resolution 3684, over Ácoma objections, to create El Malpais National Monument. He proposed that Congress create a monument of 350,000 acres, 193,000 of which would be set aside as wilderness. The monument would be managed by the Bureau of Land Management.

Congressman Richardson and Chairman John Sieberling, both of the Subcommittee on Public Lands, met with local residents in Grants on March 26, 1986, to discuss the proposal. There was general talk of additional tourism for Grants, but several landowners protested boundary conflicts. For example, the prestigious King Brothers Ranch (one of the owners was Governor Bruce King) grazed cattle and had a ranch and wells on leased lands in the planned wilderness areas. Owners requested their leased land be removed lest the workers had to enter these areas "by mule team." Another landowner who said he spoke for others in the northeast section of the proposed monument asked that 640 acres where they had their homes be removed. Also at issue were 2,700 acres owned by David and Reddy Candelaria just south of Interstate 40. The Candelarias wanted to sell while the Bureau was recommending a land swap with the State of New Mexico. Then-Governor Toney Anaya, in a prepared statement for publication, urged the public lands subcommittee to add more wilderness area on the east where off-road vehicles and woodcutting would be prohibited. Whether he knew it or not, his proposed restrictions would inhibit Ácoma's future immeasurably.[79]

During the same meeting, Governor Paytiamo set forth for its first public hearing the Ácoma position, beginning with the people's deep concerns that these lands were theirs.

> The Pueblo of Acoma people retain vested interest in these lands considered for a national monument. These lands always remain Acoma's aboriginal lands in spite of its designations as Bureau of Land Management land and/or as state school lands. Federal and state laws may take away our lands under newly instituted laws but our people remain intact with the land, as our Acoma elders say, "We are already underneath the land."

The Governor then went on to list specific points of dispute, indicating that these were paramount tribal concerns over increased unemployment, expanded tourism, or protections proposed under federal wilderness designation:

1. Acoma did not want to be constrained in any future development of its property adjacent to El Malpais.

2. Acoma must be assured continued access to the reservation.

3. Acoma would protect its water rights, both for her private deeded lands and for the surface and subsurface waters reaching the reservation.

4. Acoma wanted the religious shrines protected under the Indian Religious Freedom Act.

5. Acoma objected to attracting more visitors who would trespass on Tribal lands or damage property

6. Acoma considered the prehistoric ruins as sacred and objected to visitors disturbing them in any manner.

Ácoma's initial stand against the monument became compromised over the next year as politicians chose to ignore or failed to comprehend Indian aboriginal claims.[80]

Congressman Richardson revised the draft to exclude private and deeded lands, including those of the King Brothers Ranch and the acres of deeded Ácoma lands west of State Road 117. In response, Governor Paytiamo wrote the congressional delegation that the revision only reaffirmed the proposed exterior boundaries and that the Ácoma people were opposed to the eastern boundary coinciding with the western boundary of the reservation. "We opposed this demarcation," he continued, "and we recommend that the monument boundary be changed to the west side of State Road 117, which lies along the lava beds. We also asked that State Road 117 be the east boundary of the El Malpais monument." He and Council members concluded that the Congressman's revision offered no substantive changes. Governor Paytiamo feared that Congressman Richardson's office tried to cover up negative responses from Ácoma. In addition, the tribe received no redrafted copy of the resolution for coordination, and newspaper articles gave the impression that Ácoma had raised no further objections.[81]

Over the Ácoma protest and with no contact with the Pueblo, the House of Representatives approved House Resolution 3684 on July 30, 1986. The monument had not been reduced by 12,000 acres "to meet some of the objectives of the Ácoma and Navaho tribes plus some acreage the Bureau of Land Management wanted removed." Local news made no mention of the King Brothers Ranch affair. Congressman Richardson said that the proposal "provides some protection for the resource and at the same time would help to improve the ailing economy of Grants."

Senator Pete Domenici then took the ball: "I'm trying to put something together that would be good for Grants and could pass the Senate and be signed by the President." He foresaw a major tourist attraction for Grants.[82]

Turning to Senator Domenici, Governor Paytiamo explained again the tribe's desire to have the monument's east boundary along State Road 117. Second, he reminded the Senator of Ácoma's aboriginal claims to those western lands and that they had lost them because of incorrect federal surveys in the nineteenth century. Further, he said, the Ácoma had religious use of the area because of the American Indian Religious Freedom Act. And the Governor told the Senator that Ácoma officials were uneasy over the restrictive conditions in designated wilderness areas, particularly as they would apply to future economic development and right-of-way. These uncertainties led the Ácomas to petition for removal of Rimrock, Pinyon, Sand Canyon, Little Rimrock, and Petaca Pinta from such a designation. "Playing power politics is almost meaningless to us," Governor Paytiamo said. In a letter to the Senator he wrote:

> Albeit, we know time and right are on our side while still we want the laws of America to work for us and not against us. This is now 1986 and federal laws may have effectively blocked our legal rights to those areas at issue but we maintain that a definite wrong has been committed. We want that corrected.

Governor Paytiamo suggested that the Senator send the tribe the proposed legislation agreed upon by the New Mexico congressional delegation in order to solicit Ácoma views.[83]

Ácoma heard nothing from the delegation and two identical bills on El Malpais entered the House and Senate for "top priority" consideration in 1987. Local newspapers reported that the bills provided for:

1. A 126,000-acre El Malpais National Monument, including the Candelaria Ice Caves and Bandera Crater to be administered by the National Park Service.

2. A 253,000-acre natural conservation area to be administered by the Bureau of Land Management.

3. A 115,000-acre Bureau of Land Management wilderness authorization for an El Malpais visitor's center at the ice caves.

4. Authorization for a Masau Trail visitor's center at Grants.

5. Study of roadless areas in the national monument and a restudy of the Chain of Craters wilderness study area.

6. Protection of Native American uses of the area.

7. Continued hunting, trapping, and noncommercial fuel-

wood gathering in the Bureau of Land Management areas.

8. Direction to develop management plans for Bureau of Land Management and National Park Service areas, including plans for protection of archeological resources.[84]

Top United States officials next held a public assembly on the bills in Grants on February 10, 1987, where New Mexico Governor Garrey Carruthers enthusiastically endorsed the bills. "Our enthusiasm grows in particular when I sense we have a cooperative effort among private sector, public federal sector, and the public state sector," he told the assembly, which included Ácoma representatives. Ignoring the Indian sector he added, "Once you get one of these partnerships rolling you have a good thing going. Let me just say that this is just one more of those kinds of things that ought to be included in our desire to market the State of New Mexico." Senator Domenici credited National Park Service Director William Mott with the concept of linking major archeological attractions such as El Malpais, the petroglyphs near Albuquerque, Chaco Canyon, and others, as parts of a tourist trail to be called Masau Trail. The trail would be mostly for vehicular traffic, and, the Senator explained, "We hope to bring them [tourists] to stay longer and see the beautiful things we have." He added:

> Let me say to the Indian people, these bills do not put Acoma, something significant the Navajo Indians have, or anything else into the Masau Trail, but what it says if you want to join and be a part of the Masau Trail, you are welcome. You will have input and will be promoted, satisfactory to you, as part of this invisible linkage called the Masau Trail.[85]

Ácoma at last received an invitation to air its views before the Senate Subcommittee on Public Lands in Washington on February 19, 1987. With a briefcase full of documents and surrounded by members of the Council and Indian advisors, Governor Paytiamo repeated the tribe's objections. In the past century the tribe had lost over 1.5 million acres out of 2.5 million acres belonging to Ácoma from aboriginal times. He described how the tribe voted to accept compensation for the loss of these lands, but now had determined to buy its aboriginal lands with this same money. The bills would block the tribe's efforts to the west, and of immediate concern was the possible loss of 5,460 acres that the tribe purchased in the Berryhill Ranch as part of these aboriginal lands. Tribal members kept livestock on good grazing lands at Berryhill and had the use of many wells. Access to water and water rights in this western area were added to Ácoma's petition, which Governor Paytiamo outlined as follows:

> The Pueblo of Acoma would like the federal lands east of 117, which are controlled by the Berryhill Ranch, together with the Acoma fee lands and water rights in the Berryhill Ranch, to be placed into Trust for the Pueblo of Acoma by this Act of Congress.
>
> The Pueblo of Acoma would like the lands of the Carl Wilson Ranch and federal lands and Acoma fee lands and water rights located inside the Bar-15, or Carl Wilson Ranch, into trust, reserved for the exclusive use of the Pueblo.
>
> The ranch lands, together with existing water rights owned in fee or made available by the federal government under grazing leases currently held by the Pueblo in the Berryhill Ranch and Bar-15, or Carl Wilson, ranch, should be placed in trust for the Pueblo of Acoma.

"The United States presently controls these lands and leases them to the Pueblo of Acoma," Governor Paytiamo said. He assured the members no acquisition costs would be involved and no other owners affected. With some affirmation of trust status for these lands, the Governor believed his people would support the bills.[86]

Back home tribal officials studied the bills and began to concentrate on specific points. More determined than before, Governor Paytiamo sent word to the New Mexico delegation that Ácoma would have to have $2 million to "enable us to buy available lands now for sale. We are not demanding lands just anywhere, but rather we are trying to regain aboriginal lands which were taken from us."[87]

The Tribal Council's specific concerns were presented before members of a second House Committee on April 28, 1987. The Governor began his remarks by reminding the Committee that Ácoma considered El Malpais a "part of the lands originally exclusively occupied by our ancestors from the Pueblo of Ácoma." Ácoma's petitions were being ignored, he said, and after a review of the tribe's problems in connection with the proposed legislation, he summarized the latest plea:

1. Acoma fee lands and federal lease lands adjacent to the Berryhill Ranch boundaries east of State Road 117 be excluded from the National Conservation area and the Rimrock wilderness area.

2. The land exchange language added to this legislation indicate that placing federal lands inside the Bar-15 and Berryhill (east of State Road 117) into trust would be a fair exchange for the loss of Acoma fee lands and federal grazing rights west of State Road 117.

3. Funds [$2 million was suggested] be appropriated for additional Acoma ranch purchases.

4. Water rights of the Pueblo of Acoma will not be curtailed by this legislation.

5. *Preservation of Other Traditional Uses.*

The last point reflected growing uneasiness over management of Ácoma religious sites. Governor Paytiamo requested that the Committee include the tribe's religious authorities' approval of legislative segments on these matters.[88]

As summer approached, Ácoma heard nothing in response to the petitions. The Secretary of the Interior did support eastern boundary adjustments along State Road 117 to help resolve Ácoma's concerns. But the Ácoma heard nothing further of the hearing.

Governor Paytiamo then appealed to the entire United States Congress and each member should have received a copy of the following document dated May 18, 1987:

   I. Aboriginal and Traditional Rights

      1. These are all old Acoma lands that have been used for farming, pasturing, wood gathering, and habitation.

2. These lands were erroneously surveyed in 1876 and 1877 and Acomas have ever since pleaded that the error be corrected and have the lands there be returned to us.

3. Our time immemorial usages have existed to present day subject only to unjust land cessions.

4. Therefore, we state that the lands adjacent and around our Indian trust lands there not be declared wilderness nor conservation areas.

II. Economic Concerns

1. Grazing, wood gathering, and dry farming, are the main usages of the land now. The national monument will take grazing lands with no compensation. Our remaining lands adjacent to the monument boundary became so small they become useless for grazing.

2. Wilderness conservation laws hinder access to our lands and inhibit repair and maintenance of land and water sources. Furthermore, these stringent land laws restrict the full development of our lands for economic and beneficial purposes.

3. Water is vital to grazing and farming in the Cebollita Canyon. We have legally vested rights to develop them for our economic well-being.

4. Therefore, we oppose wilderness and conservation laws that inhibit and prohibit the economic development of those lands.

III. Preservation of Traditional Uses

1. Wood gathering, farming, and usages of natural resources all occurred there and continue today.

2. Water is precious to our physical and spiritual well-being. Kowina Spring is our main source of water in Cebollita Canyon. We have a legal established right to that water and we have plans to develop that water resource.

3. The right to protect our religious belief in private to

have our religious sites, artifacts, and objects, must all be respected.

4. Federal wilderness and conservation laws do not fully respect our traditional rights to the land there and, therefore, we oppose wilderness and conservation status for those lands.

Still, no overtures or reaction reached the tribe.[89]

Bitter and hurt upon hearing that the legislation received approval of the Interior and Insular Affairs Committee of the House, the Ácoma people demonstrated publicly for the first time in the tribe's history on May 21, 1987. Charging racism and waving protest signs, about a hundred members rallied on Ácoma lands directly west of State Road 117 and along the lava beds. They called curious reporters' attention to the fact that non-Indians' grazing rights were being spared since the original boundary for the proposed monument had been redrawn to protect the interest of Governor Bruce King and his two brothers. They also told reporters that Congress had ignored Ácoma's claim to all those lands.

Governor Paytiamo was in Washington appearing for a second time before the Committee on Interior and Insular Affairs when news of the demonstrations provoked Congressman Richardson to claim that the Ácoma charges were unfounded. "Their concerns have been addressed in the bill," he said. No doubt most congressional members who were aware of the case concurred with Congressman Richardson's statement that with the 1970 court decision, the Ácomas relinquished all claims to the lands in question. Furthermore, the bill allowed for Ácoma to take part in creating the management plans in the area, reported the Congressman's press secretary. "This office has been in constant contact with the Acomas." But the Ácoma believed the tribe was being ignored on all critical issues.[90]

Upon arriving in Gallup on May 23, Congressman Richardson said the Ácoma people stood to benefit from the bill. He suggested that the protests represented internal Ácoma politics and that the actions were attributable to certain unnamed Ácoma leaders. He and Senator Domenici were disappointed over the Pueblo's response, but the Ácomas should understand, "they are fully protected, and the bill provides for them to go to court to claim those lands. The bill does nothing to affect their lands."[91] Governor Paytiamo saw it differently: "We are a peaceable people. But, when we are up against a wall, when no one seems to be listening to our concerns, we need to attract some attention."[92]

Governor Paytiamo continued to appeal as the vote on the bill approached. He contacted all United States Senators and accused the New Mexico delegation of suppressing Ácoma concerns. Before the delegation he gave voice to the Tribal Council's latest anxieties over tribal water rights. And the Governor's office appealed to the public in a press release while the Governor entreated President Ronald Reagan for help.[93]

On June 1, 1987, the House of Representatives passed the bill unanimously and sent it on to the Senate. Governor Paytiamo was not surprised and Congressman Richardson extolled, "The real heroes are the people of Grants who labored intensively to get the legislation approved." The Reagan Administration had voiced mild opposition to the cost of a visitor's center and wanted protection assured for private landowners. In turn, the Pueblo of Ácoma joined with the State of New Mexico in voicing concerns that the legislation did not address water rights.[94]

Still firmly believing he could persuade the Senate to reject the legislation, Governor Paytiamo traveled to the nation's capital with the tribal lawyer, a hydrologist, and briefcases filled with supporting documents. They would try to get water rights written into the bill. "If we don't get water rights written into the bill," warned the Governor, "those rights will be locked in." Information from a government hydrologist had indicated there was good water to the west and that there was a very good chance "of those being alluvial supplies." The hydrologist represented the Bureau of Indian Affairs and the consensus that Ácoma did not have good control over these water resources.[95] So far as Ácoma could tell, the Senate Committee had tabled the water-rights issue for the time being.[96]

Not to delay, Ácoma continued to appeal to high places. A second petition went to President Reagan along with a similar letter to Vice-President George Bush. To Senator Daniel K. Inouye, Senate Select

Committee on Indian Affairs, Governor Paytiamo carefully listed and explained all of Ácoma's objections to the pending legislation.[97]

About this time Senator Domenici's staff offered a compromise in which the Ácoma could exchange lands that the tribe would otherwise lose to the wilderness and monument areas. The Council deliberated long over the offer but concluded no part of the Berryhill Ranch could be exchanged. The tribe's religious interests there had been major factors in the purchase of the ranch. Debate in Council also raised the vital issue of water rights, rights to the aquifer under the monument and conservation areas, plus development and continued access to Cebollita Springs. The Council urged the Senators to add a section to the bill as follows:

> All existing rights in and to the ground or surface water in the area affected by the Act, are preserved. Exploration to determine the extent of good quality groundwater shall be permitted. The federal agencies involved shall allow access to water and well sites necessary. The adequate development of the water resource by anyone establishing the right thereto, pursuant to Federal and State law. Provided, however, access and development of water resources of the area, including installation and maintenance of future pipelines, shall be conducted in a reasonable manner designed to avoid unnecessary impact on the visual character of the terrain, and unnecessary in advance with the purpose of withdrawal for the creation of the monument, conservation or wilderness area.

The tribe would accept some reasonable rewording providing this addition got into the bill.[98]

Further disappointments were in the offing. The Senate Committee on Energy and Natural Resources unanimously approved the bill on June 25, 1987, and the New Mexico delegation fully expected senate approval sometime after July 4. According to news reports, the bill had undergone adjustments to protect Ácoma land, to assure access to Cebollita Springs, and to allow for continued grazing of Ácoma livestock. Senator Domenici's offer to exchange lands was yet unresolved. And, water rights were amended in such a way as to protect valid existing or pending water-rights settlements. At issue would be un-determined claims by the State of New Mexico and the Indian tribes.[99]

Not so, declared a determined Ácoma. The Council and everyone concurred that the land issue, were not settled, water rights not clear, and religious concerns not addressed at the Berryhill Ranch or other sites in this western area. They informed the New Mexico delegation that this region had similar religious importance to the Wailing Wall in Jewish religion. The ranch contained shrines where Ácoma religious leaders offered prayers so that the rain clouds from the west would bring water and sustenance to Ácoma lands. According to ancient in-structions, divulged the Governor, annual religious ceremonies at a series of shrines beginning west of St. Johns, Arizona, established a pathway for rain clouds across the Zuñi Salt Lake, across the El Malpais, through the shrines and natural rock formations in the Berryhill area, and on to Sky City. The tenets of Ácoma religion taught that ceremonies at these shrines created a pathway for rain clouds comparable to ap-proach lights leading to an airport. Religious disclosures were rare, but Ácoma officials decided greater openness about these shrines would strengthen the Ácomas' reasons not to relinquish these lands. The Con-gressmen should know that the tribe "must maintain the position that these lands should not be locked up in wilderness area, but must be kept in that condition which will permit Acoma to acquire ownership." In other words, the Berryhill served as a gateway to the return of Ácoma aboriginal holdings out west.[100] But there was no reaction from back East to the Ácoma's religious pleas.

At this stage, the bill was before the Senate and could be voted on at any moment and the tribe offered to buy all 12,385 acres of public lands lying east of State Road 117. Ácoma sent this offer to all Senators and explained how the acquisition would allow the tribe to protect religious shrines and conduct ceremonies in private. The tribe also asked that the lands remain in trust for the Pueblo.[101]

By the end of July, Senate vote on the bill was delayed and Pueblo leaders felt lawmakers were avoiding their land and water issues. In August, New Mexico Governor Garrey Carruthers again raised objec-tions to language in the bill regarding water rights. His views on Ácoma interests were not entirely clear except that, along with the State

156

Highway Commission, he appeared to favor Ácoma's request that the monument's western boundary follow State Road 117. So the Ácoma turned to Governor Carruthers, hoping to win his influence with the New Mexico delegation.[102] Meanwhile, Governor Carruthers met with Senator Domenici to resolve the state's position on water rights and Ácoma officials attended a ceremony during which the State Land Office exchanged lands within the monument for federally owned land elsewhere. Ácoma had been to Washington fifteen times during the year and still heard nothing in response to its requests.[103]

The Ácoma offer to purchase 12,385 acres emerged as a salient issue and a major source of publicity as tribal officials hoped Congress might give them the land. Governor Carruthers was holding out for wording that subordinated federal water rights to all others. Pressed with those proposals, Senator Domenici wanted the bill to proceed with existing language lest it should fail.[104] Governor Paytiamo again notified all Senators of Ácoma's concerns over water rights, pointing out that the issues were different from the state's problems and reminding them that the lands at issue were ancestral homelands:

> We ask you to support our views. All of this land now at issue are the ancestral homelands of the Acoma people and all of the cultural resources which the El Malpais legislation seeks to protect in this area are the remains of our people. Nobody debates that. These are not just any old lands anywhere and not just Bureau of Land Management lands. They are truly aboriginal homelands of the Acoma people.[105]

In October, Governor Carruthers withdrew his objections and asked Senators Jeff Bingaman and Domenici to assure him that the language on water rights would not be used as "generic language" for any future wilderness designations in New Mexico. No mention of Ácoma water rights in these proceedings seemed to confirm rumors reaching the reservation that the New Mexico delegation refused to act on Ácoma concerns. The same rumors led Ácoma to believe its only hope for changes to the legislation at this late date was in the hands of Governor Carruthers and Senator Domenici.[106] The latter, however, was "satisfied that the bill, as is currently written, sufficiently protects the rights of the Acoma."[107]

Word finally reached Ácoma that the Senate would act within a couple of weeks. At this point, the Tribal Council authorized Governor Paytiamo to take the Abraham Lincoln cane, used by Ácoma as a traditional symbol of authority, to Washington and request the federal government to take it back and break it. "We would give them the message that they have broken the treaty," explained Governor Paytiamo. The Council had concluded that the federal government considered most of the tribe's ancestral homelands to be public domain. Indian religious shrines were no longer accepted as sacred, water rights were being ignored, and all Ácoma petitions had gone unanswered. The return of the Lincoln cane would indicate how solemnly the people believe that the land out there "is that important to us. The sacred trust between us and the federal government will be broken."[108] Ácoma leaders wanted Congress to see just how hurt and angry the people were.[109]

Other last minute attempts to amend the bill, doubtlessly inspired by the Ácoma threat to secede, also came to nothing. Senators Bingaman and Domenici met with tribal leaders on October 25, 1987, and promised to work on Ácoma requests. Senator Domenici claimed the bill had been amended nine times to meet various concerns of the Pueblo, including water rights and religious freedom.[110] Governor Carruthers responded in November to Ácoma's plea for help, stating that he had urged the New Mexico delegation to make appropriate changes to the bill, but he was told that the bill was too far along in the legislative process and that "changes will be difficult, if not impossible, to make in the current political climate that presently exists in the Congress."[111]

Governor Paytiamo continued to plead for support. Somehow the tribe's access to and eventual recovery of the vast aboriginal area to the west must remain a possibility. Amendments to this effect continued to circulate and further appeals traveled to Congressman Richardson, Secretary of the Interior Donald P. Hodel, and President Reagan. Governor Paytiamo asked four times, to no avail, for an Ácoma audience with President Reagan. Clearly, the New Mexico delegation was reluctant to make any changes and Ácoma believed the President must have known this.[112]

Compelled by growing support for Ácoma from various national groups and private citizens, Senators Bingaman and Domenici convened with Ácoma one last time on October 20, 1987. Soon after they met with Congressman Richardson to draft an amendment they believed at last addressed Ácoma's requests. Accompanied by a floor colloquy, the amendment purported to accomplish four things:

1. It assured the Ácoma people that they could continue to use El Malpais for their traditional cultural and religious activities (in language similar to the current bill).

2. The Secretary of the Interior was authorized to seek recommendations from Ácoma officials on methods of assuring access to El Malpais for religious purposes, enhancing the privacy of religious activities, and protecting religious sites.

3. The amendment permitted the Secretary of the Interior to close portions of El Malpais for reasonable periods so that the Ácoma people could conduct their cultural and religious activities in private.

4. The Secretary of the Interior would establish an advisory committee to oversee the implementation of the provisions of the bill that protected the religious rights of the Indian people in El Malpais. Committee membership would include Ácoma and other Indian people affected by the provision.

The letter to Ácoma made no mention of amendments to change boundaries or to attempt to resolve land issues. The colloquy should assure Ácoma, Senators Bingaman and Domenici wrote, that the legislation did not "preclude the Pueblo of Acoma from pursuing any available remedy under existing law relating to your settlement with the United States over the lands in question."[113]

Tribal officials continued to inform key Senators of their grievances as officials visited New Mexico several weeks before the final vote. Secretary Hodel visited New Mexico and was reminded of Ácoma's offer to purchase the 12,385 acres east of State Road 117 if necessary. No one involved with the bill could profess ignorance of Ácoma's desires at this late date.[114] The Tribal Council informed the New Mexico delegation that the proposed amendments (and colloquy) did not incorporate Ácoma's earlier proposals and that the need to discuss their religious proceedings with outsiders would interfere with actual practices, particularly if they had to announce the ceremonies long in advance.

> Acoma is hurt by the fact that laws made by the dominant society continue to oppress native people. We can no longer be pushed and required to yield to the injustice being done to us. We can only see how the whiteman's laws are so often used to the detriment of our sacred lands. We must insist that this Act is unjust.

Again, Ácoma proposed to the delegation that at least the 12,385 acres be returned to the tribe.[115]

One more last-ditch effort to amend the bill failed even with help initially from Senator Daniel K. Inouye, Chairman of the Senate Select Committee on Indian Affairs. The Senator proposed establishing a Berryhill Allotment; as a special consideration the legislation might also put the El Malpais National Conservation Area under joint management of the Pueblo of Ácoma and the Secretary of the Interior. Ácoma officials relayed this latest suggestion to President Reagan and again requested an audience with him after the Senate voted.[116] The Tribal Council unanimously, but under protest, supported the Inouye proposal:

> 1. We do not want wilderness designation for Cebolleta [sic] Canyon and for the rest of the Tribe's federally leased lands east of State Road 117.
>
> 2. We want the opportunity to regain that land by legislation or by purchase.
>
> 3. We want the land status to remain as it currently is.
>
> 4. We want the wilderness boundary moved westward.

But Senator Inouye's proposed amendments failed because the New Mexico delegation did not want to amend the bill further. Senator Inouye wrote to Ácoma:

> My position is to support the New Mexico Congressional Delegation to move ahead with Senate consideration of this bill, with the understanding that there will be future opportunities, if necessary, to amend the legislation to clarify the rights of the Pueblo to observe religious practices in the Berryhill Allotment.

At this stage none of the Senators entertained Ácoma's unanswered questions over aboriginal lands.[117]

The Senate finally voted unanimously for the bill on December 17, 1987, and sent the package on to the President who took it to his ranch in California for the Christmas holidays. With anger and despair, tribal officials once more appealed to President Reagan. They requested an audience to air their grievances in the presence of the Lincoln cane, "a symbol of mutual respect between sovereign governments." The letter went unanswered. "It is without any consciousness that Congress will not return legally stolen land, a mere 13,000 acres, to us. This is less than 4 percent of all the sacred aboriginal land included in Senate Bill 56," lamented Governor Paytiamo.[118]

Congressman Richardson anticipated the President's signature soon and without a hitch. The New Mexico congressional delegation claimed the legislation preserved the land while protecting Indian rights. Ácoma disagreed. "I heard Senator Domenici claim publicly that federal lands can never be returned to Ácoma, either by sale or by legislation," asserted Governor Paytiamo. "'We just cannot do that,'" he had heard the Senator say. "'We do not do it for other Indians around the country.'" Governor Paytiamo and Council members could not believe the Senator would make such a statement since it was common knowledge among the Indians, at least, that Congress had returned Salt Lake and other sacred lands to the Pueblo of Zuñi, and Blue Lake, with its surrounding mountains, to the Pueblo of Taos. Ácoma officials believed that Congress had the plenary power to take the land of native people and therefore had "the same power to give the land back."[119]

The Ácoma Caciques appointed Ray A. Histia to succeed Governor Paytiamo on January 1. Ironically, President Reagan signed the bill on Governor Paytiamo's last day in office. Over the holiday weekend the *Los Angeles Times* ran a lengthy cover story detailing Governor Paytiamo's fight to preserve sacred land along with many observations about the tribe and its setting. Many at Ácoma found the article offensive. The Ácoma people, including Governor Paytiamo, appeared bumbling and dull-witted and it was implied that the Ácomas neither cared for nor were able to care for what they had. Regardless of how the article might have influenced events at the time, Governor Paytiamo believed Ácoma's wishes were doomed from the start mainly because "Senator Domenici's staff advised against us and the politicos in Washington did not want to cross the Senator." Governor Paytiamo said Ácoma contacted 100 senators several times by letters and telegrams, and only a few responded.[120]

Ácoma leaders were not giving up on their quest for their aboriginal lands. The new law allowed for exchange of Ácoma lands west of State Road 117, but did not mention those at issue east of the same road. The law also permitted Indian access to the monument for religious activities, but under controlled conditions. Water-rights language survived intact—water to be used for the national monument, conservation area, and wilderness was to be held to a minimum, existing "valid or vested water rights" were recognized, and there was an allotment for pending applications for water rights. And the law further blocked future Indian ownership of these lands:

> (d)(1) Except as otherwise provided by this Act, no federally-owned lands located within the boundaries of the monument or the conservation area shall be transferred out of Federal ownership, or be placed in trust for any Indian tribe or group, by exchange or otherwise.

Non-Indians did empathize with the predicament and worried that the United States would lose an opportunity to extend a hand of friendship and understanding to Ácoma and, consequently, all Indians. V. Barrett Price, Albuquerque, wrote in the *Albuquerque Tribune:*

The Pueblo of Acoma has been deeply offended. It feels alienated from not only New Mexico's congressional leadership, which did nothing to support their demand for land, but also from state and federal governments.

It's not too late to give them back their sacred land. I am sure they will protect its "integrity," and that of the national monument, as conscientiously as any federal agency ever could.[121]

As the aboriginal lands to the west appeared lost one more time, Ácoma acquired vast aboriginal lands to the south, encompassed by the Red Lake Ranch. The Arizona-based owners had offered the ranch to Ácoma several years back but tribal funds were inadequate. After making another offer in 1988, the Tribal Council authorized Governor Histia to request federal help. Negotiations with a number of federal agencies, including the New Mexico congressional delegation, resulted in Congress approving $2 million for the purpose. The tribe raised the remaining funds from its own resources, and through bank loans it was able to purchase Red Lake Ranch on October 16, 1989.[122]

Ácoma now reached closer to the Peñol, a mesa landmark south of Sky City that the Indians always considered a southern boundary marker. There were extensive grazing areas and woods on the Red Lake Ranch, and the owners had water rights and mineral rights to 8,000 acres, which they also included with the purchase. The Tribal Council authorized the transaction, resolving to restore these lands to the Pueblo's permanently protected land base for livestock ranching and other uses to facilitate tribal self-determination. Governor Histia described the event as an enormous accomplishment for Ácoma.

The Red Lake Ranch now belongs to the Pueblo of Acoma. We had worked on this for a number of years through negotiations in efforts of regaining our original tribal lands. This is a very joyous occasion that we have experienced. We are very happy about this, that the people of Acoma have regained lands that were once held by their ancestors which includes many sacred shrines.

In the purchase, the tribe received 114,342 acres, extending through-

out Catron, Cibola, and Socorro counties. A planning committee was
exploring various uses for the ranch, but for the time being Ácoma
employed parts of the ranch for open grazing and wood gathering. On
December 13, 1989, Governor Histia, acting on behalf of the Tribal
Council, requested trust status for the ranch from the Secretary of the
Interior in order to bring the reservation to a total of 378,344.68 acres
plus 78,454.72 acres of leased lands.[123] This status was still pending.
The reservation had more than doubled in size during recent years,
but many at Ácoma viewed the accomplishment as only the beginning
to the recovery of millions of acres of aboriginal territory.

PRESERVING OUR HERITAGE

For Ácoma, preserving Pueblo lands guaranteed and protected
well-being and spiritual life. Simon Ortiz, while addressing a forum of
students and faculty at San Diego State University in April 1978, described their feelings in this way:

> All the traditions that I'm familiar with, whether they
> be dramatic rituals, anecdotal historical, narratives, cycles or
> specific incidents in history, speak about a source: where
> people came from.
> Wherever it all began, when elements came together
> there was fire, there was water, there was earth. When people
> recognize this beginning it gives them a significance.
> Land is the source of physical and spiritual life. People
> reaffirm their relationship to the land by telling of this rela-
> tionship, making the telling their document for owning, pro-
> tecting, or fighting for it. Never a moment, never a day passes
> by without telling something about the land. And not only
> how to plant it, not only its spiritual and religious nature, but
> giving it a political nature too. That's what oral tradition does.
> It constantly reaffirms, it constantly gives substance to our
> development.[124]

Over the years the Tribal Council sought to protect this "physical and spiritual life" through the development of a constitution.

The Council appointed committees from time to time to study and recommend a guiding document. As was the trend in other New Mexico Pueblos, a constitution appeared inevitable for Ácoma. The first constitution, which was never adopted by a Council, dated from 1932– 1933 and was discovered by Governor Paytiamo, who had the remnants framed for display in the Tribal Council meeting room. While it lacked the familiar complexities of modern constitutions, the document did address tribal justice, safety, welfare, and freedom. A section listed tribal officials and recommended a secretary who was a "good man that can tell all about what is being said in the letter[s] and at the meetings— good English speaking man." Another section described the Cacique as the only person who could appoint the governor and tribal officers each year and who could present the canes of authority. The constitution also recommended an oath of office to be rendered as follows:

> I do solemnly swear (affirm) that I shall faithfully execute the office of officers of the said Pueblo of Acoma, and will to the best of my ability preserve, protect, and defend the said Pueblo of Acoma constitution.[125]

At least five or six other committees have since worked on possible constitutions. Available funds to pay investigators frequently determined the committees' endurance. Defining tribal memberships in the constitution posed the toughest decision for each committee. David Garcia, Enrollment Coordinator for the Enrollment and Membership Commiteee, explained in 1990 that the current panel firmly believed that established tribal membership (enrollment) helped to maintain greater control over traditions, to promote traditions through old family lines, and to preserve the Ácoma language. Garcia's committee worked on a census, accepting all those with 25 percent Ácoma blood or more. Those people living on the reservation for over ten years and who were not enrolled would be able to apply for naturalization or enrollment in a special category. As it stood, the Tribal Court had no jurisdiction over these people.

Another major consideration was the preservation of bloodlines of

Ácoma members in the thirteen surviving clans, each who has responsibilities to perform traditional functions. The Cacique Clan, or the Antelopes, were marrying non-Indians at such a rate that within a generation or two the Antelopes would no longer qualify as Ácoma except by special dispensation. A prior committee also ran into the question of tribal membership for unknown half-Ácoma born in wartime conditions.

Another issue for the constitution committees was the old Ácoma belief that a tribal member should perform public service without pay. It was believed that making the world a better place was an ethical responsibility they all must voluntarily share.

With hope, an enrollment ordinance would be recommended to the Tribal Council and unanimously accepted by the people. Until that time the functions of government and tradition continued without a written charter. Committee members who hoped to forge Ácoma's first operative enrollment project included Juanico Sánchez, Conroy Chino, Jean Myers, Elardo Garcia, Laura Watchempino, Rosie Maupin, and Gwyndolen Garcia. The constitution would provide a basis on which tribal members had access to reservation privileges, such as the hospital, food distribution, and housing assistance, and the document would detail individual responsibilities needed to keep the reservation in order and running.[126]

ÁCOMA'S CENTERPIECE

San Estevan del Rey Mission and convent surmounted the landscape at Sky City. From the roof one could see the Pueblo world in all directions—the Peñol to the south, Enchanted Mesa off in the east-northeast, and Mount Taylor up north. Noble aspirations of the human spirit continued to converge at the mission centuries after it was built. It was central to religious life at Ácoma and perpetually awesome to visitors. After the Franciscans gave up permanent residence at the convent in the mid-eighteenth century and later, Ácoma religious and clan leaders assumed management and use of the complex, including the mission, convent, cemetery, and grounds. For Ácoma, preserving the mission was synonymous with conserving Pueblo traditions and the sacred side of life. Adding to the significance of the mission at Sky City was the large income generated in recent years by curious visitors from all over the world.

Although the mission was sacred in ways similar to their kivas and subject to concealment from public view on occasions, the Tribal Council and religious leaders accepted outside help for the preservation of the large mission complex and older dwellings in Sky City. Reservation-development surveys conducted in 1965 and 1974 warned of older houses falling into ruin because they were not being maintained by owners who stayed in them mainly during ceremonial events.[127]

In the 1970s, a serious roof leak developed in the nave of the mission, possibly from a bolt of lightning. Water washed out portions of the interior south walls and was seeping into the massive adobe walls. In December 1978, the Tribal Council authorized Pacheco and Graham Architects to conduct a structure report with a matching grant from the Historic Preservation Bureau of the State of New Mexico. They hoped to generate a guide to help in the general preservation work at the mission, and to serve in applications for funding.[128] The report done by Edna Heatherington Bergman with help from others including Frank Ortiz, then second lieutenant governor, and James Sánchez, summarized alterations described in earlier reports and those recalled by elder Ácomas. The list produced a fascinating insight to this centerpiece of Ácoma's past.

The mission and convent, according to the report, were from the beginning assembled of massive adobe walls on stone foundations covered with adobe plaster. Originally there had been a clerestory in the roof that shed light into the apse with two windows high on the south wall of the nave. Square, carved roof timbers with carved and painted woodwork introduced color throughout. There were large towers, somewhat as they appeared today, with a baptistry, sacristy, choir loft, adobe altar, altar railing, pulpit, and an altar screen in painted bas-relief within the apse to the west. (The sacristy, baptistry, and convent kitchen disappeared at some unknown dates after 1776.)[129]

As this list shows, the first major changes to the complex appeared during the Pueblo Revolt and Reconquest, 1680–1700:

Damage to roof, loss of doors and other woodwork, destruction of *convento*. Roof rebuilt without clerestory; third window added to south wall of chancel. Wood elements replaced. Bells dated 1710; approximate date of *santo* of San Estevan Rey and altar stone "given by the king." Reconstruction of *convento*.

1745–67: Addition of stairway, *sala*, and mirador [second-story additions] to *convento*.

About 1802: Altar screen dated 1802 [donated by Jose Manuel Aragon, *Alcalde Mayor* of the *Alcaldia de Laguna*]; alterations to altar and chancel. Renovation of roof.

Mid- to Late-Nineteenth Century: Periodic roof repairs. Possible installation of woodstove. Baptistry struck by lightning, allowed to collapse. Serious erosion on walls; south tower wasting away; north tower possibly rebuilt with stone. White plaster on east facade.

About 1911: Reconstruction of towers (square). Possible date of milled wood floor and chancel steps and floor; covering of columns and facia of *coro* with milled wood. Addition of wood stair to *coro*, large manufactured windows in south wall; closing of chancel window; milled woodwork of *coro* window.

After 1914: Sloped metal roof on mirador of *convento*. Faces on crenelation of cemetery. At some time, murals of the nave overpainted with white plaster and pink dado [earth colors].

1924: Reconstruction of roof with concrete slab.

1926–27: Extensive patching and repair of walls; reconstruction of both towers with stone. Discovery and reconstruction of special stair in south towers. East doors straightened and rehung. Replastering with adobe plaster.

After 1934: Veneering of west and south walls with stone begun.

Before 1939: Replacement of sloped roof [tin] of mirador with flat roof.

Early 1960: Probable date of major roof construction. Concrete slab removed; new roof with space above ceiling.[130]

Spending around $10,000 in federally matching funds, Ácoma men repaired the cemetery retaining wall from 1974 to 1976. And, with a contract from the Historic Preservation Bureau administered through the State Planning Office, Ácoma men rebuilt the *convento*, March 22, 1976 to August 31, 1977, for a total of $42,554 in matching funds, with Ácoma furnishing labor and materials. The workers replaced the roof, replaced round or milled squared vigas with hewn square vigas, installed latillas in original herring-bone design, restored soil fill in the courtyard to original ground level, replaced rejas in windows, and remudded the deteriorated and rain-damaged exterior.[131]

Lightning damage prompted emergency repairs in 1979, which were supported again with state funds. The Heritage Conservation Officer found many buildings, in addition to the mission, in need of immediate attention. Work crews were actually repairing some of these homes under a housing rehabilitation program, but many buildings were in bad shape. Crews repaired the interior of San Estevan in time to celebrate the annual feast day on September 2. Then, following recommendations of the Pacheco and Graham report in 1980, the Historic Preservation Bureau set aside $20,000 in federal preservation funds to continue priority work on the exterior walls and roof. The latest work, however, had some tragic results, according to Thomas W. Merlan, state Historic Preservation Officer.

In 1980, Ácoma had received two bronze plaques, which they never publicly displayed, that designated the Pueblo of Ácoma and San Estevan del Rey Misson natural historic landmarks.[132] However, destruction of original materials during the renovation in 1981–1982 threatened this status. Merlan discovered that all historic materials in the sanctuary of the mission had been removed, including the chancel, chancel rail, and altar. He said the new design and materials were "totally inappropriate to, and out of character with, the historic character of the church." Also lost during the work were the ancient murals on the apse walls, about which little study had been done (these were in addition to the murals of the convent). The architectural reputations of Sky City and San Estevan were blemished, Merlan wrote Governor Merle Garcia. "This will affect tourism, which is sure to drop and which is one of the Tribe's most lucrative sources of income." The Historic

Preservation Bureau consequently withheld $5,000 until the new chancel was removed and the historic chancel, rail, and altar were replaced or reconstructed.[133]

The repercussions from Merlan's letter would probably never surface, but James Sánchez claimed that all the renovation projects lacked management and that preservation was lagging. At this point, promise of help came from an unexpected source. During the mid-1980s, James Coriz, member of the Pueblo of Santo Domingo and an architect, grew increasingly zealous about preserving the Ácoma mission complex. His enthusiasm inspired a small following, and in June 1988 Coriz and his group met with the Ácoma Tribal Council and received approval for a feasibility study on the complex. The Council members were intrigued by what they proposed to do. Working with James Sánchez, Coriz completed a preliminary report that Christmas.[134]

Their initial assessments found the mission to be in good order with excellent maintenance having been done in recent years. In the report, the group offered to repair and conserve the complex much more thoroughly than previous efforts. In particular, they proposed to replace missing rooms and artifacts and, within the convent, to restore as many rooms as possible, such as the priests' cell rooms, to reflect earlier activities. The report did not recommend rebuilding a convent kitchen. The overall assessment concluded that major portions of the mission were still present and that the cemetery wall appeared to be in very good condition.[135]

James Coriz died unexpectedly in January 1989, more or less as the project got under way. Within a month Coriz's influence caused the followers to establish the Mission at Old Ácoma Foundation to continue the enterprise mainly by raising funds. Again, spokespersons appealed to the Tribal Council on behalf of the Foundation and the Council voted in March 1989 to allow them to proceed. The Foundation had proposed tackling problems individually as funds became available.[136]

During all seasons of 1990, tourists daily arrived at Sky City in larger numbers. There to mix with the Ácomas, visitors themselves were drawn to this historic mecca. "Ácoma beliefs and traditions, and in a sense a longing, draw our people back to the mesa at intervals throughout the year on particular days," explained the governor during a recent public announcement. "For this main reason families return to the Ácoma Mesa which serves to give a feeling of belonging at home."

Upon leaving Sky City the road wound past Enchanted Mesa where the Pueblo maintained inviting picnic grounds. A visit to this site by full moonlight offered one of the more arresting sights in the world.

Appendixes

APPENDIX 1

Text of Patented Grant, Ácoma

PUEBLO DE ÁCOMA. Grant. 1689. Made by Governor and Captain-General Don Domingo Jironza Petriz de Cruzate, September 20th.

1689. In the village of our Lady of Guadalupe del Paso del Río del Norte, on the twentieth day of the month of September, in the year one thousand six hundred and eighty-nine, his excellency, Don Domingo Jironza Petriz de Cruzate, governor and captain-general, stated that whereas in the overtaking which was had in the pueblo of Ácoma, and the power which he has over the Queres [Keres] Indians and over the apostates in New Mexico, he provided that an Indian named Bartolome, who was the most conspicuous in the battles, lending his aid everywhere, and surrendered, having been wounded by a ball and an arrow, and being already crippled, I ordered him to state the truth, and declare in his confession the condition of the pueblo of Ácoma and that of the other apostates in that kingdom; and as the Indian is well versed in the Spanish language, intelligent, and can read and write, he was examined before General Don Pedro Reneros de Posada, who had returned from New Mexico, having been at the pueblo of Ácoma, and the maestro de campo, Dominguez Mendoza, having also been called, in order that the Indian, Bartolome de Ojeda, might give his name.

Having been asked if he is disposed to confess the truth as to what he knew and about which he might be asked, and having been asked his name, of what place he is a native, his age and what office he has, and whether he knows the condition of Ácoma and Laguna, who are neighbors, he said that his name was Bartolome de Ojeda; that he is a native of the pueblo of Zia, in the province of New Mexico; that he is twenty-one or two years of age, more or less; that he has had no other office than that of soldier (warrior) and that he knows the condition of Ácoma and Laguna because he was an apostate in the Province of New Mexico; and this he answered.

Having been asked how it happened that Laguna and Ácoma,

175

being neighbors, disagreed so much, and how was it that they had moved to the Peñol, being much arrogant Indians, and why had they left their pueblo, he responded saying that the Ácomas had moved to the Peñol because they were very proud and had moved to the Peñol because of the many wars these Pueblos had, one with the other; and this was his answer.

Having been asked why it was that these Pueblos lived near to each other, what agreement there was between them and why they disagreed, he answered that Laguna moved close to Ácoma because of the abundance of water there was at that Pueblo, but always for the purpose of collecting the surplus remaining from the pueblo of Ácoma; and this he answered.

Having been asked what are the existing boundaries of Ácoma, and to how much is each pueblo restricted, he said that the Prieto mountain is on the north, that the Gallo spring is on the west, and that the Cubero mountain is opposite the old pueblo of Ácoma and that the Peñol is on the south side and that when the Indian Poc-Pec (Po-pé) visited the pueblos he confirmed the above because he is an Indian of the Tegua nation and a native of the pueblo of San Juan, to whom all the land gave obedience at the time of the insurrection, and was in company with Alonzo Catiti; and Don Luis Tu-pa-tu, and many other chiefs of those pueblos had declared that the water belonged to the pueblo of Ácoma, and that Laguna was to collect the surplus remaining from the pueblo; and this is his answer.

Having been asked if he knows any more than he has stated, and if Laguna has any other defense to make concerning the water, he answered that he had not; that although the pueblo had removed to the Peñol it had not lost its right to the water, and that the Laguna Indians were not ignorant of the fact as it is notorious; and that what he has stated is the truth, under the oath which he has taken, which he affirms and ratifies. This grant being read and explained to him he signed it with his excellency, the governor and captain-general, aforesaid, before me, the present secretary of government and war, to which I certify.

DOMINGO JIRONZA PETRIZ DE CRUZATE
BARTOLOME DE OJEDA

Before me:

DON PEDRO LADRON DE GUITARA,
Secretary of Government and War.

From Ralph Emerson Twitchell, *The Spanish Archives of New Mexico* (Cedar Rapids, Iowa: The Torch Press, 1914).

APPENDIX 2

Fray Francisco Atanasio Domínguez'
Description of Acoma, 1776

ÁCOMA

South of Laguna, crossing the sandy plain that lies in this direction, then the wooded hills mentioned there, and then taking a long cañada with mesas on either side which runs from south to north, at a distance of 4 leagues over the above terrain one finds the pueblo and mission of San Esteban de Acoma. It is located and established on the flat top of a mesa 80 to 100 varas high. This resembles a cliff, and for this reason they call it the Peñol of Acoma. The ascent to this is a sandy and very difficult slope (there are many footpaths leading up, which only the Indians manage with skill). It begins on the west side of the mesa, ascends almost halfway, and from there on makes a number of boxed-in turns, so difficult that in some places they have made wide steps so that the pack animals may ascend with comparative ease.

The buildings are at the top of the said mesa, almost in the center, and they resemble the little shrine to St. Michael on the hill of Guadalupe in Mexico. The said mesa stands in the middle of the plain, which has some cañadas nearby in the south, east, north, and northwest. To the west and southwest a chain of mesas runs a long distance. This mesa has some crags around it, some of which rise to a third of its height and others halfway up, and there are some corrals for livestock on them, to which they climb by little paths which the Indians have made. In other places there are such horrible precipices that it is not possible to look over them for fear of the steep drop. This Acoma is 34 good leagues from Santa Fe via the highway and lies to the southwest of this villa.

Although I have not spent so much time at the beginning of my description of other missions as I have here, it is because there is no comparison with the situation here. The little I have said to begin with at those places indicates in brief to the judicious reader the nature of

178

the buildings and transportation in relation to the nearby rivers and easy transportation of all necessities. The contrary is true here, for there is not even a brook, earth to make adobes, or a good cart road. Therefore it is necessary to prevent any preconception in order to achieve even a confused notion of this place. This makes what the Indians have built here of adobes with perfection, strength, and grandeur, at the expense of their own backs, worthy of admiration.

CHURCH

This church was inaugurated in the year 1725. Father Miranda (they say) built it, and it is of good adobe with walls nearly 2 varas thick. The main door faces east, and from there to the ascent to the sanctuary it is 36 varas long, 12 wide, and 14 high up to the bed molding. Six steps of wrought beams form the ascent to the sanctuary, which measures 6 varas from the last step to the center, with the same width as the nave. The height is the same because there is no clerestory. The choir loft is in the usual place, occupies the width of the nave, and projects 5 long varas into the church. It is supported by fourteen wrought beams which rest on a strong cross timber imbedded in the side walls with corbels. Below, two pillars of carved wood reinforce it, and their position results in a semblance of three arches.

On the right side there are three beautiful windows with wooden gratings facing south, and one in the choir facing east. The whole roof consists of fifty well wrought and corbeled beams. The main door is squared, with a strong wooden frame instead of masonry, two well-paneled leaves, no lock except the crossbar, and is 4 varas high by 2 1/2 wide. The tower buttresses jut out from the front corners and extend toward the center to hold two small towers, one on each. The one on the right contains two small bells which the King gave, and they are cracked. There is no balcony between them as in other places.

When we enter the main door, the entrance to the baptistery is under the choir to our left. It is outside the church wall and is a very spacious room with a window to the east, a door with two completely grated leaves to the church, an ordinary one without a lock. In the center stands a small wooden pillar, hollowed out for a drain, with a large earthen bowl on top for a baptismal font, covered with a board. The cemetery is enclosed by a stone-and-mud wall. It begins at the corner of the baptistery, where it juts out like a head wall, and continues around to the front corner on the Epistle side. It is 40 varas square. The wall is more than a vara high and has two gates, one on each side. The dead are buried in it, for it has been deliberately terraced up with earth because of the steepness of the slope in relation to the area in varas. There are no burials in the church because the rock prevents this, and in order to cover it, it was filled with earth to a depth of about half a vara. This is the church floor. The interior is pleasant, although bare, and the adornment is as follows.

HIGH ALTAR: The whole wall is covered, as we shall see. Beginning with the gradin, I state that it is adobe and wide. There are three ledges of the same material on it, ascending like a throne. On the top there is an ordinary painted wooden niche to hold a completely carved St. Stephen of rather medium size. The Indians bought this statue, or image, along with the niche. Above it hangs a large old painting on buffalo skin of St. Stephen's martyrdom, which Father Miranda provided in a painted wooden frame. Above this is another buffalo skin picture without a saint, but there is a beautiful gilt paper cross on it and it is all spangled with little flowers made of painted paper.

The whole area that I have been describing, up to the top, has arches painted with colored earth, executed by the Indians. The same is true of the saints at the sides which follow here. On either side of the niche hang two large oil paintings, now old. One represents St. Peter and the other St. Anthony of Padua. Above these are two paper prints surrounded by little painted paper flowers. The altar table is adobe with an altar stone given by the King on it. A cross of painted wood, two small brass candlesticks, which the King gave, and an ordinary missal stand. Below there is a small bronze bell, a board dais, and a beautiful carpet dyed with cochineal, which the Indians wove in Father Pino's time. The only thing in the nave is the confessional, which is adobe and resembles a bookstand.

SACRISTY: It is joined to the church on the Epistle side, but there is no door to the church, only to the cloister, in a corner of which it stands against the church. Running along the cloister, it is 10 varas long and 5 wide, and 3 long varas high with a good roof. The door is single-leaved, of ordinary size, and has a good key. It has two small windows, with wooden gratings and no shutters, to the west. Across the head wall there is a wooden table with two drawers, one above the other, in the middle. Both are secured by a vertical iron rod without a padlock. Some little paper prints adorned with small paper flowers are arranged on the wall above this table. The father uses the table when he vests, and the following are kept in its drawers.

Vestments: An old damask chasuble with two faces (white and crimson) will all accessories, which the King gave. A new chasuble of green ribbed silk with all accessories, which Father Pino provided. An old purple satin chasuble with accessories. Another new one of mother-of-pearl ribbed silk, which the said father provided. Another old white satin one with accessories. Another old mother-of-pearl satin one with accessories. Another very old black ribbed silk one with accessories. An old black damask cope. A green ribbed silk pall. Another mother-of-pearl one.

Linen: Three good Brittany amices. Three albs like them. Three altar cloths like the foregoing. A cloth cincture. Father Pino provided them all during the many years he lived here. Six pairs of double corporals of Brittany in fair condition. Several purificators. Four finger towels.

Silver and other metal: Chalice with paten and spoon, which the King gave. Three small vials for the holy oils, which the same lord gave. The arras and rings given by the said lord.

Thurible with accessories. Processional cross. Tin-plate box for altar breads. Mold for making altar breads, which the King gave.

Other things: A usable missal for secular priests. Another very old one. *Manual* by Osorio. Two ordinary cruets. A small gourd cup for baptizing. Many old poles, which are in the rear of the sacristy.

CONVENT

The convent is joined to the church on the left side and forms a square there, extending to the north. Its porter's lodge faces east and is an ordinary small portico with adobe seats around it and two pillars at the mouth, which divide it into three arches. The door is in the middle of the center wall. It is an ordinary single-leaf one with a crossbar for a lock. The whole convent is adobe with very good walls, all well made and very large. As we enter the porter's lodge there is a single cell on the left and then the stair well for the well-arranged stairway that leads to the choir.

The principal cell is on the right. It has a key in its door and consists of three rooms, one of which is on a corner. Around the corner is a stair well leading to a small upper story, which we shall soon see, and then two beautiful storerooms with wooden locks. Just before we turn the corner, there is a passage which leads to the corrals I shall soon describe, making two turns on the way. The kitchen is around the corner, then a storeroom, and then the sacristy. There is an enclosed cloister, lighted by three good windows on each side. On one side there is a door to the patio, in which there are some little peach trees which are watered by hand. And in one corner there is a small recess for certain necessary business. The door leading to either the sacristy or convent is on the side against the church in its very wall.

Let us proceed to the corners I left for future mention. The stair well in the first one was once a small cell, whose door remains today, but a small stairway is now fitted into the center with three short and very neatly made turns, for the steps are made of bricks with a railed banister. There is a railing at the top with a gate to match, which, when closed, prevents any sudden accident. It is all roofed over, with a closed wall to the north and completely open to the south over the whole flat roof of the first floor. As we emerge and face south over the flat roof, there is a well-arranged mirador to our left on the flat roof of the room on the corner. It faces north and east, with railings and pillars. It has an earthen floor, but hard, and on the south and west walls there are seats of well-wrought boards resting on small corbels. It has an ordinary single-leaf door without a key.

On the right there is a beautiful salon, the upper part of which is partitioned off with boards to make an inner cell. Father Pino made it all. In the other corner where the passage is, is the exit to the afore-mentioned corrals, and they are really one, with a third of it divided off. The said father made them, and they have a very high and thick stone-and-mud wall. The largest one has a good two-leaved door without a key to the north, and there are a stable and strawloft in it. The other is beside it to the south at the back of the church. It serves as a chicken yard and is narrow with a rather low door.

Its Furnishings: Two large tables. Three benches. Three armless chairs. An adobe stand for books.

Its Service: The same as has been described at Laguna, but here there are twelve Indian women who bring twelve small jars of water to be used daily. And as soon as they put them in the kitchen, they go home until the next day, when they do it again. The reason for such a large number of water carriers is that the water (as I shall explain later) is very far away, and to avoid frequent trips a good deal is brought at one time. When it is necessary to water the little trees mentioned above, the girls who come to catechism go with the weekly fiscal and bring a great deal all at once, even more than is enough.

Its Lands and Fruits: There are no lands assigned to this mission as is the case in other missions, and I will explain the reason for this in detail when I describe the pueblo lands.

MISSION FATHER

The one who exercises the ministry at this mission is Father Fray José Mariño, native of San Miguel el Grande, thirty-six years of age, seventeen in profession, three years as a missionary in the Custody, as follows: El Paso, six months; Acoma, two years, six months. He holds general faculties in Durango, revocable at will.

Administration of the Mission: The usual regime, but carried out in a most exquisite manner which Father Pino taught the Indians, and this is: Sometimes the men put the questions of the catechism, other times the women; still others, the little boys, and others the little girls, and still others, the father. Sometimes they all put the questions to the father, sometimes at random, sometimes in sequence. And when the questions are put by the respective groups, as I have said, the other groups reply in the same way. Some explanation is always made, and the said Indians have many quaint customs that the said father taught them.

183

EXPENDITURES: Food consumed by the household is not counted. About 6 pounds of wax a year, about 2 jugs of wine. A fanega of wheat is given to the chief sacristan for the altar breads used here and for those sent to Laguna when they ask for them.

HOW HE ACQUIRES NECESSITIES: In this regard I refer to what was said at Laguna in a few well-chosen words.

NOTE

I made the visitation of this mission on December 17 of the past year of 1776, and no writ of visitation was left because I did not consider it necessary. Instructions were left for Father Mariño that the convent provisions should be as follows: 4 fanegas of wheat, 4 of maize, a jar of ordinary lard, a bottle of wine, 2 wax candles.

The parish books were inspected and approved. And since they are nearly full, I ordered the said father to ask the Father Vice-Custos for three new ones from the supply that just arrived and to remit the old ones to the archive. I also ordered him to remit the old Inventory to the same place, and since the book of Patents is incorporated with it, the same is to be done with it as with its adjunct. I gave sufficient paper for new books for the Inventory, Patents, and an additional one for the Edicts of the Lord Bishop, and authorized them.

PUEBLO

Although the site of this mission was described at the beginning, it still remains to be said that west of the buildings on the adjoining surface of the mesa which I mentioned in that place, there is a cistern which God made in the rock itself. Its opening must be about 40 varas in circumference, and it must be fully as deep. Rain water is caught in it, and when it snows, the Indians take care to collect all the snow they can in it. For this purpose, and in order that the rain water may be clean when it goes in, they are careful to keep the space around it swept, and there is a guard to prevent pollution.

The water collected in this usually half fills it. Because the rock is cold, it has never been known to become fetid, and it is always fresh, although turbid. The descent to it is a little stairway in a corner, made in the rock itself and very steep. When one goes to it, one travels a quarter or a third of a league from the pueblo, because one descends by the boxed-in road mentioned above, reaches the sandy slope, and, traveling up hill over the sand again, traverses a rocky stretch to it. After getting water, one returns the same way, and so home. This trip is made constantly, for although there are other cisterns in view of the pueblo on the site where it stands, they are no bigger than a vessel of a font, and therefore do not last for more than eight or ten days.

In view of this, it is clear how much work must have been involved in building church and pueblo. The latter is north of the church, arranged and built in six tenements, or blocks, of dwellings constructed of stone and mud. Three face east, and three south, one behind another, with very wide streets between, forming, with the convent, a handsome plaza. They have upper and lower stories such as I have described in all the foregoing, and they are not as clean and well kept as at Laguna but like the rest.

ITS LANDS AND FRUITS: The Indians have lands wherever the cañadas in the south, east, north, and northwest mentioned above provide arable level ground. All are completely dependent on rain, for although there are two small springs, they only suffice as drinking water for some small livestock. They have made a low bank of earth around them for this purpose. When it rains these milpas do well, but if rain is completely lacking, there are hardships, as has been the case for three years now, when there has been great drought.

Three leagues up the cañada from Laguna and 5 or 6 north-northeast of Acoma (we shall see this again on our way to Zuñi) there is a place called Cubero in a cañada which runs between mesas from south to north. It is about a league long from south to north and about half a league wide from east to west. The Indians sow all they can in it on both sides of the river that flows to Laguna; they irrigate with it and harvest very reasonable crops. In this very place they plant for the convent wherever the father chooses, usually harvesting 40 fanegas of wheat, the same amount of maize, and a little of each kind of green vegetable. The natives are Queres (this completes the seven pueblos of this nation), whose native tongue they speak. As for everything else, they are like the Laguna Indians. With regard to these Acomas, here is this

NOTE

Father Claramonte tells me that in the year 1768, when he was missionary of Laguna and was taking care of this Acoma mission because of Father Pino's death, the census of the Acoma Indians numbered 1,114. Only those whom we shall soon see now remain in the pueblo out of so large a number. The reason for this great decrease is that many have died since then, some from natural causes in epidemics or from other diseases, others at the hands of Apaches so insolent that if this pueblo were not by nature defensible, perhaps nothing would now remain of it. The present mission father also states that still others are wandering about and that some have fled to Moqui for fear of the famines and war they have suffered in a few years. The following lists those here at present.

CENSUS

135 families with 530 persons

There is no settlement under the administration of this mission, but only the lieutenant alcalde mayor and his family live here. This note includes them.

1 family with 5 persons

Section on Ácoma in *The Missions of New Mexico, 1776, a Description by Fray Francisco Atanasio Dominguez with other Contemporary Documents*, Eleanor B. Adams and Fray Angelico Chavez, trans. and eds. (New Mexico: University of New Mexico Press, 1956, 1975).

APPENDIX 3

Ácoma Militia Muster Roll, 1839

Hombres [Men]	Cavallos [Mounted]	Infantes [On Foot]	Escopetas [Muskets]	Carcajs [Quivers]
Mateo Chapalon	00	1	00	1
José Sarracino	1	00	1	00
Visente	00	1	00	1
José	00	1	00	1
Lorenzo Candelaria	1	00	1	00
Francisco Pancho	1	00	1	00
Antonio Salvador	00	1	00	1
Ygnacio Romero	1	00	00	1
Vicente	00	1	00	1
José Leyba	00	1	00	1
José Manuel	00	1	00	1
Bartolo	00	1	1	00
Juachín	00	1	00	1
Antonio Montoya	00	1	00	1
Juanico	1	00	1	00
Bautista	1	00	1	00
José Ortiz	1	00	00	1
Antonio Luna	00	1	00	1
Lusiano	00	1	00	1
José Estevan	1	00	00	1
Juan de Dios Paseno	00	1	00	1
Antonio Contador	00	1	00	1
José Vicente	00	1	00	1
José Martin	00	1	1	00
Juan Estevan	00	1	00	1
Santiago Torres	00	1	00	1
Juan Pillito	1	00	1	00
José Ribalid	00	1	1	00
Lorenzo	00	1	1	00
Antonio Cajero	00	1	00	1
Faustino	00	1	1	00
Diego Antonio	1	00	1	00
Paulin	1	00	1	00
Juan Estevan	1	00	00	1
José Garcia	00	1	00	1
José	00	1	00	1
Santiago	00	1	00	1
Santiago Cuilluna	1	00	00	1
Juan Chávez	00	1	00	1

	Hombres [Men]	Cavallos [Mounted]	Infantes [On Foot]	Escopetas [Muskets]	Carcajs [Quivers]
	Merijildo Torres	00	1	00	1
	Eusebio Aragon	00	1	00	1
	Francisco	00	1	00	1
	Antonio	00	1	00	1
	José Belen	1	00	1	00
	José Antonio	00	1	00	1
	José Lino	1	00	00	1
	Juan Agustín	00	1	00	1
	José	00	1	00	1
	Juan Pedro	00	1	00	1
	Francisco	00	1	00	1
	Visentilo	1	00	00	1
	Juan Estevan	1	00	00	1
	José Matias	1	00	00	1
	Santiago Viejo	1	00	00	1
	Visente Chávez	1	00	1	00
	Mateo Candelaria	00	1	1	00
	José Vicente	00	1	00	1
	San Juan	00	1	00	1
	José	00	1	00	1
	Asencio	00	1	00	1
	Santiago	00	1	00	1
	Visente Gutierrez	00	1	00	1
	Juan de Dios	00	1	00	1
	Juan Cruz	00	1	00	1
	José Carrio	00	1	00	1
	Francisco	00	1	00	1
	Silviano	1	00	00	1
	Antonio	00	1	00	1
	Juaquín	00	1	00	1
	Juan Diego	00	1	00	1
	Felix	00	1	00	1
	José María Archundi	00	1	00	1
	Baltasar Perea	00	1	00	1
Teniente Cap^{tan} de Guerra	Pascual	1	00	1	00
	Francisco Lovera	00	1	00	1
	Francisco	00	1	00	1
	Juan José	00	1	00	1
	Santiago	00	1	00	1
	Geronimo	00	1	00	1
	José Guacasualla	00	1	00	1
	Juan Antonio	1	00	1	00
	José Portal	00	1	00	1
	Baltasar Zuni	00	1	00	1
	José Romero	1	00	00	1
	Santiago	00	1	00	1

	Hombres [Men]	Cavallos [Mounted]	Infantes [On Foot]	Escopetas [Muskets]	Carcajs [Quivers]
	Antonio Vivora	00	1	00	1
	Lorenzo Leon	00	1	00	1
	Antonico	1	00	00	1
	José Anaya	00	1	00	1
Cap^{tan} de la	Blas	00	1	00	1
Guerra	Juan Lovera	00	1	00	1
	Lusiano Paye	1	00	00	1
	Juan Matías	00	1	00	1
	Juan Ygnacio Chavez	1	00	00	1
	José Penco	1	00	00	1
	Miguel Correa	1	00	1	00
	José María Romero	1	00	1	00
	José Señor	00	1	00	1
	Juan Rey	00	1	00	1
	Pedro Garviso	00	1	00	1
	José Tagle [?]	1	00	00	1
	José Vigil	00	1	00	1
	José	1	00	1	00
	Lorenzo	00	1	00	1
	Antonio Romero	00	1	00	1
	Ylario	00	1	00	1
	Francisco	00	1	00	1
	Jose Chivatito	00	1	00	1
	Diego Antonio Sarracino	1	00	1	00
	Antonio Yuata	00	1	00	1
	Antonio Pena	00	1	00	1
	Toribio	00	1	00	1
	Antonio Salaises	00	1	00	1
	Bautista	00	1	00	1
	Santiago Aragon	1	00	00	1
	Torivio	00	1	00	1
	Visente Chara	00	1	1	00
	José Talero	00	1	00	1
	Alonzo Verrendo	1	00	00	1
	Antonio Grullauna	00	1	00	1
	San Juan	00	1	00	1
	Juan Ramires	1	00	00	1
	Santiago Garcia	00	1	00	1
	Lorenzo Romero	00	1	00	1
	José Lupes	00	1	00	1
	Juaquín	00	1	00	1
	José Alarid	00	1	1	00
	Antonio Pacheco	1	00	00	1
	San José	00	1	00	1
	José el fiscal	00	1	00	1
	Juan Estevan	00	1	00	1

	Hombres [*Men*]	*Cavallos* [*Mounted*]	*Infantes* [*On Foot*]	*Escopetas* [*Muskets*]	*Carcajs* [*Quivers*]
	Matías	00	1	00	1
	José Gervacio	1	00	00	1
	Antonio José	1	00	00	1
	Diego Antonio	00	1	00	1
	Mariano Ortiz	00	1	1	00
	Tomás	00	1	00	1
	Diego Antonio	1	00	00	1
	Bautista	00	1	1	00
	José Antonio	00	1	00	1
	Francisco Montoya	00	1	00	1
	Lusiano	00	1	1	00
	Antonio Bibora	00	1	00	1
	José Ortiz	00	1	00	1
	Fabian	1	00	00	1
	Estevan	00	1	00	1
	Bentura	00	1	00	1
	Juan Rosario	00	1	00	1
	Juan Chavez	1	00	1	00
	Pedro Matias	00	1	00	1
	Diego Antonio	1	00	1	00
	Blaz	1	00	1	00
	Francisco	00	1	1	00
	Lusiano	00	1	00	1
	Pascual	00	1	00	1
	Juan Isidro	00	1	1	00
	Lorenzo Romero	00	1	00	1
Governadorsillo	Juaquín Seloso	00	1	00	1
Capitan de la guerra	Antonico	1	00	00	1
	Total 96[?]	28[?]	66[?]	22[?]	72[?]

Original in Mexican Archives of New Mexico, New Mexico State Records Center.

APPENDIX 4

Boundary Agreement Between Ácoma and Laguna, 1857

Be it remembered that on the 6th day of July year of our lord 1857, the following entry was made in the words and figures following to wit.

Pueblo of Ácoma to settle boundaries and the Pueblo of Laguna to quit possession to lands.

And now on this day again came the parties of their council and say that they will no further produce testimony to the court in this case, but move the court to make and enter a decree in pursuance of an agreement mutually made between the parties and placed on file in this cause and the court having duly examined the provisions and stipulations of said agreement doth consider, order, adjudge, and decree:

1. That the Pueblo of Ácoma and its inhabitants shall have free and undisturbed possession and enjoyment of all the lands in complainants bill mentioned, opened, and irrigated by the Río del Gallo from its source to the lower part or side of the Cañada de la Cruz, including said Cañada.

2. The dividing line between said pueblo and inhabitants thereto shall be a line drawn north and south from the eastern or lower edge or side of the Cañada de la Cruz where the Gallo crosses the said Cañada leaving the said Cañada for the Pueblo of Ácoma and its inhabitants.

3. The present years crop growing upon said lands in dispute in this cause shall be gathered by the respective parties or persons who have planted and cultivated the same. It is further considered and decreed that all the controversies and disputes existing between the said Pueblo of Ácoma and the Pueblo of Laguna or the inhabitants of the said pending in this court or other . . . investigations and the same hereby are forever quieted compromised and settled. And that each of the pueblos or inhabitants thereof are hereby enjoined to conform to and faithfully abide by the said agreement and provisions of this decree. It is further ordered that the Pueblo of Laguna pay the costs in this cause laid out and expected except for the costs of the witnesses for complainants.

Original in Valencia County District Court Records, New Mexico State Records Center.

APPENDIX 5

Ácoma Ditches and Farm Lands in 1911

Territory of New Mexico,
County of Valencia,

Before me, the undersigned, a Notary Public, in and for the County and Territory aforesaid, this day personally appeared, Lorenzo Concho, Governor of the Ácoma Pueblo, Leo García, Lieutenant Governor, Ross Lowdon, 2nd Lieutenant Governor, Edward Hunt and José Andrés both officers, all Ácoma Indians, who being first duly sworn and each for himself and not for another deposes and says:

That the Ácoma Indians have occupied the present Pueblo and the land adjacent thereto, and now included in the Pueblo Grant of Ácoma for a long period of time, so great that there is no record of the time of settlement.

That they have cultivated the ground and irrigated the same, using water from the Río San José and there is no other source from which to secure water for the irrigation of their land which is desert land and upon which crops will not grow without water for generations of time past and are still using the water for such purposes.

That the land is now supplied with water through five ditches, that beyond the memory of any living man they have existed as ditches appurtenant to the Río San José, a stream running in said County, that the age of the said ditches is unknown but it is believed that they and each of them are of the age of two hundred years, and that their points of heading with the said Río San José are set forth correctly as defined in the following description.

That the Juan Sarracino Ditch has its heading on the Ácoma Grant and from which point the Northwest corner of the Ácoma Grant bears N10° W and 7000 feet distant.

That the said ditch is about 4000 feet long and from it is irrigated land on the southside of the Río San José and that the acreage cultivated is about 28 acres.

192

That the said ditch was built by the Indians and that no others but the Ácoma Indians use or are entitled to use the said ditch for the carrying of water.

That the Hunt's ditch has its heading on the Ácoma Grant, and from which point the Northwest corner of the Ácoma Grant bears N25° W and about 9000 feet distant.

That the said ditch is about 3/4 mile long and from it is irrigated land on the southside of the Río San José and that the acreage is 7 acres.

That the ditch was built by the Indians and that no other persons but the Ácoma Indians use or are entitled to use the said ditch for carrying water.

That the McCarty's ditch has its heading on the Ácoma Grant, and from which point the A.T.&S. Fe Ry. water tank bears N82° E and 1 mile distant.

That the said ditch is about 3 miles long and from it is irrigated land on the northside of the Río San José and that the acreage cultivated is about 118 acres of land.

That the said ditch was built by the Indians and that no other persons but the Ácoma Indians use or are entitled to use the said ditch for carrying water.

That the North Puncho ditch has its heading on the Ácoma Grant and from which point the 6 mile stone on the North Boundary line bears due north about 1 mile distant.

That the said ditch is 5 1/2 miles long and from it is irrigated about 232 acres of land on the northside of the Río San José.

That the said ditch was built by the Indians, and that no other persons but the Ácoma Indians use or are entitled to use the said ditch for carrying water.

That the South Candelario ditch has its heading on the Ácoma Grant and from which point the northeast corner of Joe Vallo's property bears S35° W and 350 feet distant.

That the said ditch is 6 3/4 miles long and from it is irrigated 314 acres of land on the southside of the Río San José.

That the said ditch was built by the Indians and that no other persons but the Ácoma Indians use or are entitled to use the said ditch for carrying water.

And we each of us have had the above statements interpreted to us in our language, and we each of us understand the contents thereof, and we each of us sign it of our own free will.

Lorenzo Concho

Above imprint made in my presence this 11 day of May 1911.

Howard P. Wasmer

Subscribed and sworn to before me this 11 day of May AD. 1911
My commission expires

Copy in Pueblo of Ácoma Archives.

APPENDIX 6
Ácoma Artisans and Trainees

POTTERS, 1939–1940

Mrs. Torivio Haskaya
Mrs. Marie Aragon
Mrs. Luciano Chavez

Mrs. Nicholas Lucardio

Mrs. Andres D. Vallo
Mrs. Juan E. Garcia
Mrs. Jose A. Sandoval

POTTERS, 1974

Master Potters

Stella Shutiva°
Marie Z. Chino°
Lucy Lewis°
Lois Johnson°†
Maria Antonio
Juana Lena

Jessie Garcia
Lolita Concho
Lillian Salvador
Wanda Aragon
Mrs. Lucian Garcia
Rosecinda Torivio

Mrs. Gus Keene, Sr.
Andrea Lowden
Eva Histia
Helida Antonio
Santana Cerno
Sara Garcia

Lay Potters (recognized as excellent)

Lita Garcia
Joselita Ray
Marie Miller
Mrs. Pablita Concho
Margaret Acencino
Mildred Antonio
Rebecca Lucero
Marie Garcia
Jennie Chavez
Mamie Ortiz
Edna Torivio
Nellie Garcia
Nora Aragon

Lola Gunn
Doris Patricio
Helen Patricio
Lena Torivio
Roselide Vallo
Mary Torivio
Juanita Vallo
Jennie Vallo
Lillie Vallo
Helen Vallo†
Dolores Sanchez
Santana Antonio
Lupe Paytiamo

Juanita Rinee
Linda Juanico
Elizabeth Vallo
Santana Vallo
Maria Estevan
Juanlita Ortiz
Lupe Aragon
Marie Torivio
Jessie Lewis
Josephine Garcia
Emmalita Chino
Lupe Lucero

Trainees

Regina Vicente°
Edna Chino°
Maxine Sanchez°
Lupe Lewis°
Alvina Lowden°
Florence Johnson°
Nora Wilson°

Marjie Vallo°
Elma Wanya
Ruby Keene
Dorothy Siow
Lillian Concho
Frances Sarracino
Elizabeth Garcia

Terry Lukee
Veronica Salvador
Marie Vallo
Merlinda Miller
Merlinda Trujillo
Virginia Victorino

† Ceramics.
°Winners of special recognition.

SILVERSMITHS

Master Craftsman

Gus Keene, Sr.—instructor in training program; silversmith for many years

Trainees

Joseph Garcia°	Ronald L. Charlie	Steven Antonio
Juanita Lukee°	Dina Leno	Virginia Chino
Evelyn Martinez°	Pearl Leno	Philip Lorenzo
Irene Castillo°	Peggy C. Torivio	Hanna Pasquale
Alden Keyope°	Susie H. Vallo	Simon Vallo
Barbara Miller°	Geraldine Victorino	Edward Lewis
Eleanor Antonio	Lucinda Victorino	Ella Vallo
Rafalita Antonio	Pearl Andrews	

List furnished the author by Robert J. Magirl, Director of Employment Assistance, Southern Pueblos Agency, Albuquerque, New Mexico.
°Considered outstanding.

POTTERS, 1990‡

Louise Amos	Francis Concho	Lois Johnson
Diedra Antonio	Lillian Concho	Rita Juanico
Hilda H. Antonio	Pablita Concho	Juanita T. Keene
Maria Antonio	Rachel Concho	Ruby Keene
Mildred Antonio	Darla Davis (T)	Juana Leno
Santana Antonio	Corrine M. Garcia	Andrew Louis
Steven Antonio	Elizabeth Garcia	Diane M. Lewis
Edna Aragon	Josephine A. Garcia	Grace Lewis
Florence Aragon	Lita Garcia	Lucy Lewis
John Aragon	Mrs. Lucian Garcia	Jessie G. Lewis
Wanda Aragon	Mary P. Garcia	Judy M. Lewis
Karen Aragon	JoAnn C. Garcia	Sharon Lewis
Rachel Aragon	Marie P. Garcia	Rebecca Locario
Christopher Augustine	Mary L. Garcia	Mary R. Lowden
Margaret Ascencio	Nellie Garcia	Alvina S. Lowden
Debbie Brown	Margaret C. Garcia	Lupe Lucero
Irene Castillo	Sarah Garcia	Juana Lucario
Santana Cerno	Shaytitra Garcia	Terry Lukee
Barbara Cerno	Wilfred Garcia (NT)	Emma L. Mitchell
Brenda Cerno	William Garcia	Juana Marie Miller
Joseph Cerno	Anne L. Hanson	Merlinda Miller
Edna G. Chino	Carmel Haskaya	Aurelia Pasquale
Emmalita Chino	Goldie Hayah	Camille Pasquale
Laura V. Chino	Marylan Henderson	Marcella Pasquale
Grace T. Chino	Eva Histia	Marilyn Pasquale
Rose M. Chino	Gregg Histia	Rebecca Pasquale
Corrine M. Charlie	Jackie Histia	Doris Patricio
Anthony Concho	Loretta Joe	Ella Peters
Carolyn Concho Lewis	Florence Johnson	Devine Routzen

Joselita Ray
Sandra Ray
Lillian Salvador
Earline Sanchez
Maxine Sanchez
Dorothy V. Sanchez
Margaret Seymour
Edwin Sarracino
Francis Sarracino
Ethel Shields
Brenda Torivio
Edna Torivio

James M. Torivio, Jr.
Lena Torivio
Marie Torivio
Mary Torivio
Adrian Trujillo
Merlinda Trujillo
Yolanda Trujillo
Darlene Vallo
Elizabeth Vallo
Ergil F. Vallo, Sr.
Florinda Vallo
Jennie Vallo

Lillie Vallo
Margie Vallo
Marie Vallo
Pearl Vallo
Roselido Vallo
Simon Vallo
Regina Starr Vicente
Virginia Victorino
Elma Wanya
Nora Wilson

---

‡List compiled with help from Arthur and Carol Cruz, Pueblo Pottery, Pueblo of Ácoma; Mary Lewis Garcia; and Mary Tenorio, Ácoma Visitor's Center.

APPENDIX 7
Incomplete List of Governors for Ácoma Pueblo

Year Governor	Lt. Governor	2nd Lt. Governor
1692—Mateo		
1839—Juaquin Seloso		
1857—Jose Lovato		
1877—Jose Berrendo		
1880—Martin del Vallo		
1881—		
1882—		
1883—		
1884—Martin del Vallo		
1885—Martin del Vallo		
1886—Solomon Bibo		
1887—		
1888—		
1889—[shared]		
Juan Rey		
1890—		
1891—		
1892—		
1893—		
1894—		
1895—Martin del Vallo		
1896—		
1897—		
1898—		
1899—		
1900—Juan R. Bibo		
1901—		
1902—		
1903—		
1904—		
1905—		
1906—		
1907—		
1908—		
1909—		
1910—		
1911—Lorenzo Concho		
1912—		
1913—		
1914—		
1915—		

Year	Governor	Lt. Governor	2nd Lt. Governor
1916—			
1917—	Leo Garcia		
1918—			
1919—	Leo Garcia		
1920—	Frank Ortiz		
1921—			
1922—	Juan Pablo Garcia		
1923—	Juan Pablo Garcia		
1924—	James H. Miller		
1925—	James H. Miller		
1926—	Bautisto Rey	Jose Leon Chino	Larto Garcia
1927—	Juan Pablo Garcia		
1928—	Juan Louis Haskaya	John K. Poncho	
1929—	Juan Louis Haskaya	John K. Poncho	Frank Cerno
1930—	Jose L. Vallo	Amado Garcia	Frank Estevan
1931—	Juan Pablo Garcia	Frank Estevan	Syme Sanchez
1932—	Juan Louis Haskaya	Santiago Howeya	Frank Johnson
1933—	Albert Paytiamo	Jose Leon Chino	Raymond Wanya
1934—	Bautisto Pino	John Zieu	Herbert Brown, Sr.
1935—	Bautisto Pino	Lorenzo Routzen	Antonio Garcia
1936—	James T. Vallo	Bautista Rey	Estevan Cerno
1937—	Jose Leon Chino	Bruce Vallo	Lorenzo Routzen
1938—	Syme R. Sanchez	Andres Vallo	Ramon Sanchez
1939—	Steve Orilla	Antonio Torivio	Juan Pasqual
1940—	Martin W. Pino	Estevan Cerno	Faustino Salvador
1941—	George Cerno	Lorenzo D. Vallo	Estevan Ascencio
1942—	Antonio M. Torivio	Vicente R.Chavez	John Zieu
1943—	Vicente Ray Chavez	Lorenzo Concho	Bruce Valley
1944—	Jose A. Chino	Andres T. Vallo	Estevan Cerno
1945—	Antonio M. Torivio	Joseph Lewis	Jimmy A. Vallo
1946—	Antonio M. Torivio	Joseph Lewis	Julian Chino
1947—	Antonio M. Torivio	Amado Garcia	Frank Cerno
1948—	Martin W. Pino	Lorenzo Concho	Jose A. Chino
1949—	Julian Chino	Juan Pasqual	Ross Lowden
1950—	Lorenzo Concho	Syme Sanchez	Pete Ray
1951—	Syme R. Sanchez	Jose A. Chino	Lorenzo Torivio
1952—	Albert Paytiamo	Castillo Vallo	Frank Estevan
1953—	Castillo A. Vallo	Syme Sanchez	Andres D. Vallo
1954—	Castillo A. Vallo	Syme Sanchez	Jose Estevan
1955—	Castillo A. Vallo	Syme Sanchez	Gus Keene
1956—	Henry Vallo	Henry Chavez	Lorenzo Hunt
1957—	Jose A. Chino	Joe C. Ray	Frank L. Garcia
1958—	Frank L. Ortiz	Raymond Wanya	Frank M. Torivio
1959—	Frank L. Ortiz	Raymond Wanya	Syme R. Sanchez
1960—	Sandy D. Vallo	Syme Sanchez	Frank M. Torivio
1961—	Frank Estevan	Robert Salvador	Martin Pino
1962—	Frank Torivio	Joe M. Ray	Jose A. Chino

Year	Governor	Lt. Governor	2nd Lt. Governor
1963	Jerry Garcia	Tony Chino	Walter Juanico
1964	Sam Victorino	Syme Sanchez	Sandy D. Vallo
1965	Sam Victorino	Frank L. Ortiz	Perfilio Garcia
1966	Frank L. Ortiz	Clyde Sanchez	
1967	Syme R. Sanchez	Henry L. Vallo	Joe Chino
1968	Joe Chino	Sam Victorino	Syme Sanchez
1969	Sam Victorino	Frank L. Ortiz	Mariano Chavez
1970	Sam Victorino	Frank L. Ortiz	Merle Garcia
1971	Lorenzo Toribio	James Ray	James Sanchez
1972	Harry Martinez	Joe C. Ray	Phillip Concho
1973	Clyde J. Sanchez	Joe L. Ortiz	Henry Vallo
1974	Clyde J. Sanchez	Merle Garcia	Gus Keene, Sr.
1975	Merle Garcia	Francis Wanya	Diego Vallo
1976	Merle Garcia	Harry Ascencio	Raymond Concho, Sr.
1977	Stanley Paytiamo	Frank L. Ortiz	Lorenzo Toribio
1978	Stanley Paytiamo	William Estevan	Harry Ascencio
1979	Raymond Concho	Ron Martinez	Frank L. Ortiz
1980	Raymond Concho	Ron Martinez	Frank L. Ortiz
1981	Raymond Concho	Ron Martinez	Frank L. Ortiz
1982	Merle Garcia	Harry Ascencio	Wayne Salvador
1983	Merle Garcia	Fermin Martinez	Harry Ascencio
1984	Merle Garcia	Fermin Martinez	Harry Ascencio
1985	Merle Garcia	Fermin Martinez	Harry Ascencio
1986	Stanley Paytiamo	William Estevan	Ron Martinez
1987	Stanley Paytiamo	Ray A. Histia	Everett Routzen
1988	Ray A. Histia	Robert T. Garcia	Diego Vallo
1989	Ray A. Histia	Simon Ortiz	Harry Ascencio
1990	Ray A. Histia	Tony Chino	Reginald Pasqual

List compiled by author and from information furnished by Joe C. Ray of the Pueblo of Ácoma and Robert J. Magirl, Director of Employment Assistance, Southern Pueblos Agency, Albuquerque, N.M.

APPENDIX 8

Pueblo of Ácoma Veterans of World War I, World War II, Korea, and Vietnam

Alfred Anaya (K)
Anthony Antonio (WW II)
Gary Antonio (VN)
Ira Antonio (VN)
Jack Antonio (WW II) (d)
James Antonio (WW II) (d)
James R. Antonio (WW II) (d)
Jose R. Antonio (WW II) (d)
Melfred Antonio (VN)
San Juan Antonio (POW) (WW II)
Vernon Antonio (VN)
Vicente Antonio (K)
Winfred Antonio (VN)
Calvin Aragon (VN)
Carl Aragon (VN)
Clifford Aragon (WW II)
Joe Aragon, Jr. (VN)
Joe Aragon, Sr. (WW II)
John Aragon (WW II) (d)
Leroy Aragon (WW II)
Norbert Aragon (VN)
Ernest Augustine (K)
Wilbert Augustine (K)
Edward Bailey, Jr. (K)
Angus Brown (K)
Earl Brown (K) (d)
Herbert Brown (K)
Hiram Brown (WW II)
Joseph Brown (WW II)
Matthew Brown (K)
Robert Candelaria (K) (d)
Martin Cerno (VN)
Matthew Cerno (K)
Steve Cerno (VN)
Frank Charlie (VN)
Thomas Charlie (POW) (WW II)
Emery Chavez (K)
Everett Chavez (VN)
Joseph Chavez (WW II)
Lorenzo Chavez (WW II) (d)

Marcus Chavez (VN)
Michael Chavez (WW II)
Paul Chavez (WW II) (d)
San Juan Chavez (WW II) (d)
Stanley Chavez (VN)
Timothy Chavez (VN)
Vicent Chavez (WW II) (d)
Vincent Chavez (VN)
Wilbert Chavez (WW II) (d)
Albert Chino (WW II)
Andres Chino (WW II) (d)
Chris Chino (VN)
Darlene Chino (VN)
Darrel Chino (VN)
Dominic Chino (VN)
Eddie Chino (K)
Elmer Chino (K)
Felix Chino (VN)
Francis Chino (K)
Frank Chino (WW II)
Gerald Chino (K) (d)
Gilbert Chino (VN)
Glen Chino (K) (d)
Harold Chino (VN)
Huston Chino (VN) (d)
Jimmy Chino (VN)
Lawrence Chino (K) (d)
Patrick Chino (VN)
Richard Chino (WW II) (d)
Robert Chino (VN)
Rhonda Chino (VN)
Wilbert Chino (K)
Lorenzo P. Cimerone (POW) (WW II) (d)
Kenneth Clemmons (K)
Anthony Concho (VN)
George Concho (VN)
Isador Concho (VN)
Jimmy Concho (WW II) (d)
Joseph Concho (WW II) (d)
Pasqual Concho (K)

Raymond Concho (K)
Wilford Davis (K) (d)
Timothy Dugenia (VN)
Augustine Edwards (WW II)
Harry Edwards (K)
James Edwards (K)
Lawrence Edwards (VN)
Darrell Estevan (VN)
William Estevan, Jr. (VN)
Joe Faustine (WW II)
Anthony Fernando (VN)
Calvin Fernando (VN)
Burt Felipe (WW II) (d)
Dennis Felipe (VN)
Harry Felipe (WW II)
Lloyd Felipe (VN)
William Felipe (WW II) (d)
Allen Garcia (VN)
Amado Garcia (WW I) (d)
Anthony Garcia (WW II) (K)
Arthur Garcia (K) (d)
Clifford Garcia (K) (d)
Clyde Garcia (VN)
David Garcia (WW II)
Elardo Garcia (VN)
Frank Garcia, Jr. (K)
Frank L. Garcia (WW II)
George Garcia (WW II)
Harold Garcia (K)
James S. Garcia (WW II)
Jerry Garcia (WW II) (d)
Kenneth Garcia (VN)
Mark Garcia (K)
Mark Garcia, Jr. (VN)
Merle Garcia (WW II)
Monica Garcia (WW II)
Michael S. Garcia (K)
Norman T. Garcia (K)
Perfilio Garcia (WW II) (d)
Peter Garcia (VN) (d)
Raymond Garcia (WW II)
Richard Garcia, Sr. (K)
Ronald Garcia (VN)
Roy Garcia (WW II)
Roy Garcia (K)
Thomas Garcia (WW II) (d)
Melvin Gunn (K)
Lucian Gunn (WW II)
Kenneth Hailstorm (K)
Marvin Hailstorm (K)

David Histia (POW) (WW II) (d)
Frank Histia (WW II)
Leroy Histia (K)
Paul Histia (WW II)
Ray Histia (WW II)
Elvis Howeya (VN)
Ventura Howeya (WW II)
Gilbert James (VN)
Albert Jaramillo (K)
Peter Francis Johnson (WW II) (d)
Valentino Johnson (VN)
Vanessa Johnson (VN)
Alvin Juanico (VN)
Ervin Juanico (K)
Merle Juanico (VN)
Russell Juanico (WW II)
Simon Juanico (K)
Steven Juanico (VN)
Gary Keene (VN)
Gus Keene, Jr. (VN)
Gus Keene, Sr. (WW II)
Donald Labelle, Jr. (VN)
Donald Labelle, Sr. (WW II) (d)
David Leno (K)
Lawrence Leno (VN)
Robert Leno (VN)
Thomas Leno (WW II)
Alfred Lavantonio (WW II)
Andrew Lewis (K)
Edward Lewis (WW II)
Edward Lewis, Sr. (K)
Irvin Lewis (K)
Jimmy Lewis (WW II)
Manuel Lewis (VN)
Melvin Lewis (VN)
Carl Lorenzo (VN)
Mark Lorenzo (VN)
Phillip Lorenzo, Sr. (WW II)
Jose Louise (WW II) (d)
Albert Lowden (K)
Alvin J. Lowden (K)
David Lowden (K)
Morris Lowden (VN)
Claudis Lucario (K)
Nelson Lucario (K)
Paul Lujan (WW II)
Henry Lukee (WW II) (d)
Marvin Lukee (VN)
Ramon Lukee (VN)
Sandy Lukee (VN)

Matthew Mariano (K)
Romero Martin (VN)
Fermin Martinez (K)
Frank Martinez (K)
Harry Martinez (WW II)
Lorenzo Martinez (WW II)
Phillip Martinez (WW II)
Ted Martinez (VN)
Vernon Martinez (VN)
Frank Miller (WW I) (d)
David Moussiau, Jr. (K)
Archie Ortiz (K)
Bertrum Ortiz (VN) (d)
Charles Ortiz (VN)
Earl Ortiz (VN)
Emmett Ortiz (VN) (d)
Frank L. Ortiz (WW I)
Gilbert Ortiz (K)
Joe M. Ortiz (WW II) (d)
Joe T. Ortiz (K)
Joseph Ortiz (WW II)
Juana Ortiz (K)
Lorenzo Ortiz (WW II) (d)
Molly Ortiz (K)
Paul Ortiz (VN)
Simon Ortiz (VN)
Wilma Ortiz (K)
Claudis Pasqual (WW II)
Clifford Pasqual (WW II)
Emery Pasqual (VN)
Leo Pasqual (K)
Lorenzo Pasqual (K)
Reggie Pasqual (K)
Santiago Pasquale (WW II)
Eugene Paytiamo (K)
Howard Paytiamo (K)
Ralph Paytiamo (VN)
Ray Paytiamo (VN)
Stanley Paytiamo (K)
Calvin Pedro (VN)
Juan Pedro (WW II)
Ned Phillips (VN)
Thomas Phillips (WW II) (d)
Angus Pino (VN)
David Pino (WW II)
Fabian Pino (K) (d)
George W. Pino (WW II) (d)
Harry W. Pino (WW II)
Henry Pino (K) (d)
Jake Pino (VN)

James Pino (WW II) (d)
Mike Pino (VN)
Rafael Pino (WW II)
Wilfred Pino (VN)
William Pino, Jr. (K)
Willie W. Pino (K)
Adam Poncho (K) (d)
Harrison Poncho (VN)
Hubert Poncho (WW II)
Hugh Poncho (WW II)
Jimmy Poncho (WW II) (d)
Joe Poncho (K)
Sam Poncho (K)
Samuel Poncho (VN)
Clarence Ray (WW II)
Dennis E. Ray (VN) (d)
Emmett Ray (VN) (d)
Hubert Ray (VN)
James Ray, Jr. (VN)
John Ray, Jr. (VN)
John Ray, Sr. (WW II)
John T. Ray, Jr. (K)
Leonard Ray (VN)
Michael Ray (K) (d)
Murphy Ray (WW II)
Alex Routzen (WW II) (d)
Dewey Routzen (K)
Everett Routzen (K)
Herbert Routzen (K)
Phillip Routzen (K)
Richard Routzen (WW II)
Winfred Routzen (K)
Arnold Salvador (VN)
Clarence Salvador (K)
Frank Salvador (WW I)
Lloyd Salvador (K)
Moses Salvador (VN)
Wilbert Salvador (K)
Alfred Sanchez (K) (VN)
Clyde Sanchez (K)
Hubert Sanchez (VN)
Ivan Sanchez (K)
Jackie Sanchez (VN)
James Sanchez (K)
Joe A. Sanchez (VN)
Juanico Sanchez (WW II)
Lawrence Sanchez, Jr. (VN)
Leonard Sanchez (K)
Romero Sanchez (WW II)
Chester Sarracino (K) (d)

203

Condron Sarracino (VN)
Edwin Sarracino (VN)
Elmer Sarracino (VN)
Larry Sarracino (VN)
Lloyd Sarracino (VN)
Melvin Sarracino (K) (d)
Ronald Sarracino (VN) (d)
William Sarracino (WW II)
Juanita Sautram (WW II)
Augustine Seymour (WW II)
Joseph Seymour (K) (VN)
Louis Seymour (K) (d)
John Shroulte (WW II)
Ernest Shutiva (K)
Frank Shutiva (WW II) (K)
Ronald Stokes (VN)
Arnold Torivio (VN)
Curtis Torivio (VN)
Dewayne Torivio (VN)
Emery Torivio (VN)
Emilio Torivio (WW II) (d)
Frank Torivio (WW II)
Frank Torivio, Jr. (VN)
Gary Torivio (VN)
Grace Torivio (WW II) (d)
Jimmy Torivio (K)
Lambert Torivio (VN)
Lorenzo Torivio (WW II)
Marty Torivio (VN)
Mike Torivio (VN)
Oliver Torivio (VN)
Paul Torivio (VN)
Peter Torivio (VN)
Howard Valdo (K)
Jimmy Valdo (WW II)
Larry Valdo (K)
Martin Valdo (VN)
Marvin Valdo (VN)
Mike Valdo (K)
Alfred Valley (WW II) (d)
Benny Valley (K)
Eddie Valley (VN)
Geraldine Valley (VN) (d)
George Valley (WW II)
Gilbert Valley (K)
Roy Valley (WW II)
Castillo Vallo (WW II)

Daniel Vallo (VN)
David D. Vallo (WW II) (d)
Dennis Vallo (VN)
Dewey Vallo (K)
Dwight Vallo (VN)
Earl Vallo (VN)
Elmer Vallo (K)
Emerson Vallo (VN)
Ernest Vallo (VN)
Eugene Vallo (WW II) (d)
Everett Vallo (VN)
Floyd Vallo (K)
Fred Vallo (VN)
Fred S. Vallo (VN)
Henry L. Vallo (K)
Howard Vallo (VN)
Jacob Vallo, Sr. (K)
John Vallo (K)
Joseph B. Vallo (K) (d)
Leroy Vallo (K)
Leonard Vallo (VN)
Lester Vallo (K)
Lloyd Vallo (VN)
Marvin Ike Vallo (K)
Peter D. Vallo (POW) (WW II) (d)
Phillip Vallo (VN)
Rafael Vallo (VN)
Romero Vallo (WW II) (d)
Ronald Vallo (VN)
Roy Lee Vallo (VN)
Wayne Vallo (VN)
Alfred Victorino (K)
Paul Victorino (K)
Pete A. Villarimo (VN)
Gordon Vincenti (VN)
Robert Vincenti (WW II)
Sam Vincenti (K)
Andrew Wanya (WW II) (d)
Charles Wanya (VN)
Francis Wanya (WW II)
Gerald Wanya (VN)
Jimmy Wanya (WW II)
Frank White (WW I) (d)
Thomas White (WW II)
Louis Zamora (WW II)
David Zia (WW II)

List compiled by Clyde Sanchez, Pueblo of Ácoma, with help from Pueblo of Ácoma veterans. Ninety percent on the above list are volunteers. (d) means the veteran is deceased.

Notes

NOTES, ABBREVIATIONS

Annual Report of the Commissioner of Indian Affairs: Report of the Commissioner
Ácoma Tribal Administrative files: ATA
Bureau of American Ethnology: BAE
Bureau of Indian Affairs: BIA
Bureau of Land Management: BLM
Coronado Cuarto Centennial Publications: CCCP
Mexican Archives of New Mexico, Santa Fe: MANM
National Archives, Washington, D. C.: NA
New Mexico Historical Review: NMHR
New Mexico State Records Center and Archives, Santa Fe: NMSRC
Pueblo Economic Assistant's Office files: PEA
Pueblo of Ácoma Archives: PAA
Quivira Society Publications: QSP
Records of the Pueblo Lands Board: PLB
Spanish Archives of New Mexico, Santa Fe: SANM
United States Government Printing Office, Washington, D. C.: GPO

Introduction

1. Mathew W. Stirling, *Origin Myth of Acoma and Other Records,* Bureau of American Ethnology (hereafter cited as BAE) Bulletin 135 (Washington: U.S. Government Printing Office, 1942), pp. 1–10, 13–14 (hereafter cited as GPO). Origin myths are also found in Leslie A. White, *The Acoma Indians,* Forty-Seventh Annual Report of the BAE to the Secretary of the Smithsonian Institute, 1929–1930; reprinted by the Rio Grande Press, Inc., Glorieta, N.M., 1973, pp. 142–48. White reported that there were fourteen clans in 1930.

2. *Proposed Findings and Brief for Pueblo de Ácoma Before the Indian Claims Commission,* Docket No. 266, n.d., pp. 1–4. Many of the Docket No. 266 records are on file in offices of Sam and Nicholas Dazzo, attorneys for Ácoma for many years. A complete file of the Ácoma case can be found with the Indian Claims Commission active files. The 79th Congress created the Commission by Public Law 726 (H. R. 4497), August 13, 1946, and though the Commission was to last ten years, Congress has periodically extended its existence. The law provides that its records shall be open to inspection by the public and upon the dissolution of the Commission, its records shall go to the National Archives. In 1971, the final settlement in favor of Ácoma's claims amounted to more than six million dollars before fees and expenses, one of the largest awards made by the Commission to Indians in New Mexico. The impact of this newly acquired wealth has yet to play itself out, but it will doubtless contribute to significant changes in the Ácoma way of life. The Ácomas, as a tribe, are now independently wealthy compared to a generation ago when tribal funds depended almost entirely upon revenue from tourist admission fees at Sky City.

Chapter 1

1. Reynold J. Ruppe, Jr., *The Acoma Culture Province: An Archeological Concept* (Ph.D. diss., Harvard University, 1953). See also Ruppe and Alfred E. Dittert, Jr., "The Archeology of Cebolleta Mesa and Acoma Pueblo: A Preliminary Report Based on Further Investigation," *El Palacio* 59 (1952):191–217.

Dr. Dittert testified before the Indian Claims Commission that the origin of Old Ácoma might be traced back to before the time of Christ. See transcripts of Dr. Dittert and Dr. Florence Hawley Ellis before the Commission on September 9, 1954, pp. 173, 239, in Docket No. 266, Pueblo de Ácoma v. the United States of America. The definition and English translations for the word "Ácoma" and all its forms were given the author by Syme Sanchez and Joe Ray.

2.   Robert L. Rands, *Acoma Land Utilization: An Ethnohistorical Report,* prepared for the Pueblo de Ácoma v. United States of America, Docket No. 266 before the Indian Claims Commission, n.d., pp. 5–8, summarizes the most recent archeological work by Dittert, Ellis, and Ruppe. See also Frederick Webb Hodge, ed., *Handbook of American Indians North of Mexico,* BAE Bulletin 30 (Washington: GPO, 1912), Part I, p. 11, for list of old villages identified by Hodge and Adolph Francis Alphonse Bandelier.

3.   Mrs. William T. Sedgwick, *Acoma, The Sky City, A Study in Pueblo Indian History and Civilization* (Cambridge: Harvard University Press, 1926), Chapter 10 passim. Mrs. Sedgwick condenses in this chapter all that was known or theorized about Pueblo Indian migration in her day. Regarding the Ácomas, little more can be added.

4.   This consensus was derived from the older tribespeople by members of the Ácoma Land Claims Committee Joe Chino, Joe Ray, and Syme Sanchez. A comprehensive archeological study of the Ácoma Tribe, although time-consuming and costly, could answer many long-standing questions.

5.   Adolph Francis Alphonse Bandelier, "Documentary History of the Rio Grande Pueblos, New Mexico," *New Mexico Historical Review* (hereafter cited as NMHR) 4 (1929):303–5. "The Narrative of Alvar Nuñez Cabeza de Vaca," in *Spanish Explorers in the Southwestern United States 1528–1543* ed. by Frederick Webb Hodge (New York: Charles Scribners Sons, 1907), pp. 7–8.

6.   Henry R. Wagner, "Fr. Marcos de Niza," NMHR 9 (1936):205; Albert H. Schroeder, "Fray Marcos de Niza, Coronado and the Yavapai," NMHR 30 (1955):265–96.

7.   Herbert Eugene Bolton, *Coronado on the Turquoise Trail, Knight of the Pueblos and Plains,* Coronado Cuarto Centennial Publications, 1540–1940, vol. I (hereafter cited as CCCP), ed. by George Peter Hammond (Albuquerque: University of New Mexico Press, 1949), p. 36.

8.   Ibid., p. 179. George Peter Hammond gave nearly the same version but it is not qualified by the negative: "They tell me there are some other small kingdoms not far from this settlement and situated on a river that I have seen and of which the Indians told me." The river, according to this version, would have to be the San José, tributary of the Rio Grande. Hammond and Agapito Rey, eds., *Narratives of the Coronado Expedition, 1540–1542,* CCCP, vol. 2 (Albuquerque: University of New Mexico Press, 1940), p. 173.

9.   Ibid. Hodge claimed that such a village near hot springs must be among the sites at the Zuñi salines. However, Ojo del Gallo was a "hot lake" which was much nearer the cotton-growing region at Acus than the Zuñi salines. Modern Ácomas claim Ojo del Gallo was an ancient farming site.

10.   Ibid., p. 182. Hodge had an intimate knowledge of this country and observed that no Zuñi in modern times has been known to take this route.

11.   Bolton, *Coronado on the Turquoise Trail,* p. 183.

12.   Documents from Coronado's *entrada,* along with those from subsequent *residencia* in Mexico, have been gathered, translated, and published largely through the efforts of Bolton, George Parker Winship, Hammond, Bandelier, and Hodge. Printed sources about Coronado's march can be divided into two chronologically distinct classes, the first comprised of documents written in New Mexico during the years 1540–42 which have all the advantages and disadvantages of eyewitness accounts. The earliest eyewitness reports are Coronado's own letters. His referenced letter to Viceroy Mendoza, a second letter dated October 20, 1541, and several shorter documents written in New Mexico by an unidentified author, contain the best descriptive material. Adolph Francis Alphonse Bandelier and Edgar L. Hewett, *Indians of the Rio Grande Valley, New Mexico* (Albuquerque: University of New Mexico Press, 1937), pp. 119–23.

13.   Hammond and Rey, eds., *Coronado Expedition,* p. 218.

14.   Among the various things which Castañeda thought remarkable about the pueblos were symbolic crosses. At Acuco, near a spring in the valley, there was a wooden cross 1.9 feet in height with a base one yard square. Around this base were many small sticks adorned with plumes, and many withered flowers which had been torn into small pieces. Ibid., p. 280.

15.   J. Lloyd Mecham, "Account of the Chamuscado-Rodríguez Entrada of 1581–1582 in the Second Expedition to New Mexico," NMHR 1 (1926):286; George P. Hammond and Agapito Rey, "The Rodríguez

Expedition to New Mexico, 1581–1582," NMHR 2 (1927):239–68; Herbert Eugene Bolton, ed., *Spanish Exploration in the Southwest, 1542–1706* (New York: Charles Scribner's Sons, 1916), pp. 137–60.

16. Though little was written about the area and its people, historians have stated that the Chamuscado-Rodríguez expedition is "of particular interest because it started that series of events which led directly to the permanent occupation of the Rio Grande country by the Spaniards." Hammond and Rey, "Rodríguez Expedition," 237–68; Bolton, ed., *Spanish Exploration*, pp. 137–60.

17. Bolton, ed., *Spanish Exploration*, pp. 182–83. The name "New Mexico" originated with the Espejo expedition. In some respects, Espejo's explorations exceeded those of Coronado and his army. Because earlier historians did not always find records complete and in good order in Mexico, Espejo was at one time thought by many to be the discoverer of the region and its inhabitants, including the Ácomas.

18. Ibid. Anthropologists claim the snake dance was once performed among the pueblos. Now the snake dance is associated with the Hopi Pueblo where it is primarily a prayer for rain.

19. George P. Hammond and Agapito Rey, eds., *Expedition into New Mexico Made by Antonio de Espejo, 1582–1583*, Quivira Society Publications, vol. 1 (Los Angeles: The Quivira Society, 1929), p. 87 (hereafter cited as QSP). Hammond believed that Espejo returned to the first lagoon which was probably at the modern site of Laguna Pueblo, but if the distances are measured, Espejo could not have made the trip within the time and distance stated if he retraced his steps to the original lagoon. It seems more logical to place Espejo's party at the marshy lake found by the springs from Ojo del Gallo. Ibid., pp. 110–12.

20. Ibid.

21. George P. Hammond and Agapito Rey, eds., *Obregon's History of 16th Century Explorations in Western America* (Los Angles: Wetzel Publishing Company, Inc., 1928), p. 325.

22. Bolton, ed., *Spanish Exploration*, pp. 189–92.

23. Some very fine Ácoma legends appear in Mathew W. Stirling, *Origin Myth of Acoma* and in Leslie A. White, *The Acoma Indians*, 47th Annual Report of the BAE to the Secretary of the Smithsonian Institute, 1929–1930 (Glorieta, N.M.: The Rio Grande Press, Inc., 1973), pp. 142ff.

Chapter 2

1. The Council of the Indies directed colonial affairs in the New World for the Spanish Crown from 1524 until its abolishment in 1834. George Peter Hammond and Agapito Rey, eds., *Don Juan de Oñate, Colonizer of New Mexico, 1595–1628*, CCCP, vol. 5 (Albuquerque: University of New Mexico Press, 1953), p. 60.

2. Ibid., pp. 1–38. Gaspar Costaño de Sosa made an abortive attempt to colonize New Mexico in 1590–91 but he did not visit the western pueblos. Instead he was arrested by Spanish authorities at Santo Domingo because he did not have a proper contract. See, Albert H. Schroeder and Dan S. Matson, *A Colony on the Move: Gaspar Costaño de Sosa's Journal 1590–1591* (Santa Fe: The School of American Research, 1965).

3. Hammond and Rey, eds., *Oñate*, p. 346.

4. Ibid., pp. 354–56. Oñate's scribe did not record the names of these nations but the incident relates to Coronado's account of the three kingdoms in the Province of Ácoma: Tontonteac, Marata, and Acus.

5. The reason for this attack continues to puzzle modern Ácomas. Some of the people certainly distrusted the Spanish intruders and in this instance, it is probable that the distrust was heightened by the Act of Obedience and Homage (a ceremony for which the Indians had no precedent even though they were not forced to perform it) and other seeming overbearances on the part of strangers.

6. Ibid., p. 462, Vicente de Zaldivar's Statement of Proceedings at Ácoma.

7. Gilberto Espinosa, ed., *Gaspar Perez de Villagra, History of New Mexico* (Los Angeles: The Quivira Society, 1938), pp. 267–68; George P. Hammond, "The Founding of New Mexico," NMHR 1 (1926):445–62.

8. Frederick Webb Hodge, George P. Hammond, and Agapito Rey, eds., *Fray Alonso de Benavides' Revised Memorial of 1634*, CCCP, vol. 4 (Albuquerque: University of New Mexico Press, 1945), pp. 258–89n. This may have been Kowina, a site on a mesa in Cebolleta Valley about fifteen miles west of Sky City.

9. Hammond and Rey, pp. 428–50, Trial of the Indians of Acoma, 1598.

10. Ibid., pp. 454–79, Proceedings at Acoma, decrees, proclamations, and statements, including the sentence and executions of the sentence.

11. Gilberto Espinosa, ed., *History of New Mexico by Gaspar Perez de Villagra, Alcala, 1610*, QSP, vol. 4 (Los Angeles: The Quivira Society, 1933), p. 32. Villagra appears to be the only source for the claim which is supported, however, by tradition at Ácoma.

12. Hammond and Rey, eds., *Oñate*, p. 938, Memorial on the Discovery of New Mexico, 1595–1602.

13. Ibid., pp. 1109–24, Conviction of Oñate and His Captains, 1614.

14. Ibid., pp. 850–51. Testimony of the soldier Juan de Leon is quoted from "Official Inquiry made by the Factor, Don Francisco de Valverde, by Order of the Court of Monterrey, Concerning the New Discovery Undertaken by Governor Don Juan de Oñate Toward the North Beyond the Provinces of New Mexico."

15. Ibid., pp. 508–9, 593, 630, 744–45, 1071, 1088–90. Instructions to Oñate are dated October 21, 1595; to Peralta, March 30, 1609. These instructions lay the groundwork for exploitation of the Indians but so far as is known, the *encomienda* system was never applied to Ácoma.

16. Leslie Byrd Simpson, *Many Mexicos* (Berkeley and Los Angeles: University of California Press, 1962), p. 43.

17. The decrees are found in English and Spanish in Lansing B. Bloom, "Instructions to Eulate," NMHR 3 (1928):357–80, and NMHR 5 (1930):288–98. They are best paraphrased by France V. Scholes, "Church and State in New Mexico 1610–1650," NMHR 11 (1936):78–79, 151, 154–55.

18. The mission was extensive, being to "the province of the Tzias, and the Pueblos of Tamaya, Yacco, Toxagua, and Pelcheu; also the Province of Ácoma with its surrounding and adjoining pueblos; the Province of Tzuni; and the Province of Mohoce, with all its pueblos, all lying west of the great Pueblo of Tzia." Hammond and Rey, eds., *Oñate*, p. 346, Act of Obedience and Vassalage by the Indians of San Juan Bautista.

19. Sedgwick, *Acoma*, pp. 97–101. Mrs. Sedgwick gives this and another version of the story about the child. George Kubler, *The Religious Architecture of New Mexico in the Colonial Period and Since the American Occupation* (Colorado Springs: The Taylor Museum, 1940), pp. 92–94.

20. Kubler, *Religious Architecture of New Mexico*, pp. 34, 92–94; Sedgwick, *Acoma*, pp. 97–105; "Preservation and Restoration of Sky City," *Development of Tourist Potential of the Acoma Reservation, New Mexico* (Albuquerque: Kirchner Associates, 1965), pp. 24–26. One Sunday in 1965, the Ácoma governor permitted Dr. Bainbridge Bunting and the author to inspect the older buildings at Sky City. They concluded that little construction, if any, remains from pre-Spanish times. The adobe brick common to all is unusually long and thin (10 x 20 x 2½ inches). Historians appear to agree on the early date for San Estevan although there are traces of foundations running north and south of the present church between the east facade and the cemetery. See Eleanor B. Adams and Fray Angélico Chávez, trans. and eds., *The Missions of New Mexico, 1776, A Description by Fray Francisco Atanasio Domínguez* (Albuquerque: University of New Mexico Press, 1956), pp. 189n–90n.

21. Scholes, "Church and State," pp. 33, 148.

22. Bailey W. Diffie, *Latin-American Civilization* (Harrisburg, Pa.: Stackpole Sons, 1947), pp. 65–68, 72–73, 526–29, 610–11; Simpson, *Many Mexicos*, pp. 90–91; see also, idem., *Studies in Administration of the Indians in New Spain* (Berkeley: University of California Press, 1934), pp. 29–129. Dr. Myra Ellen Jenkins has found a royal cedula of 1684 appointing General Jironza Petris de Cruzate governor and captain general of New Mexico and giving him the right to make land grants. She has concluded after extensive research that much evidence indicates a pueblo was "recognized as having the right to all lands its members effectively used and occupied." For her interpretations on the subject, see "The Baltazar Baca 'Grant': History of an Encroachment," *El Palacio* 68 (1961):47–48, and "Spanish Land Grants in the Tewa Area," NMHR 47 (1972):113–34.

23. Hodge, Hammond, and Rey, eds., *Benavides' Revised Memorial of 1634*, pp. 35, 72–73.

24. Ibid., pp. 13, 168n, 172. The editors found this document difficult to date, but apparently it was made by Benavides sometime after 1635. The notations and rubrics indicate that the authorities in Spain agreed that this cedula of 1635 would alleviate these problems, although it did not do so immediately. The cedula did result in dispatches to the viceroy in Mexico in which he was asked to do all in his power to assist the missionary work in progress on the northern frontier (New Mexico). Such sentiment for

protecting the Indian and his lands was expressed in Spanish law as early as 1530 and was included in the *Recopilación de Leyes de los Reynos de las Indias* (Book 4, tit. 12, law 9).

25. France V. Scholes and Eleanor B. Adams, "Inventories of Church Furnishings in Some New Mexico Missions, 1672," in *Dargan Historical Essays* (Albuquerque: University of New Mexico Press), p. 34. Other fathers who served at Ácoma during the interval after Fray Juan Ramirez and prior to Fray Lucas Maldonado were Francisco Muñoz, 1660–61; Fray Salvador Guerra, 1661; Fray Joseph Oñas, 1666; and Fray Fernando de Velasco, 1667.

26. That the stringent attitude of the missionaries against the Indian shamans provided motive for the uprising was supported by later testimony from the Indians and by observations made by Spanish colonists who escaped and retreated to the vicinity of El Paso.

27. An excellent résumé of the Pueblo Revolt is found in Charles Wilson Hackett, *Revolt of the Pueblo Indians of New Mexico and Otermin's Attempted Reconquest 1680–1682*, CCCP, vol. 8 (Albuquerque: University of New Mexico Press, 1942) p. xlviii. An Ácoma legend tells how Father Maldonado escaped by leaping from the east cemetery wall with his *capote*, a type of cape, serving as a sort of parachute enabling him to float to the valley floor below.

28. Ibid., pp. xxv, xxvii, xxxiii–xxxv, lvii, lxiii.

29. Ibid., pp. 60–61, Declaration of one of the rebellious Christian Indians who was captured on the road; pp. 232–34, Declaration [of the Indian Juan, Río del Norte, December 18, 1681]; pp. 238–39, Declaration of Josephe, Spanish-speaking Indian [Rio del Norte, December 19, 1681]; pp. 245–47, Declaration of Pedro Naranjo of the Queres (Keres) Nation [Rio del Norte, December 19, 1681]; and other testimonials, pp. 243–44, 249–52.

30. Ibid., pp. cxxxvii–cxxxviii.

31. The Congress of the United States confirmed the so-called Cruzate Grant on December 22, 1858; however, a surviving copy is thought by modern historians to be a forgery.

32. The spurious grant for Ácoma is located in the New Mexico State Records Center (hereafter cited as NMSRC). No copy of an original has turned up to date. A copy may also be found in the archives maintained by Ácoma Pueblo (hereafter cited as PAA). For the reasons why the document is considered a forgery, see Ralph Emerson Twitchell, *The Spanish Archives of New Mexico* (Cedar Rapids, Iowa: The Torch Press, 1914), vol. 1, pp. 456–62, and passim.

33. J. Manuel Espinosa, *First Expedition of Vargas into New Mexico, 1692*, CCCP, vol. 10 (Albuquerque: University of New Mexico Press, 1940), pp. 80, 86–97, Vargas' Campaign Journal and Correspondence, August 21 to October 16, 1692.

34. Ibid., pp. 98–104.

35. Ibid., pp. 104–34. The expedition to Pecos Pueblo is found in this section of the journal.

36. Ibid., pp. 135–46, 159–68.

37. J. Manuel Espinosa, *Crusaders of the Rio Grande, the Story of Don Diego de Vargas and the Reconquest and Refounding of New Mexico* (Chicago: Institute of Jesuit History Publications, 1942), p. 91.

38. J. Manuel Espinosa, *Crusaders of the Rio Grande*, pp. 88–91; Irving Albert Leonard, trans. and ed., *The Mercurio Volante of Don Carlos de Sigüenza y Góngora: An Account of the First Expedition of Don Diego de Vargas into New Mexico in 1692*, QSP, vol. 3 (Los Angeles: The Quivira Society, 1932), pp. 77–79.

39. J. Manuel Espinosa, *First Expedition of Vargas*, pp. 29–32.

40. Jessie Bromilaw Bailey, *Diego de Vargas and the Reconquest of New Mexico* (Albuquerque: University of New Mexico Press, 1940), pp. 89, 91, 113.

41. It is possible that Naranjo of Santa Clara may have been inciting the Indians to revolt; see Fray Angelico Chavez, "Pohe-Yemos' Representative," NMHR 42 (1967):85–126.

42. Bailey, *Diego de Vargas*, pp. 116–17.

43. Ibid., pp. 128–29, 128n.

44. Ibid., pp. 130–31.

45. Ibid., pp. 132–59.

46. Ibid., pp. 160–86.

47. Ibid., pp. 202–12.

48. J. Manuel Espinosa, *Crusaders of the Rio Grande*, pp. 274–75; Ralph Emerson Twitchell, *The Leading Facts of New Mexico History* (Cedar Rapids, Iowa: The Torch Press, 1911–17), vol. 1, pp. 51–60.

49. J. Manuel Espinosa, *Crusaders of the Rio Grande*, p. 275; Twitchell, *Leading Facts*, pp. 51–60.

50. J. Manuel Espinosa, *Crusaders of the Rio Grande*, pp. 276–77; Twitchell, *Leading Facts*, pp. 51–60.

51. Bailey, *Diego de Vargas*, pp. 243–45. De Vargas reported attacking Ácoma and capturing five Ácomas of whom four were shot.

52. Ibid., p. 252; Hubert Howe Bancroft, *History of Arizona and New Mexico* (San Francisco, 1890), p. 221; Twitchell, *Leading Facts*, vol. 1, p. 417. Historians generally accept this oversimplified account of the founding of Laguna. Also see, Lansing B. Bloom and Ralph E. Twitchell, eds., "A Campaign Against the Moqui Pueblos Under Governor Phelix Martínez, 1716," NMHR 6 (1931):158–226. Dr. Florence Hawley Ellis and Dr. Myra Ellen Jenkins testified before the Indian Claims Commission in 1957 that the Laguna settlement may be older based on archeological evidence. For their ideas on this interesting matter, see Jenkins, "The Baltazar Baca 'Grant,' " p. 51n.

53. Charles W. Hackett, ed., *Historical Documents Relating to New Mexico, Nueva Vizcaya, and Approaches Thereto, to 1773*, collected by Adolph F. A. Bandelier and Fanny Bandelier (Washington: Carnegie Institution, 1937), vol. 3, pp. 367, 376.

54. Ibid.

55. Ibid., vol. 3, p. 405, Declaration of Fray Miguel de Menchero, Santa Barbara, May 10, 1744.

56. Ibid., pp. 27–30.

57. Henry Kelley, "Franciscan Missions of New Mexico, 1740–1760," NMHR 16 (1941):42–64.

58. Testimonies of the alcalde mayor for Encinal and Cebolleta, his lieutenants, and also from the alcalde mayor of Zuñi, April 18, 1750, found in Hackett, *Historical Documents*, vol. 3, pp. 414–25, 435–38.

59. Ibid., p. 462. Fray Manuel de Trigo to Father Procurador General Fray Jose Miguel de los Rios, July 23, 1754.

60. Marin del Valle's decision of September 7, 1757, from Original Cedula in the Archivo General de la Nación, Mexico, translated by Eleanor B. Adams, cited in Rands, *Acoma Land Utilization*.

61. Eleanor B. Adams, ed., *Bishop Tamaron's Visitation of New Mexico, 1760*, Historical Society of New Mexico, Publications in History, vol. 15 (Albuquerque: University of New Mexico Press, 1954), pp. 59–70.

62. Adams and Chavez, eds., *Missions of New Mexico*, pp. 188–89.

63. Ibid., p. 195.

64. Census of the Missions of the Custody of the Conversion of St. Paul, October 30, 1795, Benjamin Read Collection, Misc. Series, NMSRC.

65. Adams and Chavez, eds., *Missions of New Mexico*, pp. 194–95.

66. "Fray Juan Agustín de Morfi's Geographical Description of New Mexico, 1782," in Alfred Barnaby Thomas, *Forgotten Frontiers, A Study of the Spanish Indian Policy of Don Juan Bautista de Anza, Governor of New Mexico, 1777–1787* (Norman: University of Oklahoma Press, 1932), p. 105.

67. Census of the Missions of the Custody of the Conversion of St. Paul, October 30, 1795, paragraph 5, Benjamin Read Collection, Misc. Series, NMSRC.

68. Thomas, *Forgotten Frontiers*, p. 105. Fray Agustin de Morfí used Governor de Anza's descriptions in *Resumen de los Padrones y Noticias del Nuevo Mexico*, November 1, 1779; see ibid., p. 371n.

69. Ibid., p. 105.

70. Alfred Barnaby Thomas, *The Plains Indians and New Mexico, 1751–1778*, CCCP, vol. 11 (Albuquerque: University of New Mexico Press, 1940), p. 173.

71. Whether this order was put into effect is not clearly shown in the documents; see Thomas, *Forgotten Frontiers*, p. 272.

72. Ibid., pp. 259–60, 269.

73. Conde de Revilla Gigedo to Señor Don Fernando de la Concha, September 4, 1792, Spanish Archives of New Mexico, Series II (hereafter cited as SANM), NMSRC.

74. Fernando de la Concha, Governor of New Mexico, to Senor Don Pedro de Nava, Commandant General, April 30, 1793, SANM II, NMSRC.

75. Fernando Chacon to Nemesio Salcedo, March 26 and 28, 1804, SANM II, NMSRC.

76. Chacon to Salcedo, May 16, 1804, SANM II, NMSRC.

77. Salcedo to Chacon, September 16, 1804, SANM II, NMSRC; Chacon to Jose Manuel Aragon,

Alcalde Mayor of Laguna, September 26, 1804, SANM I, No. 46, Surveyor General Records, NMSRC; Salcedo to Chacon, October 5, 1804, SANM II, NMSRC.

78. Lieutenant Colonel Antonio Narbona to Chacon, January 24, 1805; Governor Chacon to [Navajo Nation], March 27, 1805; Governor Joaquin Real Alencaster to Salcedo, May 15, 1805; all in SANM II, NMSRC.

79. Grant Number 104, dated 1768, Surveyor-General, and Number 114, Court of Private Land Claims; Jose Vicente Ortiz, Alcalde of Laguna, to Governor Pedro Maria de Allande, April 16, 1816, SANM I, No. 668, all in Surveyor General Records, NMSRC.

80. Jose Vicente Ortiz, Alcalde of Laguna, to Governor Don Pedro María de Allande, July 7, 1818; Governor Allande to the Alcalde of the Partido of Laguna, July 10, 1818; Governor Allande to the Lieutenant of Justice of the Pueblo of Zuñi, July 10, 1818; Ignacio Maria Sanchez Vergara, Alcalde of Jémez, to Governor Allande, July 21, 1818; Don Facundo Melgares to Alcaldes of Alameda, Albuquerque, and Belen, February 1, 1819; Captain Bartolomé Baca to Governor Melgares, July 9, 1821; and Governor Melgares to First Constitutional Alcalde of the Capital, July 16, 1821, all in SANM II, NMSRC.

81. Juan Armijo to Governor Melgares, October 23, 1821, SANM II, NMSRC. Armijo was serving as Alcalde for the Jurisdiction of Cochití at this time.

Chapter 3

1. Herbert O. Brayer, *Pueblo Indian Land Grants of Rio Abajo New Mexico* (Albuquerque: University of New Mexico Press, 1939), pp. 19–20. Brayer discusses legal aspects of the changeover. For a general description of the Pueblo Indians under the Mexican regime, see Lansing B. Bloom, "New Mexico Under the Mexican Administration, 1821–1846," *Old Santa Fe* 1 (1913):25ff. An informative contemporary account is found in Josiah Gregg, *Scenes and Incidents in the Western Prairie: During Eight Expeditions and Including a Residence of Nearly Nine Years in Northern Mexico* (New York: 1844. First edition later appeared as *Commerce of the Prairies*).

2. Records of the Bureau of Indian Affairs Field Papers, Michigan Superintendance, 1854–1871, Record Group 75, The National Archives, Washington, D.C. (hereafter cited as NA). The populations for 1821 are found in Bloom, "New Mexico Under Mexican Administration," p. 28. The earlier census figures for Ácoma come from visitors' reports coinciding with each year or from mission census. The last are probably unreliable in some cases, primarily because the mission inspectors reported Christian Indians only.

3. Books of Account (San José del Vado), Book LXVI (Box 6), Archives of the Archdiocese of Santa Fe. These records for San José del Vado, south of Pecos, clearly indicate that Pecos was abandoned by 1835 or soon thereafter.

4. Bloom, "New Mexico Under Mexican Administration," p. 28.

5. Statement by Don José Manuel Aragon, Alcalde Mayor of the pueblos of Ácoma, Laguna, settlement of Cebolleta, and their districts, SANM I, NMSRC; Marc Simmons, *Spanish Government in New Mexico* (Albuquerque: University of New Mexico Press, 1968), p. 168. Dr. Simmons quotes a 1773 report of Governor Medinueta to the viceroy in Mexico which states: "In every two, three, or more pueblos the governor names an alcalde mayor who serves the Indians as well as the Spanish citizens of that district, with the aid of one or more tenientes according to the number of pueblos and settlements of Spaniards in order that all may easily have recourse to the law when cases arise."

6. Legislative Records for New Mexico, January 4, 1823, in Mexican Archives of New Mexico (hereafter cited as MANM), NMSRC; also cited in Bloom, "New Mexico Under Mexican Administration," 157–58.

7. Minutes of the Junta Departmental, Santa Fe, May 22, 1837, MANM, NMSRC.

8. Tables of the Missions of the Custodia de la Conversión de San Pablo, 1821, in Bloom, "New Mexico Under Mexican Administration," p. 28; Ward Alan Minge, *Frontier Problems in New Mexico Preceding the Mexican War, 1840–1846* (Ph.D. diss., University of New Mexico, 1965), Part II, Governor Mariano Martinez Attempts to Salvage New Mexico.

9. Lists of the Administrador Principal de Correo, Chihuahua, 1833, in Bloom, "New Mexico Under Mexican Administration," pp. 14–15.

10. Mariano Martinez de Lejanza to the Inhabitants of New Mexico, June 17, 1844, No. 220 in the Ritch Collection, Huntington Library, Pasadena, California.

11. Governor Mariano Martinez to Sr. Presidente de la Exma. Asamblea Departmental, June 29, 1844, in Letter Book of the Governor, 1844, includes Decree establishing new justices of the peace July 5, 1844; Martinez to Sr. Presidente de la Exma. Asamblea, July 24, 1844; Martinez to Francisco Sarracino, Prefect of the Second District, September 14, 1844, in Letter Book of the Secretariat, 1844, all in MANM, NMSRC.

12. Secretaria to the Prefect D. Juan Andres Archuleta, July 17, August 17 and 23, 1844, all in Letter Book of the Secretariat, 1844, MANM, NMSRC.

13. Miguel Montoya, Juzgado de Paz de Cochití, to Governor Martinez, Cubero, June 1, 1844; Secretaria to Montoya, June 1, 1844, the latter in the Letter Book of the Secretariat, both in MANM, NMSRC.

14. Secretariat to the Prefect of the First District, April 6, 1844; Secretaria to Sr. Vicario Incapita y Juez Ecro. de esta Ciudad, April 6, 1844, Letter Book of the Secretariat, 1844, MANM, NMSRC. Mariano Martinez, serving as Captain General doubtless formulated this plan not only as a convenient way to help Zuñi but also to secure Mexican boundaries.

15. Governor Martinez to Sarracino, April 24, 1844; Governor Martinez to Sr. Juez de Paz de Jémez, April 25, 1844, Letter Book of the Secretariat, 1844, MANM, NMSRC.

16. Governor Martinez to Sarracino, September 23, 1844, Letter Book of the Secretariat, 1844, MANM, NMSRC. Very little more is known about formal education in New Mexico during the Mexican Period and yet this episode suggests school teachers existed as professionals in primary and secondary school systems.

17. Governor Facundo Melgares to the First Alcalde of the Capital of Santa Fe, April 24, 1822; Governor Melgares to all Alcaldes, May 6, 1822; Manuel Armijo to Governor Facundo Melgares, Santa Fe, June 30, 1822; Antonio Chavez, Belen, to Governor Melgares, September 21, 1822. Chavez reported that his man followed the Navahos to the Puerto de los Ojos de Toribio, where he and his man gave up the chase; Copy of Peace Treaty with Navahos and the terms thereof as recommended by Governor Jose Antonio Vizcarra, New Mexico, February 5, 1823; Record of Meeting between Governor Vizcarra and the Navaho Tribe, Camp at Paguate, New Mexico, February 12, 1823, all in Myra Ellen Jenkins and Ward Alan Minge, *Record of Navajo Activities Affecting the Acoma-Laguna Area, 1746–1910*, Ácoma-Laguna Exhibit Number 530 in Docket No. 229, Pueblo de Ácoma v. United States of America, 1961, pp. 43–46, on file with the Indian Claims Commission.

18. Ibid., pp. 49–55; Blas Antonio Chaves, Alcalde of Jemez, to Governor Don Francisco Sarracino, Santa Fe, February 6, 1834.

19. Ibid., pp. 57–58; Manuel Garcia, Jémez, to Blas de Hinojo, Comandante General of this Territory, January 12, 1835; J. F. Baca, Jurisdiction of Socorro, to the Political and Military Leader of the Territory of New Mexico, Albino Perez, Santa Fe, June 7, 1835.

20. Ibid., pp. 58–59; Military personnel records of the men who participated in this campaign, March 13, 1835; military personnel records of Lieutenant Colonel José Silva, October 13 to December 13, 1839; Noriega, Minister of War and Navy, to the Comandante General of New Mexico, December 11, 1843.

21. Ibid.; [Governor] to the Alcalde Don Julian Tenorio [at Albuquerque], September 3, 1837; Governor to the Prefect of the Second District, Don Antonio Sandoval, June 19, 1839.

22. Ibid., p. 94; [Governor Armijo's Letter Book, 1846] _____ to the Prefects of the Central, Northern, and Southeastern Districts.

Chapter 4

1. Lieutenant James William Abert's Report for October 21, 1846, in William Hensley Emory, ed., *Notes of a Military Reconnaissance, from Fort Leavenworth, in Missouri, to San Diego, in California*, 30th Cong., 1st Sess., Senate Executive Document No. 7 (Washington: 1848), pp. 470ff.

2. Lieutenant Abert's Report for October 21, 1846, in Emory, ed., *Notes of a Military Reconnaissance,* pp. 470–71.

3. Ibid., pp. 472–73.

4. James H. Simpson, *Journal of a Military Reconnaissance from Santa Fe, New Mexico, to Navajo Country* (Philadelphia: 1852), p. 113.

5. Lieutenant A. W. Whipple et al., *Report upon the Indian Tribes* in *Reports of Explorations and Surveys, to Ascertain the Most Practicable and Economical Route for a Railroad from the Mississippi to the Pacific Ocean,* made under the direction of the Secretary of War, in 1853–54, 33rd Cong., 2nd Sess., Senate Executive Document No. 78 (Washington: Beverly Tucker Printer, 1856), vol. 3, p. 61.

6. The above resume is taken from the case files of Victor de la O v. The Pueblo of Ácoma. Privilegio del Pueblo de Ácoma [copies], 20 September and 28 September 1689; Proceedings of the United States District Court for the 3rd Judicial District, The Pueblo of Ácoma v. Vicente Avilucia, Ramon Sanchez, and Victor de la O, starting August 26, 1854, Territorial Records of State Supreme Court, Santa Fe.

7. Victor de la O v. The Pueblo of Ácoma Opinion by Justice K. Benedict, February 20, 1857, in Territorial Records of the State Supreme Court, Santa Fe. An easier reading copy can be found in Ralph Emerson Twitchell, "Chief Justice Kirby Benedict," *Old Santa Fe* 1 (1913):75–82.

8. Annie Heloise Abel, ed., *The Official Correspondence of James S. Calhoun while Indian Agent at Santa Fe and Superintendent of Indian Affairs in New Mexico* (Washington: GPO, 1915), p. 88.

9. James S. Calhoun to Hon. L. Lea, Commissioner of Indian Affairs, March 31, 1851, in ibid., p. 307.

10. Calhoun to Orlando Brown, Commissioner of Indian Affairs, February 3, 1850, in ibid., pp. 139–41.

11. Ward Alan Minge, *Historical Treatise in Defense of the Pueblo of Ácoma Land Claim,* Plaintiff's Exhibit 104 in Pueblo de Ácoma v. United States of America, Docket No. 266 before the Indian Claims Commission, September 1957, pp. 59–61. The historic ruling of 1913 was U.S. v. Sandoval, 231 U.S. 28.

12. Minge, *Historical Treatise in Defense of the Pueblo Land Claim,* p. 59; Twitchell, *Spanish Archives of New Mexico,* vol. 1, p. 478; Ácoma Patent signed by President Rutherford B. Hayes, November 19, 1877, contains data of the survey and confirmation.

13. William Watts Hart Davis, Actg. Gov. and Supt. of Indian Affairs, to Hon. George W. Manypenny, Commissioner of Indian Affairs, March 29, 1856, copy in PAA.

14. Ibid.

15. Edwin D. Tittman, "The First Irrigation Lawsuit—Acoma vs. Laguna," NMHR 2 (1927):363–68. Originals are in Valencia County Territorial District Court Records, NMSRC.

16. John M. Gunn, *Schat-chen; History, Traditions and Narratives of the Queres Indians of Laguna and Acoma* (Albuquerque: Albright and Anderson, 1917), pp. 98–99.

17. Benjamin M. Thomas, U.S. Agent Pueblo Indian, to Messrs. Marmon and Menaul, Laguna, New Mexico, August 17, 1876, copy in BIA Archives and in PAA.

18. Thomas to Commissioner of Indian Affairs, Santa Fe, August 20, 1877, in *Annual Report of the Commissioner of Indian Affairs to the Secretary of the Interior for the Year 1877* (hereafter cited as *Report of the Commissioner*) (Washington: GPO, 1877), p. 161.

19. Thomas to Asst. Adjutant General, Dist. of New Mexico, Santa Fe, March 20, 1877; Thomas to Juan Analla, Governor of Laguna, February 27, 1877; Thomas to Walter E. Marmon, Esq., Laguna, New Mexico, February 28, 1877; all in BIA Archives, copies in PAA. Unless otherwise indicated the B. M. Thomas letters are from these collections.

20. Thomas to Jose Berrendo, Governor of Ácoma, February 20, 1877, and February 27, 1877.

21. Thomas to Marmon, March 12, 1877.

22. Thomas to Colonel P. T. Swaine, Commandant, Fort Wingate, April 21 and May 9, 1877.

23. Thomas to Reverend J. Menaul, Laguna, March 12, 1877; Thomas to Don Juan Analla, Governor of Laguna, March 17, 1877.

24. Thomas to Hon. Thomas Benton Catron, U.S. District Attorney, Albuquerque, October 1, 1877.

25. Thomas to Hon. J. C. Smith, Commissioner, Washington, July 4, 1877.

26. Thomas to Marmon, Laguna, February 28, 1877; the Hon. J. C. Smith to Secretary of the Interior, Office of Indian Affairs, Washington, August 28, 1877; Thomas to the governor, Pueblo of Ácoma, December 10, 1877. A copy of the patent can be found in the PAA.

27. Thomas to the Commissioner of Indian Affairs, August 14, 1879, in *Report of the Commissioner,*

1879 (Washington: GPO, 1879), p. 120; Thomas to Commissioner of Indian Affairs, September 1, 1880, in *Report of the Commissioner* (Washington: GPO, 1880), p. 133.

28. Sanchez to the Honorable H. Price, Commissioner of Indian Affairs, June 10, 1884, in PAA.

29. Romero to Agent A&P RR, Albuquerque, February 22, 1886, in PAA.

30. Thomas, Indian Agent, to the Honorable Hiram Price, Commissioner, December 13, 1882; License to Trade with Indians, Cosmos Mindeleff, July 1, 1885, in PAA. Bibo family activities in and around Laguna and Ácoma are described in Frank McNitt, *The Indian Traders* (Norman: University of Oklahoma Press, 1962), Chapter 8 passim.

31. T. M. Pearce, ed., *New Mexico Place Names, A Geographical Dictionary* (Albuquerque: University of New Mexico Press, 1965), pp. 2, 98.

32. *Sixteenth Annual Report of the Board of Indian Commissioners, 1884* (Washington: GPO, 1885), p. 17.

33. Report by Clarence Pullen, Surveyor General, and report by William White, U.S. Deputy Surveyor, and William Patterson, Special Agent, Surveyor General's Office, to Surveyor General Pullen, Santa Fe, October 21, 1884, both recorded in Record Book Auxiliary No. 7, U.S. Department of Interior, Bureau of Land Management (hereafter cited as BLM), pp. 372, 375.

34. George W. Julian, Surveyor General to the Hon. William H. J. Sparks, Commissioner, General Land Office, Washington, D.C., November 14, 1885, copies in BLM records, NMSRC, and PAA.

35. Catron, Thornton & Clancy, Attorneys for the Ácoma Indians, to the Honorable Commissioner of the General Land Office, Washington, D.C., January 4, 1886, copies in BLM records, NMSRC, and PAA.

36. Statement filed by H. M. Atkinson, Attorney for Settlers and Protestants, in the Surveyor General's Office at Santa Fe, January 18, 1886, copies in BLM records, NMSRC, and PAA.

37. Reply and Statement of the A&PR Co. to the Appeal on the part of the Indians of the Pueblo of Ácoma for a resurvey, February 1, 1886, copies in BLM records, NMSRC, and PAA.

38. William H. J. Sparks, General Land Office, Department of the Interior, to the Honorable George W. Julian, U.S. Surveyor General, Santa Fe, June 10, 1886, in BLM records, NMSRC.

39. Surveyor General Julian to the Honorable William H. J. Sparks, June 16, 1886, and August 21, 1886, copies in BLM records, NMSRC, and PAA.

40. Pedro Sanchez, Agent, Pueblo Agency, to Solomon Bibo, Grants, N.M. May 20, 1884; Sanchez to the Honorable Hiram Price, Commissioner of Indian Affairs, Washington, D.C., June 4, 1884, copies of both in PAA. McNitt describes this lease in *The Indian Traders*, pp. 117–18.

41. Sanchez to Martin del Vallo, Governor of the Pueblo of Ácoma, June 28, 1884, copy in PAA.

42. Sanchez to Commissioner Price, July 14, 1884, copy in PAA.

43. Governor Vallo to Commissioner Price, July 22, 1884, with attached petition addressed to the Commissioner, July 21, 1884, PAA.

44. Sanchez to Governor Vallo, July 26, 1884, PAA.

45. Sanchez to Bibo, July 30, 1884, PAA.

46. Sanchez to the Honorable G. W. Prichard, U.S. District Attorney, Santa Fe, August 1, 5, and 13, 1884, PAA.

47. Solomon Bibo, Grants, New Mexico, to Gen. Whittlesby, Washington, D.C., July 23, 1884; E. Whittlesby to the Honorable H. Price, July 31, 1884, PAA; James E. Miller, Ácoma, to Commissioner Price, August 12, 1884, PAA.

48. Sanchez to Commissioner Price, September 4, 1884; Sanchez to Alexander de Armand, Cubero, N.M., September 22, 1884, PAA.

49. Indian Agent to Governor of Ácoma Pueblo, June 13, 1896; S. L. Taggert, Special Indian Agent, to the Honorable Commissioner of Indian Affairs, February 8, 1898; Pueblo Memorials relating to Citizenship, December 20 and 24, 1904, PAA.

50. Sanchez to the Honorable H. Price, December 11, 1883, PAA. This is probably Goomi Springs, north of the Ácoma Mesa, a place where there are some stone houses and foundations.

51. *Report of the Commissioner, 1885* (Washington: GPO, 1885), pp. 156–57; Sanchez to Martin del Vallo, Governor of Ácoma, February 7, 1885, PAA.

52. *Report of the Commissioner, 1888* (Washington: GPO, 1888), p. 198, PAA.

53. *Report of the Commissioner, 1890* (Washington: GPO, 1890), p. 173; *Report of the Commissioner,*

1891 (Washington: GPO, 1891), p. 311; Captain John L. Bullis, Agent, to Dr. W. N. Hidman, Superintendent Indian Schools, Santa Fe, June 2, 1884, PAA.

54. *Annual Reports of the Department of the Interior for the Fiscal Year Ended June 30, 1899*, Part I, Indian Affairs (Washington: GPO, 1899), pp. 249–51, PAA.

55. N. S. Walpole, U.S. Indian Agent, to Governor of Pueblo of Ácoma, October 7, 1899; Acting President, U.S. Civil Service Commission, to the Honorable Secretary of the Interior, June 16, 1902, both in PAA.

56. *Report of the Commissioner, 1864* (Washington: GPO, 1865), p. 199, PAA.

57. *Annual Reports of the Department of the Interior for the Fiscal Year Ended June 30, 1898* (Washington: GPO, 1898), p. 206, PAA.

58. Jose Segura, U.S. Indian Agent, to Governor of Ácoma, June 25, 1890, PAA.

59. *Annual Reports of the Department of the Interior for the Fiscal Year Ended June 30, 1900* (Washington: GPO, 1900), pp. 293–94; *for the Fiscal Year Ended June 30, 1904* (Washington: GPO, 1905), p. 157, both in PAA.

60. M. Stack, Superintendent of Indian Affairs, to the Honorable William P. Dole, Commissioner of Indian Affairs, in *Report of the Commissioner, 1864* (Washington: GPO, 1865), p. 181.

61. J. L. Collins, Superintendent of Indian Affairs, to the Honorable C. E. Mix, Commissioner of Indian Affairs, September 27, 1858, in *Report of the Commissioner, 1858* (Washington: Wm. A. Harris, Printer, 1858), p. 192.

62. John Ward, Special Agent for the Pueblos, to the Commissioner of Indian Affairs, September 7, 1868, in *Report of the Commissioner, 1868* (Washington: GPO, 1868), p. 177.

63. Thomas to the Honorable E. P. Smith, Commissioner, September 8, 1875, in *Report of the Commissioner, 1875* (Washington: GPO, 1875), p. 333; Thomas to the Commissioner of Indian Affairs to the Secretary of the Interior for the Year 1878 [*sic*] (Washington: GPO, 1878), p. 110.

64. Thomas to the Commissioner of Indian Affairs, September 1, 1880, in *Report of the Commissioner, 1880* (Washington: GPO, 1880), pp. 133–34.

65. Id. to id., September 1, 1881, in *Report of the Commissioner, 1881* (Washington: GPO, 1881), pp. 140–41.

66. Id. to id., September 1, 1882, in *Report of the Commissioner, 1882* (Washington: GPO, 1882), p. 130.

67. Thomas to G. S. Sands, Division Superintendent, Atchison, Topeka and Santa Fe Railroad, Las Vegas, N.M., September 28, 1882, PAA.

68. Pedro Sanchez to Honorable H. Price, December 11, 1883; Superintendent R. Bryan, Albuquerque Indian School, to Sanchez, August 4, 1884, PAA; Dolores Romero, Indian Agent, to the Commissioner of Indian Affairs, September 10, 1885, in *Report of the Commissioner, 1885* (Washington: GPO, 1885), pp. 157–58.

69. Romero to Solomon Bibo, January 4, 23, and February 3, 1886; Romero to Edward Walsh, March 17, 1886; Romero to Bibo, March 25, 1886, all in PAA.

70. Romero to the Honorable J. D. C. Atkins, Commissioner, April 7, 1886; Atkins to Romero, April 17, 1886; Atkins to Romero, May 5, 1886; Romero to Atkins, August 27, 1886, all in PAA.

71. M. C. Williams, Indian Agent, to the Honorable Commissioner of Indian Affairs, October 9, 1886, PAA.

72. Atkins to Melmoth C. Williams, January 18, 1887; Confirmation of Teacher Appointments at Ácoma by the Department of Interior, February 10, 1887; Atkins to Williams, February 10, 1887; Williams to Atkins, June 15, 1887; Atkins to Williams, June 25, 1887, and August 25, 1887; Williams to Honorable Commissioner of Indian Affairs (re. Page Trotter's pay during leave of absence), February 24, 1888, all in PAA.

73. Williams to Solomon Bibo, August 29, 1887; Atkins to Williams, February 17 and March 19, 1888, in PAA.

74. Charles S. Cooper, Captain, 10th Cavalry, Acting Indian Agent, to Governor of the Pueblo of Ácoma, March 25, 1888; Cooper to Miss Cora A. Taylor, March 25, April 20, and May 30, 1888, in PAA.

75. This remarkable policy originated with a letter from Acting Commissioner A. B. Upham, to Melmoth C. Williams, U.S. Indian Agent, June 27, 1888, in PAA.

76. Captain and Superintendent R. H. Pratt to the Honorable Commissioner of Indian Affairs, September 10, 1889, PAA.

77. Captain Pratt to the Honorable Commissioner of Indian Affairs, September 10, 1889; Solomon Bibo to Captain Pratt, September 3, 1889; Frank D. Lewis, U.S. Special Indian Agent, to the Commissioner of Indian Affairs, November 25, 1889, all in PAA.

78. Lewis to the Commissioner, November 25, 1889, copy in PAA.

79. Jose Segura, U.S. Indian Agent, to Honorable Commissioner of Indian Affairs, September 27, 1890, PAA.

80. Segura to Solomon Bibo, February 9 and 16, 1891; Segura to Honorable Commissioner of Indian Affairs, April 6, 1891; T. J. Morgan, Commissioner, to John H. Robertson, U.S. Indian Agent, December 29, 1891, all in PAA.

81. Robertson to the Commissioner of Indian Affairs, August 30, 1892, in *Report of the Secretary of the Interior Being Part of the Message and Documents Communicated to the Two Houses of Congress at the Beginning of the Second Session of the Fifty-Second Congress*, Senate Executive Document No. 1, Part 5 (Washington: GPO, 1892), pp. ii, 334.

82. Indian Agent to the Governor of Ácoma Pueblo, N.M., December 22, 1896; C. E. Nordstrom, Captain, 10th Cavalry, Acting Indian Agent, to the Commissioner of Indian Affairs, August 16, 1897, in *Annual Reports of the Department of the Interior for the Fiscal Year Ended June 30, 1897. Doc. No. 5, Report of the Commissioner, 1897* (Washington: GPO, 1897), pp. 194–95; Captain Nordstrom to Miss Taylor, November 2, 1897; Miss Taylor to U.S. Indian Agent, October 5, 1898; N.S. Walpole, Indian Agent, to Commissioner of Indian Affairs, October 13, 1898, all in PAA.

83. Thomas to the Commissioner of Indian Affairs, August 14, 1879, in *Report of the Commissioner, 1879* (Washington: GPO, 1879), p. 119; draft, Sophie D. Aberle, "Pueblo Indian Canes," 1950, in PAA. The Spanish canes are traced back to the early eighteenth century, according to New Mexico's State Historian, Dr. Myra Ellen Jenkins, and indications are they may date earlier.

84. James K. Allen, Superintendent of Albuquerque Indian School, to the Commissioner of Indian Affairs, April 19, 1904, in *Annual Reports of the Department of the Interior for the Fiscal Year Ended June 30, 1904*, Doc. No. 5, *Report of the Commissioner, 1905* (Washington: GPO, 1905), p. 256.

Chapter 5

1. Annual Report of the Superintendent for the Southern Pueblos Indian Agency, Albuquerque, New Mexico, prepared by Leo Crane, Superintendent, 1920, RG 75, Records of the BIA, Southern Pueblos Agency, Decimal 051-Statistics; Annual Report 1920, in Federal Records Center, General Services Administration, Denver, Colorado, hereafter cited as GSA.

2. Hiram Jones to Superintendent P. T. Lonergan, Albuquerque, N.M., January 5, 1915, PAA.

3. Jones to Superintendent Lonergan, June 16, 1915, including "Property Roll of Hiram Jones, Acomita, New Mexico," PAA. Farmer Jones did loan equipment to the Ácomas if they asked; see Jones to Lonergan, December 14, 1915, PAA.

4. Superintendent to Station Agent, McCarty's, September 22, 1916; Superintendent to Mr. Leo Garcia, Governor, Pueblo of Acomita, Acomita, New Mexico, January 14, 1919, in RG 75, Records of the BIA, Pueblos Indian Agency, Copies of Miscellaneous Letters Sent, January 1919–April 1919, GSA.

5. Annual Report of the Superintendent for the Southern Pueblos Indian Agency for the Fiscal Year NINETEEN TWENTY, prepared by Leo Crane, August 18, 1920, 11, copy in PAA.

6. Annual Report of the Superintendent for the Southern Pueblos Indian Agency for Fiscal Year NINETEEN TWENTY, 53–54, copy in PAA.

7. Crane to the Commissioner of Indian Affairs, August 2, 1920; Crane to the Commissioner of Indian Affairs, July 1, 1921, both in RG 75, Records of the BIA, Southern Pueblos Agency, Decimal 934.0-Stock Raising Wool, GSA. The same records show Ácoma's clip to be 11,863 gross weight in pounds. Laguna's was 86,234 pounds. From these weights, the company deducted a tare to arrive at a net poundage. Ácomas total revenue for pooled wool in 1920 appears to be $1,825.07 although Superintendent Crane's arithmetic does not extend correctly.

8. Carl Seligman, Bernalillo Mercantile Co. of Grants, to Leo Crane, July 8, 1921; Crane to Wallace C. Wilson [farmer], Laguna, N.M., July 7, 1921; Crane to Bernalillo Mercantile Company, Grants, N.M., Attention: Mr. Carl Seligman, July 11, 1921, all in RG 75, Records of the BIA, Southern Pueblos Agency, Decimal 934.0-Stock Raising Wool, GSA.

9. Crane to Wilson, June 20, 1921; Wilson to Crane, June 22, 1921, in RG 75, Records of the BIA, Southern Pueblos Agency, Decimal 934.0-Stock Raising Wool, GSA.

10. Crane to Wilson, November 2, 1921; Crane to the Commissioner of Indian Affairs, Washington, November 2, 1921, both in RG 75, Records of the BIA, Southern Pueblos Agency, Decimal 934.0-Stock Raising Wool, GSA.

11. Crane to the Commissioner of Indian Affairs, November 2, 1921; Commissioner to Crane, November 23, 1921, in ibid.

12. Memo for Inspector Dorrington in *re* sale of wool 1921 for Laguna Indian Pueblo, no author, January 24, 1922, in RG 75, Records of the BIA, Southern Pueblos Agency, Decimal 934.0-Stock Raising Wool, GSA. Internal information makes it clear that Crane was the author of the memorandum which for some reason he did not sign.

13. Crane to Wilson, May 10, 1922; Wilson to Crane, May 10, 1922; Crane to Wilson, May 11, 1922; Wilson to Crane, May 12, 1922, in RG 75, Records of the BIA, Southern Pueblos Agency, Decimal 934.0-Stock Raising Wool, GSA.

14. The buyers who indicated a desire to appear and bid included the Mauger and Avery firm; W. F. Warner of Gallup, represented by C. F. Gorman and backed by the State National Bank of Gallup; L. B. Putney Mercantile Company; C. N. Cotton, also of Gallup; Charles Chadwick from 205 W. Gold, Albuquerque; Louis Ilfeld of Albuquerque; Bond, Cornell Company in Albuquerque; Siegried Abraham, Laguna; The Bernalillo Mercantile Company; and Frank Hubbell of Albuquerque. Wilson to Superintendent H. P. Marble, June 11, 1922, includes "List of prospective bidders for Laguna and Acoma wool"; Wilson to Marble, June 12, 1922, in RG 75, Records of the BIA, Southern Pueblos Agency, Decimal 934.0-Stock Raising Wool, GSA.

15. *To Whom It May Concern*, prepared by Marble, June 12, 1922; Wilson to Marble, June 14, 1922; Marble to Governor Frank Paisano and Wilson, June 15, 1922; Commissioner Charles H. Brookes to Senator H. O. Bursum, June 23, 1922, all in RG 75, Records of the BIA, Southern Pueblos Agency, Decimal 934.0-Stock Raising Wool, GSA.

16. Wilson to Marble, June 21, 1922; message, Marble to Indian Office in Washington, June 24, 1922; message, Assistant Commissioner E. B. Meritt to Marble, June 26, 1922; Wilson to Marble, June 27, 1922, all in RG 75, Records of the BIA, Southern Pueblos Agency, Decimal 934.0-Stock Raising Wool, GSA. This correspondence has the lists of Indian shippers.

17. Report, "Final Payment on Acoma Wool (1922) Figured at .1011 per lb.," by Wilson, n.d., in RG 75, Records of the BIA, Southern Pueblos Agency, Decimal 934.0-Stock Raising Wool, GSA.

18. Marble to Roscoe Rice, Agency Farmer Ácoma, May 21, 1923; Marble to Rice, June 15, 1923, RG 75, Records of the BIA, Southern Pueblos Agency, Decimal 934.0-Stock Raising Wool, GSA.

19. Reports, "Acoma Pueblo Livestock Production and Value Thereof, 1923," prepared by Roscoe Rice, Agency Farmer at Ácoma, n.d., in RG 75, Records of the BIA, Southern Pueblos Agency, Decimal 934.0-Stock Raising Wool, GSA.

20. "Annual Narrative Southern Pueblos 1924," no author [Superintendent's annual report], 10; Superintendent C. J. Crandall, Northern Pueblos Agency, to C. E. Faris, Special Supervisor, Albuquerque, February 26, 1925, RG 75, Records of the BIA, Southern Pueblos Agency, Decimal 052.9-Statistics Other Statistical Reports, 1925, GSA.

21. Juan P. Garcia, Governor of Ácoma, to Superintendent T. F. McCormick, February 28, 1927; McCormick to Governor Garcia, March 2, 1927; Superintendent Leon A. Towers to Honorable E. B. Meritt, Assistant Commissioner of Indian Affairs, June 13, 1925, in RG 75, Records of the BIA, Southern Pueblos Agency, Decimal 934.0-Stock Raising Wool, GSA.

22. Superintendent B. P. Six to Commissioner of Indian Affairs, April 3, 1930; Commissioner C. J. Rhoads to Special Commissioner H. J. Hagerman, April 10, 1930, both in RG 75, Records of the BIA, Southern Pueblos Agency, Decimal 934.0-Stock Raising Wool, GSA. Antonio Torivio, Pueblo of Ácoma, to S. D. Aberle, United Pueblos Agency, February 26, 1941. Mr. Torivio states that he bought a registered

bull in 1935 to improve his herd, document in RG 75, Records of the BIA, United Pueblos Agency. Decimal 924-Ácoma, GSA.

23. "Program for Ácoma Pueblo Fiscal Year 1938," no author [United Pueblos Agency], n.d., in RG 75, Records of the BIA, United Pueblos Agency, Decimal file 184–Ácoma, GSA.

24. Ibid.; "Estimated Livestock as of June, 1939, Acoma Pueblo," report prepared by Robert C. Hanston, RG 75, Records of the BIA, United Pueblos Agency, Decimal 924–Ácoma, GSA, includes record of sales to individual Ácomas.

25. Dr. S. D. Aberle, to E. R. McCray, Superintendent, San Carlos Indian Agency, April 4, 1940; Memorandum from Dewey Dismuke, Acting Unit Conservationalist, to Dr. Aberle, April 4, 1940; Memorandum from Dismuke to Mr. Liljenquist, Soil Conservation Service, April 18, 1940; Memorandum prepared by James T. McBroom, Assistant Field Aide, April 25, 1940; Dr. Aberle to John A. Krall, Credit Agent, May 9, 1940, all in RG 75, Records of the BIA, United Pueblos Agency, Decimal 924–Ácoma, GSA.

26. Memorandum from W. R. Centerwall, Associate Regional Forester, to Dr. Aberle, May 9, 1940, in RG 75, Records of the BIA, United Pueblos Agency, Decimal 924–Ácoma, GSA.

27. Memorandum, Centerwall to Dr. Aberle, May 9, 1940; Memorandum, Dismuke to Claud E. Humphreys, United Pueblos Agency, subject: Bulls Purchased from Zia Pueblo by the Ácoma Indians, March 26, 1941; Ordinance of the Pueblo of Ácoma, signed on April 21, 1941, by Governor Cerno and Council members, all in RG 75, Records of the BIA, United Pueblos Agency, Decimal 924–Ácoma, GSA.

28. Annual Report of Extension Work for the United Pueblos Agency on Ácoma, N.M., January 1, 1941, to December 31, 1941, prepared by Floyd Farrell and Dr. Aberle; January 1, 1943, to December 31, 1943, prepared by C. Paul Goodrich and Dr. Aberle; 1945, no author, all in RG 75, Records of the BIA, United Pueblos Agency, Decimal 042–Reports, GSA. Annual income reports show a small income from these items. Florence Hawley Ellis, "The Very Irregular Production of Nuts by Piñon Trees," unpublished manuscript, n.d., records New Mexico and Arizona piñon nut crops between 1916 and 1931 and concludes that they are undependable. Wild horses brought $3.00 per head for yearlings in 1935 and 50 cents for colts. See Individual Weekly Report for Extension Workers, prepared by Steve Orilla, stockman, June 29, 1935. He notes that a Miss I. P. Riedling of Albuquerque bought 140 head. Annual Income Report for Ácoma, Fiscal Year Ended June 30, 1940; Report, Reservation Program, United Pueblos Agency, March 1944, Part One Basic Data: Resources and Services, Pueblo of Ácoma, in RG 75, Records of the BIA, United Pueblos Agency, Decimal 045–Agency Program GSA; Benjamin J. Taylor and Dennis J. O'Connor *Indian Manpower Resources in the Southwest,* (Tempe: Arizona State University, 1969), pp. 192–93.

29. The same survey showed that Isleta, Santo Domingo, and Zia Pueblos had a money-making pottery industry, but identified only two Laguna women who still made pottery and sold it at the railway station: Mrs. Francisco Mooney living at Laguna Pueblo and Mrs. Pedro Pino at Seama. See, Director of the United States Geological Survey to Superintendent P. T. Lonergan, February 21, 1919; Manuel Baca to Superintendent Lonergan, April 25, 1919; L. R. McDonald to Superintendent Lonergan, May 1, 1919; Ned W. Caufield, Laguna Farmer, report on pottery, May 7, 1919; Roscoe Rice, Acomita, to Superintendent Lonergan, May 24, 1919, all in RG 75, Records of the BIA, Southern Pueblos Agency, Decimal 963–Manufacturing, GSA.

30. Annual Narrative Southern Pueblos 1924, Albuquerque, New Mexico, no author, n.d.; Narrative Section of Annual Report, 1929, Southern Pueblos Agency, Albuquerque, New Mexico, prepared by Lem A. Towers, Superintendent, n.d., both in RG 75, Records of the BIA, Southern Pueblos Agency, Decimal 051–Statistics, GSA.

31. Dr. Aberle to Commissioner of Indian Affairs, Attention: George M. Weber, Statistician, March 20, 1940; Annual Income Report for Acoma compiled by Walter O. Olson and Dr. Aberle, Fiscal Year ended June 30, 1940; the reports of earnings on pottery by Fiscal Year are in RG 75, Records of the BIA, United Pueblos Agency, Annual Statistics and Decimal 042–Reports, GSA. Steve Orilla, Government Stockman, to Towers, July 15, 1932; Towers to Mrs. Marion S. Norton, 32 West Tulpehocken Street, Germantown, Philadelphia, Penna., July 18, 1932, in RG 75, Records of the BIA, Southern Pueblos Agency, Decimal 963–Manufacturing, GSA. Orilla writes, "I am mailing you a list of names of pottery makers who are considered the best among the Acoma Tribe." Report, "Potters (Ácoma)," compiled by Ácoma officials, October 1974; Report, "Silversmiths (Ácoma)," compiled by Ácoma officials, October 1974; both in Appendix 6: ÁCOMA ARTISANS AND TRAINEES IN 1974.

32. Governor Juan Luis Huskay to Towers, May 3, 1928; Towers to Governor Huskay, May 10, 1928, in RG 75, Records of the BIA, Southern Pueblos Agency, Decimal 060—Tribal Relations, GSA.

33. Rice to Special Supervisor C. E. Faris, July 23, 1924; Rice to Superintendent Lawson L. Odle, May 27, 1925, in RG 75, Records of the BIA, Southern Pueblos Agency, Decimal 124—Policy Trading with Indians, GSA.

34. Surviving Annual Income Reports show the amount to vary between $100 and $250.

35. Annual Income Report for Fiscal Year 1940, prepared by Walter O. Olson and Dr. Aberle, BIA.

36. Taylor and O'Connor, *Indian Manpower Resources*, p. 201. Please see updated discussion of employment at Ácoma in chapter 6.

37. Ibid., pp. 193, 201; *Development of Tourist Potential Acoma Indian Reservation, New Mexico*, Table 18.

38. Some of these schools were the Sherman Institute, Riverside, California; the United States Indian Industrial School at Phoenix, Arizona; the United States Indian School, Albuquerque; St. Catherine's, a mission school in Santa Fe; Presbyterian at Jémez; and Loretto Convent school for girls at Bernalillo, N.M.

39. Calendar for Acomita Day School 1913–1914, no author, n.d.; Calendar for McCarty's Day School 1913–14, no author, n.d.; letter, J. K. Grimm to Philip T. Lonergan, Supt., Pueblo Day Schools, July 31, 1916; Daily Program of Acomita Day School, no author, n.d.; all in PAA; Narrative Section of the Annual Report 1919, Pueblo Day Schools, P. T. Lonergan, Superintendent, in RG 75, Records of the BIA, So. Pueblos Agency, Decimal 051—Statistics, GSA.

40. R. Perry, Superintendent, to Superintendent Lonergan, Farmers, Day School Teachers and Other Employees in the Western Portion of the Pueblo Agency, April 3, 1916; Superintendent to Mr. Louis Hashkoya, Acomita, October 10, 1916; Day School Inspector to Lonergan, May 22, 1917, all in PAA; "Narrative Section of the Annual Report, 1919," RG 75, Records of the BIA, So. Pueblos Agency, Decimal 051—Statistics, GSA. Superintendent Lonergan's letter to Mr. Hashkoya stated in part: "This is to inform you that unless these children [Maria, age 13, and Juana, age, 9, and son Jose, age 8] are placed in school within ten days you will be arrested and tried before the Judge, under the law which provides that you must send your children to school."

41. Perry to Lonergan, May 9, 1914; Superintendent to the Commissioner of Indian Affairs, April 27, 1916, both in PAA; Annual Report of the Superintendent for the Southern Pueblos Indian Agency, Albuquerque, New Mexico, for Fiscal Year 1920, Narrative Section, in RG 75, Records of the BIA, Southern Pueblos Agency, Decimal 051—Statistics, GSA.

42. Annual Report of the Superintendent for the Southern Pueblos Indian Agency, 1920, pp. 44–48, copy in PAA.

43. Annual Narrative Southern Pueblos 1924, Albuquerque, New Mexico, no author, n.d., in RG 75, Records of the BIA, Southern Pueblos Agency, Decimal 051—Statistics—Annual Report 1924, GSA; Monthly Reports of Indian Schools: Acomita Day School, for the months of September and October 1925, prepared by Mrs. K. L. Mehrens, Teacher, September 30 and October 31, 1925, in RG 75, Records of the BIA, Southern Pueblos Agency, Decimal 820.0—Pupils Attendance and Reports, GSA; Gladys June Chaves to Southern Pueblos Agency, February 28, 1925, in RG 75, Records of the BIA, Southern Pueblos Agency, Decimal 806.2—Education, GSA. Miss Chaves explains how she will go on to school over her parents' objections.

44. Reports of Children Eligible for Transfer to Nonreservation Schools, Ácoma, June 30, 1925, in RG 75, Records of the BIA, Southern Pueblos Agency, Decimal 820.0—Pupils, GSA; report [list of Ácoma students and their respective schools], no author, n.d., in RG 75, Records of the BIA, Southern Pueblos Agency, Decimal 806.1—Education, GSA; School Enrollment Work Report, McCarty's Day School, prepared by T. F. McCormick, Superintendent, to C. E. Faris, District Superintendent, September 10, 1926, in RG 75, Records of the BIA, Southern Pueblos Agency, Decimal 806—Education, GSA.

45. Narrative Section of Annual Report 1929, Southern Pueblos Agency, Albuquerque, New Mexico, prepared by Homer L. Morrison, Day School Inspector, n.d., Section III, Schools, in RG 75, Records of the BIA, Southern Pueblos Agency, Decimal 051—Statistics, GSA.

46. Lem A. Towers, Superintendent, to the Commissioner of Indian Affairs, Washington, D.C., September 17, 1931, in RG 75, Records of the BIA, Southern Pueblos Agency, Decimal 806—Education, 1930–33, GSA.

47. The annual reports from 1915 state the superintendent's need for guidelines: "As the state laws

do not apply on the reservations of this jurisdiction, it is necessary for complete Federal legislation to meet the law and order situation in these pueblos," wrote Superintendent Lem A. Towers in 1930. See Narrative Section of Annual Report 1929, Southern Pueblos Agency, Albuquerque, New Mexico, RG 75, Records of the BIA, Southern Pueblos Agency, Decimal 051—Statistics, GSA.

48. White, *The Acoma Indians*, pp. 42, 45–51.

49. Annual Report of the Superintendent for the Southern Pueblos Agency for the Fiscal Year 1920, 21–23.

50. Hiram Jones, Pueblo Farmer, to Superintendent Lonergan, Acomita, N.M., January 26, 1916, PAA.

51. Annual Report of the Superintendent for the Southern Pueblos Indian Agency for the Fiscal Year NINETEEN TWENTY-TWO, 9, in RG 75, Records of the BIA, Southern Pueblos Agency, Decimal 051—Statistics, Annual Report 1922, GSA.

52. Ibid., pp. 9–10.

53. Narrative Section of Annual Report 1929, Southern Pueblos Agency, Section I, Law and Order, RG 75, Records of the BIA, Southern Pueblos Agency, Decimal 051—Statistics, GSA.

54. White, *The Acoma Indians*, pp. 60–63. White's descriptions of Ácoma officials and their duties are recommended reading.

55. Warren A. Beck and Ynez D. Haase, *Historical Atlas of New Mexico* (Norman: University of Oklahoma Press, 1969), pp. 41–42.

56. Annual Report of the Superintendent for the Southern Pueblos Indian Agency for the Fiscal Year NINETEEN TWENTY-TWO, p. 3, copy in PAA.

57. Annual Report of the Superintendent for the Southern Pueblos Indian Agency for the Fiscal Year NINETEEN TWENTY, pp. 30–31, copy in PAA.

58. Annual Report of the Southern Pueblos Indian Agency for the Fiscal Year NINETEEN TWENTY-TWO, pp. 5–8, copy in PAA.

59. White, *The Acoma Indians*, pp. 107ff. This section includes a comprehensive description of medicine societies and curing ceremonies. White found that although a sick person was not obligated to submit to treatment from a medicine man, the medicine men were obligated to treat any person applying to them for help. In 1925 there were four medicine societies: Flint (Hictian), Fire (H'a-k'an'), KaBina, and Thundercloud (Shiwanna). The Ácomas were not certain what KaBina means precisely. White states that this society disappeared and the Flint society took over its functions in 1926.

60. Early records indicate a loss of some 3,000 Pueblo Indians during smallpox epidemics occurring between 1779 and 1881, without taking into account similar ravages before and after that period. The 1900 census showed that other pueblos suffered similar population setbacks: Zia and Sandia had only 140 and 90 persons remaining, respectively. The Ácoma people numbered 4,305 in January 1990. Please see chapter 6 for a full discussion of population changes at the Pueblo.

61. Narrative Section of the Annual Report, 1919; Annual Report of the Superintendent for the Southern Pueblos Indian Agency for the Fiscal Year NINETEEN TWENTY, pp. 34–37, copy in PAA.

62. Annual Report of the Superintendent for the Southern Pueblos Indian Agency for the Fiscal Year NINETEEN TWENTY, p. 40, copy in PAA.

63. Annual Report of the Superintendent for the Southern Pueblos Indian Agency for the Fiscal Year NINETEEN TWENTY, pp. 37–39, copy in PAA. Ácoma had a field matron sporadically.

64. Ibid., 40; Annual Report of the Superintendent for the Southern Pueblos Agency for the Fiscal Year NINETEEN TWENTY-TWO, pp. 17–18, copy in PAA.

65. Narrative Section of Annual Report 1929, Southern Pueblos Agency, Albuquerque, New Mexico, Section II, Health, prepared by Dr. R. D. Holt. White describes the Ácoma medicine cult and practices in *The Acoma Indians*, pp. 107–25.

66. Senate Bill 5-2241 (May 26, 1969).

67. Resolution No. TC-DE-23-69-A, made by Pueblo of Ácoma, Tribal Council, San Fidel, December 23, 1969; Preliminary Facility Justification Survey, Indian Community Hospital, Acomita, New Mexico, no author, n.d., both in Pueblo Economic Assistant's Office files (hereafter cited as PEA), BIA.

68. "Montoya Cites Indian Health Danger," *Navajo Times*, April 16, 1970; "$70,000 for Planning Acoma School," Grants *Daily Beacon*, June 18, 1970; Resolution No. TC-NO-AP-14-71, made by Pueblo of Ácoma, Tribal Council, San Fidel, New Mexico, April 14, 1971; Justification of the Pueblo of Laguna for a Hospital at a Site Near the I-40 Interchange at Casa Blanca, New Mexico, the last two in PEA, BIA.

69. Cubero Resolution, Cubero, Valencia County, New Mexico, April 13, 1971; petition signed by residents of San Fidel, New Mexico, April 14, 1971; San Fidel Resolution (Cañoncito Navahos), San Fidel, Valencia County, New Mexico, April 14, 1971; Governor Lorenzo Toribio and Governor Tom Dailey, Ácoma and Laguna, respectively, to Dr. Kazumi Kasuga, IHS Area Director, April 20, 1971; Governor Toribio to Dr. Kasuga, April 25, 1971; Dr. Kasuga to Governor Toribio, May 28, 1971, all in PEA, Southern Pueblos Agency, BIA.

70. Justification of the Pueblo of Ácoma for a PHS Indian-Community Hospital on the Ácoma Grant About One-Half Mile Southwest of the Acomita Interchange on Interstate 40, prepared by the Public Health Service, n.d.; Justification of the Pueblo of Laguna for a Hospital at a Site Near the I-40 Interchange at Casa Blanca, New Mexico, prepared by the Public Health Service, n.d., in PEA, Southern Pueblos Agency, BIA.

71. In brief, the Lagunas argued that their site would be more centrally located and also five miles closer for the Cañoncito Navahos, although either site required emergency transportation. They also claimed that construction would be more economical and offered to develop a nursing home, a day-care center, and staff residences. They believed they were entitled to equal employment opportunities as well. The Ácomas were greatly perturbed by the Laguna appeal because the Laguna governor had given them his solemn promise to support the decision for Ácoma. See, Dr. Emery A. Johnson, Assistant Surgeon General, Director, Indian Health Services, to Director, Albuquerque Area Indian Health Services, subject: Site Selection for the Proposed Hospital to Serve the Acoma-Laguna-Canoncito Communities, July 14, 1971; Richard Schifter, Attorney, to Dr. Emery A. Johnson, subject: Proposed Ácoma-Laguna Hospital, August 3, 1971; Governor Toribio et al., to Dr. Johnson, August 20, 1971, all in PEA, Southern Pueblos Agency, BIA; Site Evaluation Survey Report for a New Ácoma-Laguna-Canoncito Health Center, prepared by the Regional Office, Facilities Engineering and Construction, Region VI, Dallas, Texas, December 22, 1971.

72. Message, H. V. Chadwick, Acting Director, IHS, to Governor Harry Martinez et al., February 7, 1972; Governor Martinez to Governor Timothy P. Analla, Laguna Pueblo, March 7, 1972; Senator Joseph M. Montoya to Arturo Ortega, Attorney for Ácoma, March 3, 1972; "Ácoma-Laguna-Canoncito Hospital," statement by Governor Clyde Sanchez, Pueblo de Ácoma, April 4, 1974, all in PEA, Southern Pueblos Agency, BIA. The hospital was eventually built and is operating successfully. Please see chapter 6 for all the details.

73. Indenture, signed by Martin del Vallo (governor), Jose Antonio, Jose Lujan, Santiago, Jose Saavedra, Pauline Torres, Jose Manuel Sarracino, Antonio Candelario, and Jose Antonio. On the same day, the Ácomas agreed to allow the Atlantic and Pacific Railroad Company to quarry all the stone needed to build the railway bed, and for other purposes, for the sum of one dollar. Both documents in records of the field office of the BIA, Albuquerque.

74. Leo Garcia, Governor of Ácoma, to Judge Hanna, Pueblo Attorney, Albuquerque, December 17, 1919; Frank Ortiz, Governor of Ácoma, to Leo Bibo, Pueblo of Ácoma, January 13, 1920, in RG 75, Records of the BIA, United Pueblos Agency, Decimal 003-General & Statistical, Miscellaneous Correspondence, GSA.

75. Solomon Bibo, San Francisco, California, to Hon. Frank Ortiz, January 13, 1920; Bibo to Hon. Pueblo Indian Agency, Albuquerque, January 14, 1920, both in RG 75, Records of the BIA, United Pueblos Agency, Decimal 003-General & Statistical, Miscellaneous Correspondence, GSA.

76. Governor Garcia to Judge Hanna, December 17, 1919; Special Attorney for the Pueblo Indians in New Mexico to Governor Garcia, Albuquerque, December 19, 1919, in RG 75, Records of the BIA, United Pueblos Agency, Decimal 003-General & Statistical, Miscellaneous Correspondence, GSA.

77. Governor Ortiz and principals, Acomita, _____ [to Superintendent], February 24, 1920, in RG 75, Records of the BIA, United Pueblos Agency, Decimal 003-General & Statistical, Miscellaneous Correspondence, GSA. That Solomon Bibo monopolized the Ácoma lands with his grazing permits was the accusation of Walter G. Marmon during the controversies raised by Bibo's offer to lease the Ácoma grant already discussed in the previous chapter. Marmon stated that Bibo rustled cattle as well, through a company called Saint and Cleland. These and other statements are found in Walter G. Marmon, Marmon Bros. & Pratt, U.S. Deputy Surveyors, Laguna, to Hon. Pedro Sanchez, U.S. Indian Agency, July 31, 1884, in Office of Indian Affairs, Department of the Interior, 1884, NA.

78. Leslie A. White, *New Material from Acoma*, Anthropological Papers, No. 32, BAE Bulletin No. 136 (Washington: GPO, 1943), p. 315.

79. Report No. 1, *Ácoma Pueblo,* prepared by Pueblo Lands Board, 1610 Miscel. filed October 7, 1929; E. A. Meritt, Assist. Comm., U.S. Department of the Interior, Office of Indian Affairs, Washington, D.C., to Lawson L. Odle, Superintendent, Southern Pueblos Agency, August 17, 1925, Records of the Pueblo Lands Board (hereafter cited as PLB), Southern Pueblos Agency, BIA, Albuquerque.

80. Leo Garcia, Governor of Ácoma, to Superintendent of Southern Pueblos, July 23, 1917; Governor Garcia to Commissioner of Indian Affairs, Washington, D.C., September 9, 1917, PLB.

81. E. B. Meritt, Assistant Commissioner, to Messrs. Leo Garcia and James Miller, Indians of Ácoma Pueblo, November 28, 1917; Meritt to Odle, Superintendent, Southern Pueblos Agency, August 17, 1925, PLB.

82. Charles H. Burke, Commissioner, Office of Indian Affairs, to Odle, September 2, 1925, in PLB.

83. James H. Miller, Governor of Ácoma, to Commissioner of Indian Affairs, March 27, 1924; Governor Miller to Odle, May 23 and July 14, 1925, PLB.

84. H. J. Hagerman, Special Commissioner to Negotiate with the Indians, Representative of the Secretary of the Interior on the Pueblo Indian Land Board, Santa Fe, New Mexico, to Honorable Charles H. Burke, Commissioner of Indian Affairs, November 2, 1925, PLB.

85. C. E. Faris, Special Supervisor in Charge, Southern Pueblos, to Honorable Charles H. Burke, Commissioner of Indian Affairs, May 24, 1924, PLB.

86. Ibid.; H. J. Hagerman, Special Commissioner to Negotiate with Indians, Santa Fe, New Mexico, to the Honorable Burke, November 25, 1925.

87. Report No. 1, *Ácoma Pueblo,* October 7, 1929, and miscellaneous papers. The Ácomas feel they were never compensated for the loss of the use of this land.

88. Ibid.

89. Ibid.; Towers, Superintendent, to Juan Louis Haskaya, Governor of Ácoma, October 12, 1929, and attached report, "Compensation to Pueblo Indians of New Mexico," shows Ácoma with no compensation for loss of lands and in settlement for damages for land and water rights lost, RG 75, Records of the BIA, Southern Pueblos Agency, Decimal 381-Allotment of Lands, GSA.

90. Governor Haskaya and Head Councilman Antonio Garcia to John Collier, March 12, 1932; Commissioner Collier to William A. Brophy, U.S. Indian Service, September 18, 1934; Pueblo Attorney to Honorable John Collier, September 25, 1934; Special Attorney for Pueblo Indians to Honorable John Collier, September 29, 1934; Memo., "In Connection with the letter of November 20, 1934, from William A. Brophy, Special Attorney for the Pueblos, to Mr. Mark Radcliffe, relative to certain conditions of the Ácoma Pueblo Grant," prepared by Guy P. Harrington, District Cadastral Engineer, Santa Fe, November 22, 1934, all in RG 75, Records of the BIA, United Pueblos Agency, Decimal 053.0-Ácoma, GSA.

91. "Reservation Progress," report compiled by United Pueblos Agency and dated March 1944, in RG 75, Records of the BIA, United Pueblos Agency, Decimal 050.0-General Ácoma, GSA. Augmentation of lands under the Reservation Program started in 1934 and involved four separate agencies—the Submarginal Land Board, the Federal Surplus Relief Corporation, the Federal Emergency Relief Administration, and the Resettlement Administration. They sought to alleviate the drouth conditions and extreme poverty of the Depression years.

92. All odd-numbered sections in the Ácoma Purchase Area (Eleven Township) were purchased by the United States from the New Mexico and Arizona Land Company, by warranty deed dated October 27, 1936, at a cost to the Government of $1.50 an acre. The New Mexico and Arizona Land Company reserved all oil, gas, and minerals. In addition to the resettlement lands, the United States also purchased the holdings of John William Brown by deed dated July 25, 1941, amounting to approximately 200 acres. Kenneth L. Payton, Superintendent, United Pueblos Agency, to Land and Natural Resources Division, Department of Justice, Attention: Mr. Walter A. Rochow, Attorney, June 11, 1968, in files of Dazzo, Dazzo and Ashby, Claims Attorneys, for Ácoma Pueblo, Albuquerque, N.M.

93. Before the Indian Claims Commission, Pueblo de Acoma v. U.S.A., Docket No. 266, A Summary, prepared by Sam Dazzo and Nicholas C. Dazzo, March 3, 1970, in files of Dazzo, Dazzo and Ashby, Claims Attorneys for Ácoma Pueblo, Albuquerque, N.M.

94. These were Jose Ulario Garcia, San Juan Shutiva, Santiago Juanico, Bautista Rey, Santiago Heweya, San Juan Sanchez, Jose Leon Chino, Santiago Pino, Bautista Pino, Joe Chino, Syme Sanchez, and Joe C. Ray. Dr. Ellis and the author presented archeological and historical evidence for Ácoma. Dr. Ellis

and Dr. Myra Ellen Jenkins served as Laguna's archeologist and historian, respectively, throughout the case.

95. Resolutions prepared by Sam Victorino, Governor of Ácoma; Frank L. Ortiz, Lieutenant Governor; Frank L. Garcia, Head Councilman; Fermin H. Martinez, Councilman, April 19, 1970; Resolution, prepared by same officials, May 9, 1970; Before the Indian Claims Commission, Pueblo de Ácoma v. the U.S.A., Docket No. 266, Stipulation for Entry of Final Judgment, all in files of Dazzo, Dazzo and Ashby, Claims Attorneys for Ácoma Pueblo, Albuquerque, N.M.

96. Gary L. Tietjen, *Encounter with the Frontier* (Los Alamos, N.M.: 1969), pp. 77–82. The Tietjens were among the early settlers in the area and helped to construct the first earthen dam; Before the Indian Claims Commission, Pueblo de Ácoma, Pueblo of Laguna et al., The Navaho Tribe of Indians v. The United States of America, Dockets 266, 227, and 229, "Findings of Facts," March 31, 1967, in files of Dazzo, Dazzo and Ashby, Claims Attorneys for Ácoma Pueblo, Albuquerque, N.M.

97. Paraphrased notes prepared by author from spontaneous speech by Governor Lorenzo Toribio at the occasion of a Pueblo Governor's luncheon hosted by Colonel Algernon G. Swan, Kirtland Air Force Base, N.M., June 21, 1971.

Chapter 6

1. "The Pueblo of Ácoma's Commentary on the Wilderness Study Effecting Ácoma Lands in the Valencia County." June 11, 1981, in Ácoma Tribal Administrative files (hereafter cited as ATA files), under subheadings: Natural Resources-Land-Wilson Ranch Land.

2. The Council's older members were being succeeded by Ácoma with broad experience, but also by some who could no longer speak Keres, the tribal language.

3. Tribal members gathered at the author's home after that May meeting. Some expressed mixed reactions as they worried that the compensation was not enough, and worse, that the lost lands should have been returned as well. Both issues persist today but back then all were elated when more than twenty years of litigation ended auspiciously.

4. Public Law 93-638, Indian Self-Determination and Education Assistance Act, January 4, 1975, in *Indian Self-Determination Reference Materials*, prepared by the Sterling Institute, Washington, D.C., no date; Public Law 100-472, Indian Self-Determination and Education Assistance Act Amendments of 1988, October 5, 1988.

5. Visitors used to be allowed to climb the trail in their own vehicles, but moving the Visitor's Center from the top of the rocks enabled the tribe to control access and large numbers much more efficiently. Report, "Calendar of Events," by the Office of the Governor, Pueblo de Ácoma, no date.

6. All Cacique appointments are male. Report, "Introduction to The Pueblo of Ácoma," no author, no date, in ATA files; Velma Garcia-Mason, "Acoma Pueblo," in *Handbook of North American Indians*, Vol. 9, *Southwest* (Washington: Smithsonian Institution, 1979), p. 463.

7. Ibid., "Introduction to the Pueblo of Ácoma." For further discussion of a tribal constitution see pp. 164–166.

8. See pertinent sections in this chapter for further information on these organizations.

9. Data furnished by Laura Watchempino, Tribal Records Administration Officer, July 2, 1990.

10. See Chapter 2, page 36.

11. See Appendix 6, Ácoma Artisans and Trainees. Information on Ácoma pottery from Arthur and Carol Cruz, owners of Pueblo Pottery, June 1, 1990; Mary Lewis Garcia, June 20, 1990; and May Tenorio, Ácoma Visitor's Center, June 20, 1990.

12. Information from Laura Watchempino; Garica-Mason, "Ácoma Pueblo," p. 451.

13. Garcia-Mason, "Ácoma Pueblo," p. 452; Raymond B. Farnsworth, "Evaluation and Investigation of Damage to the Agricultural Lands of the Ácoma Pueblo from Use of Water Polluted by Sewage from Grants' Sewage Treatment Plant," Provo, Utah, 1985, p. 20.

14. Ibid., Farnsworth, pp. 25–26; Resolution No. TC-DEC-10-82-03-0-1, Ácoma Tribal Council, December 10, 1982, ATA files. Lawsuit, *Acoma v. Grants and NMWDCC*, 1982, ATA files, Case No. CIV-82-15040-M.

15. Memorandum, "Brief in Opposition to the Motion to Dismiss Filed by the City of Grants and the State of New Mexico," Case No. CIV-82-15040-M, *Pueblo of Ácoma and Pueblo of Laguna vs. City of Grants, State of New Mexico, and United States Environmental Protection Agency, et al.*, April 4, 1983, ATA files; "First Amended Complaint for Declaratory Relief Injunction and Money Damages," Case No. CIV-82-15040-M, *Pueblo of Ácoma, et al.*, August 29, 1985, ATA files 1985; Brief Description of Nature of Action and Results," ATA files, Correspondence, 1988–90.

16. Final Judgment, Case No. CIV-82-15040-M, *Pueblo of Acoma and Pueblo of Laguna vs. City of Grants, et al.*, May 14, 1990, ATA files, correspondence-1990.

17. Press Release, Ácoma Pueblo, August 18, 1987, prepared by Danny Sanchez, Tribal Secretary; Governor Stanley Paytiamo to New Mexico Water Quality Control Commission, subject: Amendment to the Water Quality Standards of the Rio San Jose, August 27, 1987; "Final Hearing on WWTP Draws Comment from 35; Site Decision Expected Thursday," Grants *Daily Beacon*, February 9, 1990. All in ATA files, Case No. CIV-82-15040-M. Correspondence-1987–1990.

18. Memorandum, to Governor Stanley Paytiamo and the Ácoma Tribal Council from the Ácoma Advisory School Board, subject: Endorsement of Board Recommendations and By-Laws, February 29, 1978, Approval by the Ácoma Tribal Council to Endorse the By-Laws of the Ácoma Advisory School Board, both in ATA files, Education, Ácoma Advisory School Board By-Laws.

19. Laura V. Garcia, Acting Agency Superintendent of Education, to Governor Stanley Paytiamo, December 18, 1986; Christine P. Sims, Title VII Bilingual Programs, to Governor Stanley Paytiamo, Ácoma Tribal Administration, November 18, 1986, ATA files, Education, Title VII Bilingual Program, General Correspondence, 1987. Title VII Bilingual Program Funding accounted for the shift in agency sponsors.

20. Cyrus J. Chino, Principal, Sky City Community School, to Title VII Project Officer, subject: Verification of Standard Fee, September 17, 1986; Christine P. Sims, Director, Ácoma Bicognitive Learning Program, to Ms. Anna Johnson, United States Department of Education, Contracts and Grants Services, April 3, 1987, both in ATA files, Education, Title VII Bilingual Program, General Correspondence, 1987. A three-year funded effort in fiscal year 1987 (October 1986–September 1987) meant over $110,000 for the program each year.

21. Interview with Juan Steven Juanico, Title VII Bilingual Program Director, Sky City Community School, July 2, 1990.

22. *AAK'UM'E DZEENI, A Topical Dictionary*, Ácoma Bilingual Program, Sky City Community School, Ácoma Pueblo, New Mexico, 1982.

23. *AA'UM'E USUMEESHTAAN'I, A Bilingual Resource Book*, Christine P. Sims and Carmen Sánchez, Acoma Bilingual Program, Sky City Community School, Ácoma Pueblo, New Mexico, 1982.

24. *AAK'UM'E UBEETAAN'I, A Collection of Acoma Stories*, Christine P. Sims, ed., Ácoma Bilingual Program, Sky City Community School, Ácoma Pueblo, New Mexico, 1982.

25. Richard Danek, Chairman, Ácoma Scholarship Program, to Janice Pilcher, November 7, 1985, ATA files, Higher Education Program, General Correspondence.

26. Charles E. Antonio, Director, Division of Student Services, to Students and Counselors, 1983; Memorandum, Charles E. Antonio, Ácoma Higher Education Director, to William Estevan, First Lieutenant Governor, Pueblo of Ácoma, subject: Ácoma Higher Education Findings and Progress Report, February 5, 1986; "Acoma Higher Education," List of Students, School, Etc., no date; Governor Ray Histia to Reginald Rodriguez, Education Specialist, Bureau of Indian Affairs, subject: FY 1988 Ácoma Higher Education Funding Level, Contract No. MOOC14204774, January 5, 1988, all in ATA files, Higher Education Program.

27. Merle L. Garcia, Governor, Pueblo of Ácoma, to Betty Walter, Agency Superintendent, Bureau of Indian Affairs, July 29, 1985 and passim, ATA files, Contracts/Grants Adult Education.

28. Resolution No. TC-SEPT-28-85-8, Position of The Pueblo of Acoma Tribal Council on Indian Health Care, September 28, 1985; Quarterly Program Report FY 1984/1985, Fourth Quarter, October 15, 1985, and passim, ATA files, Ácoma Social Services, General Correspondence. The Bureau of Indian Affairs grant for fiscal year 1985 amounted to $201,201. Funds were reduced by $31,000 in 1985, see Omar Bradley, Acting Superintendent, Bureau of Indian Affairs, to Merle L. Garcia, Governor, Pueblo of Ácoma, April 10, 1985, same files.

29. Interviews with Caroline Torres, Director, Ácoma Senior Center, May 23, 1990. Funding for the Center came mainly from Title VI Older Americans Act.

30. Ordinance Prescribing a Code of Law and Order for the Pueblo de Ácoma Indian Reservation, enacted by the Council of the Pueblo de Ácoma on April 13, 1971, ATA files, Ácoma Law and Order Code.

31. Ibid.; Resolution No. TC-FEB-25-81A, Revision of the Code of Law and Order for the Pueblo of Ácoma, February 25, 1981, ATA files, Tribal Court.

32. Dwain Clark, Tribal Judge, to Ron Martinez, Director, Bureau of Indian Affairs, subject: Annual Report, Contract #MOOC14202439, November 20, 1978, ATA files, Tribal court, 1978; interviews with Clyde Sánchez, Advocate General, Pueblo of Ácoma, May 16, 1990.

33. Charles Histia, Personnel Specialist, to Merle L. Garcia, Governor, subject: Tribal Judge Duties and Rate of Pay for FY 84, August 23, 1983, ATA files, Law Enforcement, Tribal Court, General Correspondence, 1983.

34. Contract for three years, October 1, 1988, through September 30, 1991. Resolution No. TC-AUGUST-4-88-1, Application for Funds through the Department of Interior, Bureau of Indian Affairs, in Support of the Ácoma Tribal Courts, P.L. 93-638, August 4, 1988, ATA files, Tribal Court, 1988.

35. Contract form for Professional Technical Services to the Pueblo of Ácoma, Contract No. MOOC14203284, between Pueblo of Ácoma and Dwain Clark, October 29, 1981, ATA files, Tribal Court Monthly (Quarterly Reports, *passim.*)

36. Ácoma Tribal Courts/Angelo Skelares, to Governor Garcia and Tribal Council, subject: Degrees of Blood, February 28, 1983, ATA files, Law Enforcement, Tribal Court, General Correspondence, 1983.

37. Floyd J. Kezele, Tribal Judge to Governor Merle Garcia and Tribal Council, subject: Jury Trial, March 20, 1984, ATA files, Law Enforcement, Tribal Court, 1984,

38. Merle L. Garcia, Governor, to Sam R. Montoya, Superintendent, Bureau of Indian Affairs, subject: Tribal Courts Proposals for FY 85, September 26, 1984; Pueblo of Ácoma Monthly Reports for 1988, all in ATA files, Law Enforcement, Tribal Court, General Correspondence, 1984 and 1985.

39. Angelo Skelares, Tribal Judge, to William Johnson, Chief of Police, subject: Prisoners Working for the Tribe, May 11, 1983, ATA files, as above in General Correspondence for 1983.

40. Interview with Clyde Sánchez, May 16, 1990.

41. Memorandum, Ácoma Tribal Court to Tribal Administration and Council, subject: Tribal Court Report from 1983–1990, April 10, 1990, ATA files, Law and Order, General Correspondence, 1990.

42. Ibid.

43. Proposed Program for Ground-Breaking Ceremony, June 26, 1976, Ácoma-Canoncito-Laguna Hospital, in Ácoma Tribal Administration files, IHS-ACL Hospital, Correspondence, 1978, hereafter cited as Tribal ACL files.

44. Tribal Council Resolution No. TC-NO-AP-14-71, April 14, 1971, subject: Community Hospital Facilities to serve Indian and non-Indian Residents of Central Valencia County, in Tribal ACL files.

45. Report, *"Funding for the Acoma-Laguna-Canoncito Hospital,"* 1972 or 1973, in Tribal ACL files.

46. From the start, an entry posed the only real drawback to the Ácoma proposal because reservation boundaries required passage through steep, rugged terrain. Fortuitously, the tribe was able to gain a right-of-way easement across the Cubero Land Grant to gain access to the hospital site with a paved road. For the most part, James Toya and Calvin J. Aragon, Director and Assistant Director of the hosptal, respectively, furnished the author information from memory as well as from personal notes. Victoria E. Johnson, Medical Records Librarian, provided statistical data.

47. "Indian Leaders Tell Kennedy of Troubles," *Albuquerque Tribune*, November 11, 1977; "Indian Hospital Help for Health and Area Economy," Grants *Daily Beacon*, November 16, 1977.

48. George Pearl of the Albuquerque architectural firm of Stevens, Mallory, Pearl, and Campbell designed the hospital building, including this room.

49. "Indian Hospital Help for Health and Area Economy," Grants *Daily Beacon*, November 16, 1977.

50. Report, "Ácoma-Canoncito-Laguna Hospital Opened Its Doors," February 27, 1978, no author, typed notes from Tribal ACL files. The report described Veronica Salvador as the first outpatient and six-year-old Frederick Torivio, Ácoma from McCarthy's, as the first dental patient that day.

51. Memorandum, prepared by Michael H. Trujillo, M.D., Acting Clinical Director, to Nicholas T.

Redeye, Director, subject: Management Fact Sheet, October 27, 1978, Tribal ACL files.

52. "Indian Hospital Help for Health and Area Economy," Grants *Daily Beacon*, November 16, 1977.

53. The Ácoma-Canoncito-Laguna Hospital Board charter exists as a Memorandum of Agreement, Ácoma-Canoncito-Laguna Tribes, January 26, 1979.

54. The Indian Health Service listed kidney dialysis as an important adjunct to the proposed hospital services being considered by planners. Other health problems plaguing these Indian tribes included heart disease, cancer, cirrhosis of the liver and alcoholism, and homicides. "Indian Hospital Help for Health and Area Economy," Grants *Daily Beacon*, November 16, 1977.

55. See section on legal services for additional information on Ácoma's approach to the problem.

56. Chapter V of the Tribal Code adopted by the Council in 1971 made failure to send children to school an offense punishable by confinement and fines.

57. "Pueblo of Ácoma Deeded and Lease Acreage," prepared by Ácoma Land Office, 1989. Acreage figures include adjustments that reflect recent surveys, land exchanges, etc.

58. Council Resolution TC-JA-04-88-0, January 4, 1977, authorizing purchase of the Berryhill Ranch, ATA files, Natural Resources-Berryhill Ranch Land Purchase of 1977.

59. Agreement signed by Gladdus T. Berryhill and co-executors for the Estate of Adrian Berryhill, and Merle Garcia, Governor, Pueblo of Ácoma, March 10, 1976; Lotario D. Ortega, Area Director, Bureau of Indian Affairs, to Superintendent, Southern Pueblos Agency, subject: Final Title Opinion, Land Acquisition, Pueblo of Ácoma-Berryhill Ranch, May 31, 1977; Tribal Resolution No. TC-FEB-28-80B, adopted February 25, 1980; Omar Bradley, Agency Realty officer, Bureau of Indian Affairs, to Governor Raymond Concho, June 3, 1981, all in ATA files, Berryhill Ranch Land Purchase.

60. Tribal Resolution No. TC-MAY-30-70-D, May 30, 1979; Raymond Concho, Governor, to Samuel Montoya, Superintendent, Southern Pueblos Agency, May 16, 1980, ATA files, Natural Resources-Kowina Purchase.

61. Sale of Kowina Foundation, signed by Governor Raymond J. Concho and Henry H. and Sue M. Elkins, July 5, 1979, in ATA files, Kowina Purchase.

62. Interview with Joe C. Ray, December 31, 1978.

63. Minutes, General Meeting, Office of the Governor, Pueblo of Ácoma, September 5, 1978, ATA files, Natural Resources-Wilson Ranch Purchase of 1978.

64. Resolution No. TC-JUL-19-780, July 19, 1978, Approval of the Ácoma Tribal Council to Purchase the Wilson Ranch, ATA files, Wilson Ranch Purchase.

65. Purchase and Sale Agreement, signed by Carl W. Wilson, President, and Laurence L. Wilson, Secretary of Wilson Cattle Company, and Governor Stanley Paytiamo, June 20, 1978, ATA files, Wilson Ranch Purchase.

66. Lotario Ortega, Office of the Solicitor, to Superintendent, Southern Pueblos Agency, subject: Land Purchase, Pueblo of Ácoma, from Wilson Cattle Company, October 3, 1978, ATA files, Wilson Ranch Purchase.

67. Resolution No. TC-NOV-8-78-D, November 8, 1978; Wilson Ranch (BAR FIFTEEN) Purchase Agreement, October 20, 1978, and Cattle Purchase, November 1, 1978, all in ATA files, Wilson Ranch Purchase. The inventory further described an adobe house with six rooms, bath, and two porches; a rock bunkhouse with three rooms; a mobile home with four rooms and two baths; a tool shed; a rock feed barn; ten wells and windmills; corrals; ten springs; fourteen fenced pastures; numerous livestock reservoirs; and stock ponds.

68. Charles P. Reynolds, Attorney at Law, Ortega and Snead, Albuquerque, to Governor Raymond Concho, Pueblo of Ácoma, February 23, 1979, in ATA files, Wilson Ranch Purchase.

69. Ácoma Tribal Council, Resolution No. TC-SEPT-16-86-13a, September 16, 1986; Purchase and Sale Agreement, signed by Frank and Mabel Analla, Pueblo of Laguna, and Stanley Paytiamo, Governor, Pueblo of Ácoma, October 3, 1986, both in ATA files, Natural Resources-Mabel and Frank Analla Purchase in Bar-15.

70. Ray A. Histia, Governor, Pueblo of Ácoma, to Eunice Gunn, subject: Pueblo of Ácoma Proposed Purchase of Ranch Land, June 23, 1988; Governor Histia to Samuel R. Montoya, Superintendent, Southern Pueblos Agency, subject: Pueblo of Ácoma Proposed Purchase of Eunice Gunn Property, June 23, 1988; Peter C. Chestnut, Attorney-at-Law, to Governor Histia, subject: Eunice Gunn Property, June 23, 1988;

Warranty Deed, December 5, 1988, all in ATA files, Natural Resources-Land-Eunice Gunn, General Correspondence, 1988.

71. Resolution No. TC-AUG-16-88-2, Request to Declare Reservation Status for Eunice Gunn Tract, August 16, 1988; Governor Histia to Samuel R. Montoya, subject: Eunice Gunn Property, August 16, 1988, ATA files, Gunn, General Correspondence.

72. Resolution No. TC-AUG-24-82-03-0-02, August 24, 1982; Warranty Deed, signed by Governor Merle Garcia and Pete Baca, Jr., December 6, 1982, both in ATA files, Pete Baca, Jr., Ranch Purchase of 1983.

73. Merle L. Garcia, Governor, Pueblo of Ácoma, to Vince Little, Albuquerque Area Director, Bureau of Indian Affairs, January 24, 1984, ATA files, Natural Resources-Los Cerritos Purchase of 1983.

74. Charles E. Barnhart, Attorney for Marie S. Bibo, to Merle L. Garcia, Governor, Pueblo of Ácoma, subject: Los Cerritos Trading Post and adjacent property, May 16, 1983; Purchase Agreement between Marie S. Bibo and the Pueblo of Ácoma, December 22, 1983, and Warranty Deed, December 22, 1983, all in ATA files, Los Cerritos Purchase.

75. Merle L. Garcia, Governor, Pueblo of Ácoma, to Vince Little, January 24, 1984; Information on Los Cerritos Projects 1986, Keystone Enterprise, Inc., p. 2, ATA files, Los Cerritos Purchase.

76. "Acoma Announces Plans for Self-Sufficiency," Gallup *Independent*, October 22, 1983; "Acoma Seeks State Funds for Multimillion Dollar Development," Grants *Daily Beacon*, December 1, 1983; "Acoma Readies for Bingo Fans," *Albuquerque Journal*, October 29, 1983.

77. Lee Peters, Assistant Attorney General, Department of Justice, Santa Fe, New Mexico, to Honorable Toney Anaya, Governor of the State of New Mexico, December 19, 1983; "Information on Los Cerritos Project 1986," pp. 1–2, 28, and 45, both in ATA files, Los Cerritos Purchase. Governor Garcia accused the Bureau of Indian Affairs of "holding Indians back economically." See, "Acoma Leader Says BIA Blocking Indians," Gallup *Independent*, June 14, 1984.

78. "Malpais Lava Flow Belongs to Acoma Pueblo, Indian Leaders Tell BLM," *Albuquerque Tribune*, May 23, 1979; Resolution No. TC-JUN-25-79B, Commentary Submitted by the Pueblo of Ácoma to the El Malpais Proposed Wilderness Study, June 25, 1979; Raymond L. Concho, Governor, to Paul Tanner, Bureau of Land Management, June 15, 1981, the last two are in the Ácoma Land Office, Malpais Papers.

79. Bruce King to Bureau of Land Management–Rio Puerco Resource Area, subject: Proposed WSAs–Rimrock, Little Rimrock, Sand Canyon, Rincon, February 2, 1986 in Malpais Papers; "Area Likes Park Idea," Gallup *Independent*, March 27, 1986.

80. "The Pueblo of Ácoma's Statement of Concern on the Proposal to Declare El Malpais a National Monument," prepared by Governor Stanley Paytiamo for hearing on House Resolution 3684, El Malpais Badlands, Grants, New Mexico, March 26, 1986, in Malpais Papers.

81. Governor Paytiamo to the Honorable Bill Richardson, July 9, 1986, in Malpais Papers.

82. "House Approves El Malpais Monument," *Albuquerque Journal*, July 30, 1986.

83. Governor Paytiamo to the Honorable Senator Pete Domenici, August 19 and October 13, 1986, Malpais Papers.

84. "N.M. Congressional Delegation Introduces El Malpais Bills," Grants *Daily Beacon*, January 1, 1987.

85. "The Pueblo of Ácoma's position on the legislation to establish the El Malpais National Monument and the Grants National Conservation Area," statements prepared by Governor Paytiamo, February 10, 1987, in Malpais Papers; "Carruthers Adds His Support to El Malpais–Masau Trail Bills," Grants *Daily Beacon*, February 11, 1987.

86. Governor Paytiamo to Chairman [John Sieberling], Subcommittee on Public Lands, February 17, 1987; Statement of Governor Paytiamo before the Subcommittee on Public Lands, National Parks and Forests of the Senate Committee on Energy and Natural Resources Concerning Senate Bill 56, a bill to establish the El Malpais National Monument, the Masau Trail, and the Grants National Conservation Area in New Mexico, and for other purposes, February 19, 1987, Malpais Papers.

87. Governor Paytiamo to the Honorable Pete V. Domenici, April 6, 1987, Malpais Papers.

88. Memorandum, Governor Paytiamo to Whom It May Concern, subject: Summary of Testimony of El Malpais National Monument for Delivery April 28, 1987; Testimony before the Congress of the United States by Governor Paytiamo, presented Tuesday, April 28, 1987, Malpais Papers.

89. William P. Horn, Assistant Secretary, United States Department of the Interior, to Honorable Morris K. Udall, Chairman, Committee on Interior and Insular Affairs, May 15, 1987; Governor Paytiamo to the Honorable Donald P. Hodel, Secretary for Indian Affairs, May 15, 1987; Ácoma Pueblo's Statement on El Malpais National Monument, La Ventana National Conservation–Cebolla Wilderness Area, May 18, 1987; Memorandum, Governor Paytiamo to Honorable Bruce F. Vento, Chairman, Subcommittee on National Parks and Public Lands, May 8, 1987; Memorandum, Governor Paytiamo to United States Senators and Representatives, subject: summary of Ácoma's Statement of Concerns on the Proposal to Establish El Malpais National Monument, La Ventana National Conservation Area, and Cebolla Wilderness Area, May 18, all in Malpais Papers.

90. "Acoma: We Don't Like Malpais Deal," Gallup *Independent*, May 21, 1987; "Acoma Protest at Malpais," Gallup *Independent*, May 21, 1987; "Indians Protest Malpais Bill," *Albuquerque Journal*, May 21, 1987.

91. "Acoma Protest Draws Fire," Gallup *Independent*, May 23, 1987.

92. "Acoma Protest Was a New Twist to a Centuries Old Conflict," Grants *Daily Beacon*, May 22, 1987.

93. Governor Paytiamo to Senators Domenici and Jeff Bingaman and Congressman Richardson, subject: El Malpais National Monument House Resolution 403-5856, June 3, 1987; Press Release, prepared by Governor Paytiamo, June 8, 1987; Governor Paytiamo to the Honorable Ronald Reagan, June 9, 1987; all in Malpais Papers.

94. "House Oks El Malpais Over Reagan Administration's Objections," Grants *Daily Beacon*, June 2, 1987; "House Votes Status at Lava Sites," *New York Times*, June 2, 1987.

95. "Water Rights New Barb in Proposed El Malpais Monument," Grants *Daily Beacon*, June 8, 1987; "Water Rights Questions Postpone Senate Action on El Malpais," Grants *Daily Beacon*, June 11, 1987; "Water Debate Slow El Malpais Bill," *Albuquerque Journal*, June 11, 1987.

96. "Acomas Claim Malpais Nixed," Gallup *Independent*, June 12, 1987; "El Malpais Bill Remains Stalled in Senate Comm.," Grants *Daily Beacon*, June 18, 1987.

97. Western Union Mailgram, Alvin Lowden, head councilman, to President Reagan; Jennifer A. Fitzgerald, assistant to the vice-president for legislative affairs, to Governor Paytiamo, June 16, 1987; Governor Paytiamo to Senator Daniel K. Inouye, June 19,, 1987, all in Malpais Papers.

98. Western Union Mailgram, Governor Paytiamo to Dear Pete, June 22, 1987, Malpais Papers.

99. "Senate Comm. Gives El Malpais Go-Ahead," Grants *Daily Beacon*, June 25, 1987; "El Malpais Bill Goes to Senate," *Albuquerque Journal*, June 26, 1987; "El Malpais Bill Protects Acoma," Gallup *The Independent*, June 26, 1987.

100. "New Bill Angers Acomas," Gallup *Independent*, June 27, 1987; Governor Paytiamo to Senator Domenici and Staff, et al., subject: El Malpais National Monument House Resolution 403-SB56, June 30, 1987; Governor Paytiamo to New Mexico Congressional Delegation, July 8, 1987, Malpais Papers.

101. Governor Paytiamo to Senators, July 9, 1987, Malpais Papers.

102. Governor Paytiamo to Governor Garrey Carruthers, August 3, 1987; Press Release, Pueblo of Ácoma, August 19, 1987, both in El Malpais; "Acomas Press Carruthers on El Malpais," Grants *Daily Beacon*, August 21, 1987; "Acomas Claim Wilderness Will Disturb Religious Sites," Grants *Daily Beacon*, September 2, 1987.

103. "N.M. Water Rights Snag Malpais Bill," *Albuquerque Journal*, September 6, 1987; "Carruthers' Concerns Stall El Malpais Land Bill," Gallup *Independent*, September 11, 1987; "Malpais Land Swap Completed," Gallup *Independent*, September 16, 1987; "Carruthers Position on El Malpais Rejected by N.M. Delegation," September 21, 1987.

104. "Carruthers to Consult Experts Before Deciding on El Malpais," Grants *Daily Beacon*, September 22, 1987; "Governor to Review Malpais," Gallup *Independent*, September 23, 1987; "Governor Needs to Get Behind Malpais," Grants *Daily Beacon*, September 24, 1987.

105. Governor Paytiamo to Senator Paul Simon, October 6, 1987; Governor Paytiamo to all Senators, October 6, 1987, both in Malpais Papers.

106. Governor Paytiamo to Governor Carruthers, October 2, 1987; Western Union Mailgram, Governor Paytiamo to Senator J. Bennett Johnson, et al., October 15, 1987, both in Malpais Papers; "El Malpais, Governor Carruthers Withdraws Water Objections," Gallup *Independent*, October 10, 1987.

107. "Malpais Passage Likely," Gallup *Independent*, October 16, 1987.

108. "El Malpais Bill Gets the Green Light," Grants *Daily Beacon*, October 19, 1987; "Acomas to Make a Symbolic Gesture Protecting El Malpais," Grants *Daily Beacon*, October 20, 1987; Press Release, Pueblo of Ácoma, October 21, 1987, Malpais Papers.

109. "Acomas Threaten to Return Symbol," *Albuquerque Journal*, October 22, 1987. The threats were not carried through and the Ácoma governor still uses the Lincoln cane as a symbol of office.

110. Proposed Amendment by Staff of the Senate Select Subcommittee on Indian Affairs, October 24, 1987; The Pueblo of Ácoma's Amendments to Senate Bill 56, El Malpais National Monument, October 25, 1987; Opening Statement by Governor Paytiamo, October 25, 1987, Malpais Papers; "Senators Meet with Acomas on Malpais," Grants *Daily Beacon*, October 26, 1987.

111. Governor Carruthers to the Honorable Stanley Paytiamo, November 2, 1987, Malpais Papers.

112. Governor Paytiamo to Congressman Bruce F. Vento, October 29, 1987; Governor Paytiamo to Sidney R. Yates, October 29, 1987; Governor Paytiamo to Congressman Richardson, November 12, 1987; Governor Paytiamo to Chistena L. Bach, Special Assistant to the President for Intergovernmental Affairs, November 13, 1987; Governor Paytiamo to Donald P. Hodel, Secretary, Department of the Interior, November 13, 1987, all in Malpais Papers.

113. "Senators Promise 'Protection' for Acoma," Grants *Daily Beacon*, November 10, 1987; Senators Bingaman and Domenici to Governor Paytiamo, November 19, 1987, Malpais Papers.

114. Press release, Governor Paytiamo, November 22, 1987; Governor Paytiamo to Donald P. Hodel, Secretary, Department of the Interior, November 22, 1987, both in Malpais Papers.

115. Memorandum, Governor Paytiamo to Senator Domenici et al., subject: El Malpais Monument Legislation, Senate Bill and House Resolution 403, November 23, 1987, Malpais Papers.

116. Governor Paytiamo to the Honorable Ronald Reagan, November 28, 1987; Governor Paytiamo to Joe Trujillo, November 30, 1987; Governor Paytiamo to Senatory Inouye, December 1, 1987; Governor Paytiamo to Senator Bingaman, December 2, 1987; Governor Paytiamo to Senator Domenici, December 2, 1987; Senator Inouye's Proposal as Amended by Ácoma Pueblo Council, December 3, 1987, all in Malpais Papers.

117. Pueblo of Ácoma Press Release, December 4, 1987; Alan R. Parker, Staff Director, Senate Select Committee on Indian Affairs, to Governor Paytiamo, December 4, 1987; Governor Paytiamo to Honorable Daniel K. Inouye, December 10, 1987; Senator Inouye to Governor Paytiamo, December 11, 1987, all in Malpais Papers; "Acoma Council OK on Malpais," Gallup *Independent*, December 4, 1987; "Malpais Compromise Accepted by Acomas," Grants *Daily Beacon*, December 7, 1987.

118. Governor Paytiamo to President Ronald Reagan, December 17, 1987, Malpais Papers; "Acomas Want Malpais Land," Gallup *Independent*, December 17, 1987; "Acomas Would Meet Reagan on Malpais Bill," Gallup *Independent*, December 18, 1987.

119. Interview with Stanley Paytiamo, Pueblo of Ácoma, July 25, 1990; "Richardson Expects Reagan to Sign El Malpais Legislation," Grants *Daily Beacon*, December 21, 1987; Press Release, Governor Paytiamo, December 24, 1987, Malpais Papers; "Acoma Christmas, Officer Says Malpais Bill Veto Would Make It Merry," Gallup *Independent*, December 24, 1987.

120. "Acoma Governor Criticized El Malpais Approval," *Albuquerque Journal*, December 25, 1987; "Tribe Fights to Preserve Sacred Land," *Los Angeles Times*, December 26, 1987; "President Reagan Will Not Likely Veto El Malpais Legislation," Grants *Daily Beacon*, December 31, 1987; "Reagan Signs Bill Creating El Malpais," *Albuquerque Journal*, January 1, 1988; "Acoma Administration Taking Quiet Approach to Problems," Grants *Daily Beacon*, January 7, 1988; interview with Stanley Paytiamo, July 25, 1990.

121. Public Law 100-225 [House Resolution 403], December 31, 1987; "Give the Acomas Their Land Back," *Albuquerque Tribune*, January 22, 1988; "Acoma's Land Was Stolen—Now We Want It Back," *Albuquerque Tribune*, January 26, 1988.

122. Sidney L. Mills, Area Director, to Deputy to the Assistant-Indian Affairs (Trust and Economic Development) attention: Real Estate Services, Code 220, subject: Approval of Trust Land Acquisition–Ácoma Pueblo, no date; Tribal Council Resolution No. TC-FEB-11-88-3, February 15, 1988; Ácoma Pueblo Tribal Resolution No. TC-DEC-12-89-1, December 12, 1989, all in ATA files, Land Purchases, Attempts to Gain Trust Status Approval.

123. Governor Ray A. Histia, Pueblo of Ácoma, to Mrs. Jeanne J. Jones, Mrs. Margaret J. Delph, Mr. Edwin K. Delph, and the Valley National Bank of Arizona, as Co-Trustees Under the Last Will and

229

Testament of Suzanne Jacobs Orth, deceased, and the Valley National Bank of Arizona, as Trustee of Trust B. Under the Last Will and Testament of John M. Jacobs, Deceased, December 7, 1988 (purchase offer); Governor Histia to Sidney L. Mills, Area Director, Bureau of Indian Affairs, Albuquerque Area Office, subject: Federal Trust Status for the Red Lake Ranch on Behalf of the Pueblo of Ácoma, December 13, 1988, ATA file, Land Purchases; "Acoma Buys Red Lake Ranch," Grants *Daily Beacon*, October 18, 1989.

124. Simon Ortiz, "The Last Word," in *Indian Tribal Sovereignty and Treaty Rights* (Albuquerque: La Confluencia, P.O. Box 409, 1978), p. S59. Transcript of proceedings of a forum held April 12–14, 1978, at San Diego State University. The forum was sponsored by the Cultural Arts Board of the Associated Students of San Diego State University, the California Council for the Humanities in Public Policy, The National Endowment for the Humanities, and the Department of American Indian Studies at the university.

125. Draft Constitution from 1932–1933, on Ácoma Tribal Council Meeting Room wall.

126. Interview with David Garcia, Pueblo of Ácoma, June 20, 1990; interview with Governor Paytiamo, Pueblo of Ácoma, July 25, 1990.

127. Kirshner Associates, *Development of Tourist Potential of the Acoma Reservation, New Mexico*, Albuquerque, 1985; *Overall Economic Development Program, Acoma Indian Pueblo*, January 1974, p. 93, both in Acoma Land Office files.

128. Governor Stanley Paytiamo to Pacheco and Graham Architects, December 12, 1978; Thomas W. Merlan, State Historic Preservation Officer, to the Hon. Stanley Paytiamo, May 9, 1978, offers to support the study with $5,000 of state funds, both in ATA file, Preservation Projects at Ácoma-Grants, Ácoma Tribal Administration Funds: San Estevan del Rey Mission. Standards for Historic Preservation Projects, etc.

129. Edna Heatherington Bergman, *Historic Structures Report, Mission San Estevan Rey, Pueblo of Ácoma, New Mexico*, Pacheco and Graham Architects, March 1980, p. 39.

130. Ibid., pp. 39–40.

131. State of New Mexico, State Planning Office, and Pueblo of Ácoma made and entered into a contract agreement relating to Project Number 35-75-00048 on March 22, 1976, providing Phase II Pueblo de Ácoma Restoration, as amended and appended, ATA files, San Estevan del Rey Mission—Restoration Phase II, Grant #35-75-00048-00, NM/Acoma, 1977. Working with the Ácoma on the convent was Mike Marshall, contract archeologist, who recorded artifacts from the earth fill and analyzed and recorded, in color, Indian murals that had been painted over on the exterior convent walls along its corridors. See Michael Marshall, "Investigations at the Mission of San Estevan Rey, Acoma Pueblo, New Mexico: A Preliminary Report," Thomas W. Merlan, ed., Historic Preservation Program, Department of Education Finance and Cultural Affairs, Santa Fe, New Mexico, 1975.

132. Although identified as an historic site by the National Park Service after the Historic Sites Act of 1935, Ácoma received the plaques upon being declared a National Historic Landmark by the Secretary of Interior in 1969, acting under the National Historic Preservation Act passed by Congress in 1966. See, *The National Register of Historic Places, 1969* (Washington, D.C.: United States Department of Interior, National Park Service), pp. vii, xi, and 197.

133. Merlan to the Honorable Merle L. Garcia, July 14, 1982, ATA files, San Estevan del Rey Mission-Restoration Phase II.

134. Kenneth Bateman to Governor Ray Histia, February 17, 1989, ATA files, Preservation Projects and Grants, San Estevan del Rey Mission Church-Restoration-Preservation Project 1989. Aiding Coriz on the report were Toni Prestupa and Stan Davis of Davis and Associates, Inc., Santa Fe.

135. Victor J. Chavez, Chavez-Grieves Consulting Engineers, Inc., to Toni Prestupa, concerning Preliminary Report for Ácoma Church, December 22, 1988, ATA files, Preservation Projects and Grants, San Estevan del Rey Mission Church-Restoration.

136. "Restoration Plans for the Mission at Old Acoma," The Mission at Old Ácoma Foundation, Inc., no date; Minutes, Council Meeting, Acomita, New Mexico, March 28, 1989; Governor Histia to Board of Directors, Mission at Old Ácoma Foundation, Inc., May 17, 1989; Bateman to the Honorable Ray A. Histia, November 2, 1989, all in ATA files, Preservation Projects and Grants, San Estevban del Rey Mission Church. Initial Board members: Kenneth Bateman, Presient; Peter Gould, Vice-President; Caroline Cochener, Secretary; Ann B. Ness, Treasurer; Stan Davis and Toni Prestupa.

230

About the Bibliography

Research for the Ácomas included an attempt to locate and identify source records for the tribe and to use primary references as much as possible. The notes identify the documents as they appear in the text along with other information such as persons and dates. Whenever possible correspondence and reports show place of origin and always where they are currently located. This should afford the Ácomas and their friends a ready guide to primary sources. Copies of these are now residing with the tribe and are so indicated in the notes as Pueblo of Ácoma Archives. The collection is newly established and will grow in size as the Ácomas are able to add items of interest to the pueblo.

The Indian Claims Commisson assembled a major collection of documents about Ácoma and these may be found with the United States Department of Justice under Docket Number 266 for the Commission. The important documents would be in the records of hearings and include maps (some quite recent to correspond with archeological findings), depositions, and experts' reports, among other things. Aside from the judicial proceedings of the Commission, which form a unique historical record unto themselves, the report of Robert L. Rands, *Acoma Land Utilization: An Ethnohistorical Report* (n.d.) stands above the others. Additionally, these records contain testimonials made by Ácomas, some no longer living. Nicholas and Sam Dazzo accumulated many documents of historical value and they plan to transfer these to the tribe.

Archeological information about Ácoma is still somewhat confusing. Studies on the province remain sketchy. The spadework by Alfred E. Dittert, Jr., Florence Hawley Ellis, and Reynold J. Ruppe, Jr., resulting from problems arising within the definitions of the claims problem, produced some very interesting results but much more is required. Such is the case, for example, to render a better understanding of what constituted the Kingdom of Acus, as reported by the early

Spanish. Origins of the tribe, particularly as they relate to migrations, remain a puzzle, largely because what has been passed down among them by tradition does not always match the archeological reports. Mathew W. Stirling's *Origin Myth of Acoma and Other Records*, Bureau of American Ethology Bulletin 135 (Washington: U.S. Government Printing Office, 1942) contains the more acceptable version of the origin myth but by no means should be considered definitive.

Starting with early history down to Mexico's independence from Spain in 1821, the Spanish documents assembled and translated in the Coronado Cuarto Centennial Publications, 1540–1940, edited by George Peter Hammond and published by the University of New Mexico, are undoubtedly the finest collection of historical sources. They should be of interest to all Indians in the Southwest. Earliest materials are found in Herbert Eugene Bolton, *Coronado on the Turquoise Trail, Knight of the Pueblos and Plains* (1949), volume 1 of the series, along with *Narratives of the Coronado Expedition, 1540–1542* (1940), volume 2, edited by Hammond and translated by Agapito Rey. *Don Juan de Oñate, Colonizer of New Mexico, 1595–1628* (1953) volume 5, contains Indian names, depositions, and testimonials relating to Oñate's settlement policies. The volume actually appears in two parts (two thick volumes) and holds the bulk of the documents from the Ácoma troubles with the Zaldivar brothers.

Articles containing documents of the Chamuscado-Rodriguez party in New Mexico are found in the *New Mexico Historical Review:* J. Lloyd Mecham, "Account of the Chamuscado-Rodriguez Entrada of 1581–1582 in the Second Expedition to New Mexico" 1 (1926):265–91; and Hammond and Rey, "The Rodriguez Expedition to New Mexico, 1581–1582" 2 (1927):239–68, 334–62. Some of this material was included in Bolton's *Spanish Exploration in the Southwest, 1542–1706* (New York: Charles Scribner's Sons, 1916).

The Quivira Society of Los Angeles also published important documents showing Spanish contacts with Indians in New Mexico. The first volume, edited by George P. Hammond and Agapito Rey, was *Expedition into New Mexico Made by Antonio de Espejo, 1582–1583* (1929). *Gaspar Perez de Villagrá, History of New Mexico* (1938), edited by Gilberto Espinosa, contains a contemporary version of the Ácoma battle with the Zaldivars.

In addition to the Oñate documents, the Coronado Cuarto Centennial Publications include documents of the seventeenth century and the Pueblo Revolt, with references to Ácoma. *Fray Alonso de Benavides Revised Memorial of 1634* (1945), volume 4, must be read in context with Lansing B. Bloom, ed., "A Glimpse of New Mexico in 1620," *New Mexico Historical Review* 3 (1928):357–89 and "The Royal Order of 1620 to Custodian Fray Estéban de Perea," *New Mexico Historical Review* 5 (1930):288–98, for background on the introduction of Spanish political institutions into the pueblos.

An unusually large number of references to Indians are found in documents relating to the Pueblo Revolt of 1680. These are gathered and translated in several volumes, starting with Charles Wilson Hackett, *Revolt of the Pueblo Indians of New Mexico and Otermin's Attempted Reconquest*, CCCP, vol. 8 (Albuquerque: University of New Mexico Press, 1942). This collection should lead one to J. Manuel Espinosa, *First Expedition of Vargas into New Mexico, 1692* (1940), volume 10 of the same series. The last significant collection would be Jessie Bromilaw Bailey, *Diego de Vargas and the Reconquest of New Mexico* (Albuquerque: University of New Mexico Press, 1940). All three have excellent introductory observations, especially Hackett, which must not be overlooked when using the documents. Finally, the entire period should be supplemented with documents now residing in the New Mexico Records Center and Archives, Santa Fe, including those listed in Ralph Emerson Twitchell, *The Spanish Archives of New Mexico* (Cedar Rapids, Iowa: The Torch Press, 1914), volume 1, and which were formerly deposited with the Bureau of Land Management in Santa Fe. The most readable account of the reconquest is J. Manuel Espinosa, *Crusaders of the Rio Grande, the Story of Don Diego de Vargas and the Reconquest and Refounding of New Mexico* (Chicago: Institute of Jesuit History Publications, 1942).

For eighteenth-century New Mexico there is no single definitive history. While we wait for one, there are some useful collections of documents, also translated and published in book form. The documents in Charles Wilson Hackett, ed., *Historical Documents Relating to New Mexico, Nueva Vizcaya, and Approaches Thereto, to 1773,* collected by Adolph F. A. Bandelier and Fanny Bandelier (Washington: Carnegie Institution of Washington, 1937), correspond chronologically to the two now classic volumes of Alfred Barnaby Thomas, *The Plains Indians and New Mexico, 1751–1778,* CCCP, vol. II (Albuquerque: University of New Mexico Press, 1940) and *Forgotten Frontiers, A Study of the Spanish Indian Policy of Don Juan Bautista de Anza, Governor of New Mexico, 1777–1787* (Norman: University of Oklahoma Press, 1932).

The eighteenth century lacked an artist, apparently, and photography was nonexistent. So far as we know there are no graphics of life in New Mexico during the often-called colonial period other than what may have been translated into religious art. Until now, however, nothing descriptive has survived to equal Fray Francisco Atanasio Domínguez' piece on Ácoma, reproduced in *The Missions of New Mexico, 1776, A Description by Fray Francisco Atanasio Domínguez,* Eleanor B. Adams and Fray Angelico Chavez, trans. and eds. (Albuquerque: The University of New Mexico Press, 1956; reprinted 1975), and included as an appendix to this volume.

The primary sources are supplemented with Spanish Archive documents found in the New Mexico Records Center and Archives. They may be found in Twitchell, *The Spanish Archives of New Mexico,* but one should not rely on Twitchell solely. More current is the *Guide to the Microfilm of the Spanish Archives of New Mexico, 1621–1821* (Santa Fe: State of New Mexico Records Center, 1967).

The laudable record keeping of the Spanish bureaucracy all but disappears with the Mexican Revolution. There has been no project such as the centennial series to ease the problems of translating difficult script. Marc Simmons introduces the reader to the period in *Spanish Government in New Mexico* (Albuquerque: University of New Mexico Press, 1968), by describing the structure of the local government before the revolution.

For the Mexican period in New Mexico, the text again relies principally on primary sources. The only overview and best guide through the next twenty-five years is Lansing B. Bloom's series, "New Mexico Under the Mexican Administration." This was published in *Old*

234

Santa Fe, starting with 1 (July 1913):3–49, and continuing as follows: 1 (October 1913):131–75; 1 (January 1914):235–87; 1 (April 1914): 347–68; 2 (July 1914):3–56; 2 (October 1914):119–69; and 2 (April 1915):351–80. Some documents he used, the author is no longer able to find.

Of the primary sources, however, the bulk are located in the New Mexico Records Center. A milestone was reached when that institution's *Calendar of the Microfilm Edition of the Mexican Archives of New Mexico, 1821–1846,* compiled by Myra Ellen Jenkins, appeared in 1970. With a grant from the National Historical Publications Commission, the New Mexico Records Center reorganized and microfilmed documents covering the entire Mexican period, greatly facilitating research into these items.

Unfortunately, the Mexican records contain fewer references to Pueblo Indians. Raids on them by unfriendly Indians are listed for the years 1746–1910 in Myra Ellen Jenkins and Ward Alan Minge, *Record of Navajo Activities Affecting the Acoma-Laguna Area* (Ácoma-Laguna Exhibit Number 530 in Docket No. 266, Pueblo de Ácoma versus United States of America, 1961). Much of this information appears in John P. Wilson, *Military Campaigns in the Navajo Country, Northwestern New Mexico, 1800–1846* (Santa Fe: Museum of New Mexico Press, 1967).

Several military expeditions visited Ácoma just after the United States took over New Mexico in 1846. From them, the Lieutenant James H. William Abert report is the finest and can be found in William Hensley Emory, ed., *Notes of a Military Reconnaissance, from Fort Leavenworth in Missouri to San Diego, in California* (30th Cong., 1st Sess., Senate Executive Document No. 7, Washington: 1848). A Mexican visitor, Victor de la O, about this time attempted to extort money from the Ácomas for what he claimed was their grant papers. The resulting suit and case files deeply involve Ácoma and are to be found in the records of the New Mexico Supreme Court. The correspondence of the first Indian Agent at Santa Fe is invaluable for studying the period following United States occupation of New Mexico. See Annie Heloise Abel, ed., *The Official Correspondence of James S. Calhoun while Indian Agent at Santa Fe and Superintendent of Indian*

Affairs in New Mexico (Washington: U.S. Government Printing Office, 1915).

From this point, the records of the Bureau of Indian Affairs become most important because of the almost daily reports on economics, health, education, and law and order. There are numerous letters and reports from the Indians themselves. These documents deal mainly with secular matters and do not in any way include religion.

Bureau of Indian Affairs documents regarding Ácoma were found in three separate repositories. For the period between 1854 and 1871, they are in the National Archives, Washington, D.C., under the heading Record Group 75, Records of Indian Affairs Field Papers, Michigan Superintendancy. Microfilm copies are located in many institutions, including the University of New Mexico. The Pueblo of Ácoma Archives contain true copies. Records for succeeding years were found at the General Services Administration regional building in Denver and they are filed under Records of the Bureau of Indian Affairs, Southern Pueblos Agency, with various subtitles under the general heading of Ácoma and again Record Group 75. There were some photos appended to economic reports which were also very interesting and will become even more so with age. For current years, similar documents are being accumulated by the various departments of the Southern Pueblos Agency in Albuquerque.

The Annual Reports of the Commissioner of Indian Affairs contain some information found nowhere else. This is especially true for census data and for those problems—such as financial ones—requiring congressional action. S. Lyman Tyler has written a general survey of congressional relations with the United States Indians in *A History of Indian Policy* (Washington: United States Department of Interior, Bureau of Indian Affairs, 1973). Information on specific government relations with the Ácomas is found in the annual reports and correspondence of Indian agents.

Other references are indicated in the notes which should also serve as bibliography. There are a few recent studies on Ácoma worth noting. An overview by Bertha P. Dutton, *Indians of the American Southwest* (Englewood Cliffs, N.J.: Prentice Hall, Inc., 1975), describes the Pueblo Indian (including Ácomas) and distinguishes him from other Indians in

236

the Southwest. Benjamin J. Taylor and Dennis J. O'Connor, *Indian Manpower Resources in the Southwest* (Tempe: Arizona State University, 1969), contains a section on Ácoma which will remain an economic yardstick for many years. Another study being used more and more on the reservation is *Development of Tourist Potential of the Acoma Reservation, New Mexico* (Albuquerque: Kirschner Associates, 1965). The report consists of many suggestions for economic improvements. Both studies are available at the Southern Pueblos Agency. If you can find a copy, Gary L. Tietjen, *Encounter with the Frontier* (Los Alamos, N.M.: n.p., 1969), has many descriptive items for part of New Mexico surrounding the Ácoma reservation. And finally, reports from the State Planning Office, Santa Fe, include sections on Ácoma. *Historic Preservation: A Plan for New Mexico* (1971), places Ácoma in a long-range program. *The Historic Preservation Program for New Mexico*, volume 1, *The Historic Background* (1973), and volume 2, *The Inventory* (1973), include references to Ácoma.

Index

242